Echoes of Eternity: Discovering the
Mahabharata's Resonant Truths

THE MAGNIFICENCE OF THE MAHABHARATA

Sitansu Ghosh

BLUEROSE PUBLISHERS
India | U.K.

Copyright © Sitansu Ghosh 2023

All rights reserved by author. No part of this publication may be reproduced, stored in a retrieval system or transmitted in any form or by any means, electronic, mechanical, photocopying, recording or otherwise, without the prior permission of the author. Although every precaution has been taken to verify the accuracy of the information contained herein, the publisher assume no responsibility for any errors or omissions. No liability is assumed for damages that may result from the use of information contained within.

BlueRose Publishers takes no responsibility for any damages, losses, or liabilities that may arise from the use or misuse of the information, products, or services provided in this publication.

For permissions requests or inquiries regarding this publication, please contact:

BLUEROSE PUBLISHERS
www.BlueRoseONE.com
info@bluerosepublishers.com
+91 8882 898 898
+4407342408967

ISBN: 978-93-5819-586-6

Cover design: Muskan Sachdeva
Typesetting: Pooja Sharma

First Edition: December 2023

Contents

The Beginning 1

The Birth Of Satyavaty 13

The Tale Of Parashara 23

Ganga, Shantanu & The Vasus 35

The Sons Of Satyavaty, Shantanu 49

Vyasa And Devavrata 60

The Birth Of Kuru Princes 64

The Marriage Of Kuru Princes 69

Pandu's Conquest, Forest Life, Despondency,
Getting Of Sons And Death 78

Karna — The Son Of Virgin Kunti 102

The Birth Of A Hundred Sons And A Daughter
Of Gandhari 112

The Application Of Poison To Bhima 118

The Birth Of Kripa, Kripee And Drona 123

Drona, The Military Teacher 129

Drona And Drupada 133

The Burning Of The House Of Lac 137

The Tale Of Bhima & Hidimba 142

The Sacrifice Of Drupada For A Son 148

The Pandavas' Journey To Panchala 152

Draupadi's Marriage	158
Arjuna's Abstinence & Self-Imposed Exile	164
The Conflagration Of The Khandava Forest	183
The Royal Court Of Yudisthira And The Rajasuya Sacrifice	200
The Game Of Dice In The Kaurava Court	216
The Exile Of The Pandavas	230
The Life Of The Pandavas In Exile	246
Interaction Of Yudhisthira With Draupadi & Bhimsena	254
Arjuna Receives Celestial Weapons	261
Arjuna In Heaven And The Love Tryst Of Urvashi	268
The Thoughts Of Armed Conflict In The Kaurava And Pandava Camps	273
The Tale Of Bhima, Nahusa And Yudhisthira	280
Duryodhana's Expedition To Dvaitavana	286
Karna, Duryodhana And The Vaishnava Sacrifice	297
Rishi Durvasa And The Forest-Dwelling Pandavas	307
The Abduction Of Draupadi By Jayadratha	313
The Unrevealed Exile Of The Pandavas	320
The Theft Of Bovine Herd Of Virata	330
The Embassy Of Krishna In The Kaurava Court	346

The Beginning

The Mahabharata needs no introduction; but it deserves some commendatory remarks. Prior to writing this epic poem Vyasa divided the Vedas, wrote Brahma-sutra and the Puranas. Even after completing such monumental works he felt at heart the inspiration to write this epic poem the huge mass of which appears to be confounding to the readers in general. The scholars and researchers are still engaged in finding out the different facets of truth in this great work of Vyasa which is regarded as history as well as myth that appears to be one of the finest works of art by any standard of aesthetics in the annuls of human civilization. Like all other great works of art this epic too has three layers of understanding — physical, intellectual and spiritual. On the physical plane there is a story attractive to the readers told on the basis of the prevalent political, social and moral ambience whereas on the intellectual plane Vyasa has demonstrated his marvellous acumen in using imagery, metaphors, allegories along with deep-rooted symbols and suggestions in weaving the fabric of his argument so dexterously that it appears to be a perennial source of relish to an ardent reader. On the spiritual plane the author by dint of his extra-ordinary wisdom, has showed his readers the way to be established in their own Dharma to attain peace and tranquility here on earth. But what is Dharma?

Faith or religion is the means to meet the end but Dharma is the end in itself being the means too. Faiths were established by some divine personae responding to the demands of the prevalent conditions of a particular point of time in human history but that is not true in respect of Dharma. Dharma is unborn, all pervasive and imperishable. It is eternal. As Consciousness is omnipresent, so also is Dharma in things and beings as the inherent nature of them all. Even a grain of sand has its own nature, similarly an ocean has its own nature too. Dharma is the nature intrinsic to every object and every existence that determines their course of action so long they exist.

Now, in case of living beings including the vegetation Dharma is determined by the way of their birth (yonigata) and they are divided in four categories, viz (1) The vegetation, (2) The mites and insects, (3) Those born of egg and (4) Those born of the womb. Although the humans fall under the fourth category yet they are completely different from other members of it. Having been endowed with conscience as well as the capability of realizing truth at heart to the highest degree, the human beings are distinctly different and their dharma is manhood which is synonymous with Godhood. Hence the humans are termed as the crown of creation being the finest product of evolution since the cosmogenesis.

We have been taught since our childhood that man is mortal and everything perishes in death. Is it so? Had it been the truth then how was a multicell human body possible from a single cell ameba in the course of evolution? Everything does not perish with death. The physical body contains two other bodies within this one and only the physical body perishes in death while the other two bodies remain in Nature as a seed awaiting assumption of a new physical body. As those two bodies turn a seed devoid of the physical body and protected by Nature Herself. At an appropriate time for rebirth this seed is allowed to have a refuge in the father's head and at a propitiated moment the father throws the seed into the mother's womb in course of his union with her. So sexual behaviour of men and women has found a place in this epic tale but enshrouded with highly pregnant metaphors and also some symbols are there. Now having the seed the mother carries it in her womb for ten months and ten days and gives birth to the baby. The life on earth again continues as before with a new physical body. Therefore death does not steal away life but physical body only and life remains in continuum beyond our physical vision. In fine, life is perennial that can defy death.

There are people who do not believe in rebirth and existence of life beyond the physical death, but they too await the Judgment on the Doomsday. If there remains no life after physical death for whom the seat of judgment be arranged in the other world? The life is a continuous flow of consciousness and man is not mortal but immortal. His life flows on and on being punctuated by death and rebirth assuming a new form from time to time. Long before this epic tale came into existence the Rishi of the Upanishads gave a clarion call to the humans to be the sons of Immortality (Amrita) and the apple tree will surely bear apples for you and never shall it offer you bramble berries.

Again, the Dharma India used to profess and does so till date, is known to be Sanatana (Eternal) Dharma which is unborn and imperishable and not founded by any human being. With the passage of time it has been identified as Hinduism as India is known to be the land of the Hindus. Though there exists no dharma in the name of Hinduism, some scholars do call it so. Without getting to the depth of its very existence they call it as such and define it to be the symbiosis of cultures which is but a fallacy. It is true that the Sanatana Dharma is as liberal as the endless sky and since the time immemorial many a faith, many a culture has come to this land which has been assimilated here. The scholars come to their conclusion on their observation of social and sometimes religions rituals at modern times in which the influence of various cultures is discernible in the so-called Hinduism although the nature of performing such rituals varies much from region to region. More so, the rituals performed in religious and social functions should not be termed as Dharma which is the inherent nature of men and women that sustains them, protects them and also manifests itself through them in their actions.

The Mahabharata is a deep rooted allegory having a basis of history and myth as well to a serious reader. But to an ordinary reader its storyline sometimes presents problems that cannot be solved with a common understanding such as (1) the birth of human babies in the womb of a fish which swallowed the human semen borne on a leaf by a hawk that fell in the water of the Yamuna while fighting with another hawk, (2) Gandhari's having one hundred sons and a daughter of a hard lump of flesh, (3) Drupada's having offspring from the flaming fire of sacrifice, (4) the miraculous deliverance of four fledglings of Mandapala and Jarita from the blazing fire of the Khandava forest and many other such instances.

The epic including the Geeta holds a mirror upto the realties (tattva) of the human body. The author invites us to visualize them in our own body showing them in their ture nature (dharma) within us and expecting us to be rich with their knowledge to decide our course of action vis-à-vis behaviour to have a peaceful life to the aim of Ananda in this mundane world amidst the lure to enjoy innumerable sense-objects. Readers may ask as to how could one visualize the realities of the body by studying an epic tale? The answer is, yes, it is possible as the Mahabharata is a treasure-trove but locked. The readers are required to unlock it and the keys to the locks have been provided by the author in a subtle way in the epic itself. Consider the title of this epic first, the Mahabharata. In Sanskrit the term 'maha' is an adjective meaning transcendent, exalted, majestic etc, the term 'bha' means knowledge and the term 'rata' means engaged in, devoted to etc. So, the title means one who is engaged in that exalted knowledge, not a tale of a great geographical land mass, Bharata which was much larger a land than what it is now. But what is that exalted knowledge and how to attain it? In this phenomenal world we lead a life armed with phenomenal knowledge which is termed as maya jnana or jada jnana. This is the lowest state of knowledge and there are six other states of it. They are the knowledge of realities (tattva jnana), the pure knowledge (Vishuddha jnana), the knowledge of the Self (atma jnana), the knowledge of Brahman (Brahma jnana), the divine knowledge (Divya jnana) and the maha jnana (Exalted knowledge). The humans have the potentiality to attain this great or exalted knowledge passing through other states of it and that had unequivocally been proclaimed by Lord Krishna in His song sung by Him before Arjuna (known to be the Bhagavat Geeta) in the Bhishma Parva of the epic.

Secondly, there is a myth that after resolving to write this epic Vyasa was in search of a writer to take down his dictations. He was advised by Brahma to take the help of Lord Ganesha, the god of knowledge and success. But when the god was approached he said that he would not pause for a while even in course of writing, rather continue. This reply from Ganesha posed a problem for Vyasa. He then asked Ganesha to write down his slokas (couplets) fully understanding them and Ganesha agreed. Then he began to dictate some critical slokas off and on which compelled Ganesha to pause for some time to understand them and meanwhile Vyasa could prepare some other slokas to dictate. Those critical slokas are known to be the 'Vyasa Kuta' (critical ones by Vyasa). The myth may be true or not but they say, Vyasa Kuta is there in the text. The readers should be mindful of it.

Thirdly, the epic is divided in eighteen Parvas (cantos). The War of Kurukshetra continued for eighteen days and the men fought the war were eighteen aukshahini in number. So there is a clear emphasis on the number eighteen. But why this emphasis on the number eighteen? There are eighteen centres of eros in the human body which stand in the way of austerity of men and women to attain Truth. Hence they require to be dominated by the austerer by restraining them. So this emphasis on the number eighteen.

Fourthly, to dominate over the centres of eros one needs to identify them first in one's own body and then to take steps to contain them. So one is required to know of the realities of the body to identify them in the body. Anyone aspiring to realize Truth is expected to know the realities of the body — their beneficence and malfeasance, actions and reactions etc. Added to this the basic knowledge of the reality of creation (srishtitattva) is also necessary.

Fifthly, relying on the phenomenal knowledge only one cannot be endowed with the realization of the ultimate Truth. So there is the necessity to strive for the progression of understanding passing through the layers of knowledge and this journey through knowledge is known to be austerity that is necessary to be endued with knowledge for which there are three ways — of yoga, of knowledge and of devotion and also that of karma (action) common to former three. But those ways are not known to you nor can you independently perform your austerity in a way that in necessitated.

Sixthly, if you aspire to undertake this journey to achieve the goal you are to seek the guidance of one to know the ways, who happens to be your Guru and you are to obey his dictates in letter and spirit to be successful in your bid. But you are not required to go here and there in search of your Guru, rather he himself will knock at your door to grace you if your quest is earnest enough.

Seventhly, we, the beings lead our life depending upon our material cognizance. So in general, most of us live a three dimensional life pertaining to food, sleep and coition. These three are not unknown to us but there are other dimensions of which most of us know very little or nothing. Such a dimension is time. We build the edifice of time present upon the scaffolding provided by the time past to be successful and happy in the time future. Therefore, the time past and the time future play a significant role for our time present. But what is the time present? Every moment of time future is becoming the time present to turn to be the time past in a wink. Yet we talk of time present taking a greater part of the time past into account to identify our time present while the time future ceaselessly is turning to be the time past. So the time present appears to be a mysterious non-existent existence, if not a conundrum. Again, we cannot draw a dividing line between time present and time future nor can we do so between time past and time present; yet we are very much accustomed to the three states of time viz. past, present and future.

Then what is time? Time is an absolute existence, indefinable, imperishable and all pervasive that monitors the progressive evolution of matter and devours the consequences of it and sustains them as their repository. It is imperceptible by the senses nor can the sense-organs touch or grasp it, but to be perceived by intellection only. Who then created the states of time? The answer is the man and under his own compulsion. Otherwise, it is absolute, a complete whole, all pervasive and indivisible existence being unborn as Consciousness is.

Had this been so, why then the man was impelled to divide this absolute and all pervasive existence into three states? What were the principal considerations to do so? Those who did it, did on the prime consideration that time moves and moves forward to the immeasurable future. But does time really move or has its own motion? The answer is an emphatic no. One of the preconditions of motion is space, but as time is omnipresent no space could be available for its movement from one point to another. Again, time itself is another precondition of motion. How time would measure the motion of it in no space provided to it. Therefore the concept of motion of time is not correct but fallacious.

On the other hand, it is matter that has motion and matter moves in time and space. The matter gained its motion since the cosmogenesis and the transformation of matter through the course of evolution is monitored by time. This act of monitoring has been erroneously taken by us to be the motion of time. Time is formless, it is not a matter, it is absolute and omnipresent.

The belief in the motion of time is a notional one and a fallacy too. The motion of matter in course of evolution is an undeniable fact. So long the matter exists, it is bound to evolve by Natural Law and at the same time its progress in course of evolution is monitored by all pervasive time which stores all previous states of matter to be sustained in its womb. Hence the time past is the repository of all the previous states of matter including its primordial state i.e. the seed. And human wisdom is capable of reaching that state of 'seed' retracing the steps in time past and at the same time the wisdom may move forward in time future to visualize its culmination. Then and then only one can properly realize that time is indivisible, all pervasive and constant. This time is the fourth dimension of life. This absolute, eternal time is symbolized as the third of the Hindu Trinity — Mahakala (The Destroyer of all forms). Lord Shiva.

Eighthly, Consciousness is Omnipresent, unborn and imperishable. The energy of Consciousness is responsible for creation, evolution and culmination of matter and beings that have been created of that Golden Egg. Consciousness and its energy are inescapable and hence they are synonymous. Consciousness incarnates itself as and when necessary for the creation. In Sanatana Dharma such incarnations are known to be Avataras who through their Leela uphold Dharma from time to time as a Universal Teacher to mankind. Consciousness is there in this epic in the form of Krishna being the Teacher, the Guide and Guru to mankind being the fifth dimension of life of beings. This Consciousness is not only a dimension of life of beings alone but also the dimension of matter. One may question as to how could Consciousness be the dimension of matter? It is a fact that in case of absence of Consciousness in it, the matter is sure to disintegrate for lack of bonding between the molecules of it and resultantly matters would have been non-existent. So Consciousness is not only responsible for the existence of matter but it settles also for the shape and size and its existence as such.

To comprehend the epic in its proper perspective one is required to keep in mind these points discussed heretofore as they are the keys to unlock this treasure trove.

Taking the cue from history Vyasa has authored this epic, of course, using myths as well. But the epic is highly allegorical and full of symbolism. As we have said earlier that the characters though seem to be historical, actually they are not humans but the realities of the human body. They have been provided with flesh and blood along with the attributes of human character to manifest their dharma under the given circumstances exposing the dimensional attitude and behaviour which may be evident to the readers while going through the text.

Now, one may question that if the characters manifest their own dharma why then we hear, "where Dharma prevails, there victory smiles" from time to time? We should not forget that though the characters appear before us in human form in the tale, actively they are not humans but realities of the human body and must manifest the dharma of the realities. When it is said, "Where dharma prevails, there victory smiles", the term 'dharma' pertains to the dharma of mankind. But alas, the realities are not humans and they stick to their own dharma which in many cases becomes antagonistic to the dharma of man. On the other hand, the realities are of two kinds. On the one, there are realities pertaining to knowledge and morality regarded to be divine, on the other, those pertaining to ignorance and demoniac qualities and the two sides are antagonistic to each other. The former group represents the divine qualities of human life while the latter group represents the demoniac qualities. The former group is represented by the realities of (1) the earth (Sahadeva), (2) the water (Nakula), (3) the fire (Arjuna), (4) the air (Bhima) and (5) the ether (Yudhisthera) led by the Solver, Krishna, the Incarnation of Supreme Consciousness. The other group is represented by cardinal passions viz. (1) Kama (desire-Duryodhana), (2) Krodha (wrath-Duhshasana), (3) Lobha (avarice-Karna), (4) Mada (assertiveness — (1) Drona, (2) Kripa and (3) Ashvathama), (5) Moha (delusion – Shakuni) and (6) Matsarya (ego – Bhishma). This group is led by the grandsire Bhishma. These two sides are antagonistic to each other and hence the conflict that ensues the war of Kurukshetra. It is noteworthy that while the divine side is established in the dharma of divinity, the other side manifests the demoniac dharma which is not congenial to manhood, while they all are present before us in human forms and expected to manifest manhood but they cannot do that as they are not humans but realities of the body and they stick to their own dharma which is demoniac. In this perspective the axiom said earlier be considered.

Again, like the epic poets of olden days, poet Vyasa himself is a character in the tale influencing the turns and twists in the progress of the argument. Vyasa, the character and Vyasa, the author do not of course, perform in the same way. The author is a visionary who envisions his creation as he likes to draw a final conclusion of the tale upto his delightful satisfaction while Vyasa the character plays the role of the fourth dimension of beings which is time. Whenever there arises any crisis he is present there to solve the problem and to ease the flow of events in the argument playing a vital role, be it Gandhari's motherhood or having her children from a hard block of flesh or the security of the Pandavas while they were running for safety consequent of the burning of the house of lac or inspiring them to have Draupadi by marriage etc. It is Vyasa the character, who is the symbol of Time Eternal and the fourth dimension of beings' life.

Again, Lord Krishna being the Supreme Consciousness incarnate is also a character in this epic. He is the embodiment of universal Guru who is Imperishable, Omnipresent and Eternal being the fifth dimension of beings.

We raised a question earlier regarding the inspiration that prompted Vyasa to write this epic poem even after completion of so many great works. Now we assume that with a view to offer to the human race a picture of the journey of life especially the human life evolving through the different stages of knowledge starting with the phenomenal knowledge to its ultimate culmination in the exalted knowledge to attain durable peace and eternal tranquility in the Ananda of Immortality.

Lastly, notwithstanding the indisputable greatness and importance of his earlier works, the Mahabharata appears to be Vyasa's magum opus and rightly regarded as the Fifth Veda by the wise.

The Birth Of Satyavaty

Now let us plunge into story starting with the birth of Satyavaty. She was born in the womb of a fish and was brought up by her foster father who was a fisherman. She was to ferry passengers and travellers from one bank to the other propelling her boat on the river Yamuna. She was to transport the passengers free of cost as ordered by her father; but she did never alight from the boat. One day she met with the great muni Parashara on board. The muni became charmed on seeing her beauty although the fisherman's daughter used to emit fishy smell from her body, yet the muni proposed to have her body to enjoy. Satyavaty though not unwilling altogether to the proposal, expressed her unwillingness feebly on two grounds that her virginity was sure to be impaired and the open ambience around. Parasara instantly refuted them saying that even after union with him her virginity would remain unimpaired and at the time of union he would create a mist to envelope them in such a way that they would not be visible by others. The union took place and as a result of which Krishna Dwaipayana was born. After his birth Dwaipayana left for austerity with his father leaving Satyavaty. On the other hand, Matsyagandha (of fishy smell) become Padmagandha (of lotus smell) being blessed by the muni and her virginity remained intact.

We have already said that in this epic tale all the dramatis personae are the realities (tattvas) which have been given human form and human character and this fact requires to be kept in mind, otherwise, we may err here and there. On the other hand, we should note that to present a human life complete in all respects, the author has used different terms in different circumstances to present the same truth in accordance to his requirement to fulfil his purpose using imagery and symbols, but in all cases the truth remains the same. This would be evident while we would discuss the birth of Satyavaty. As she is a human child, her birth should have been like other human children; but it has been described by the author allegorically using peculiar imagery although in all cases the same technique has not been applied. Yet the significance of the realities remain the same even in different perspectives. An eternal truth has been expressed in case of the birth of Satyavaty though veiled under an allegory while that of Parasara was also enveloped in another kind of allegory; in this case also the same eternal truth is there which we could see analyzing the birth of both of them.

Now we are to analyse the events relating to the birth of Girika, the so called step-mother of Satyavaty. Thus goes the tale: In the Puru dynasty there was a very religious king named Uparichara. His other name was Vasu. The king was very much fond of hunting. On the advice of Indra Uparichara acquired and became the king of the kingdom of Chedi. Indra advised him also to become a votary of his own dharma and then he would be pure and pious. Indra promised to give him a chariot made of crystal and on boarding it he could travel in the sky like the gods being a human though. He used to do this and hence his name was Uparichara.

There was a river named Suktimati near the capital of the kingdom. There was a conscious hill, Kolahala (cacophony) by name, which was very much lascivious and eager to enjoy that river Suktimati. This appeared to the king to be audacious and he kicked on his head as a result of which the hill was bifurcated and forthwith the stream of the river began to flow with a greater speed. Then a son and a daughter were born in the river bed. The river offered them to the king satisfactorily. The king appointed the son in his army and accepted the daughter as his wife.

How strange is it that a hill is desirous to have coition with a river!

The story says, there was a river near the capital of Chedi Kingdom and its name was Suktimati. Oyster is called 'Sukti' in Sanskrit that contains mother of pearls in it. In terms of the realities of human body Suktimati is the feminine genital organ that has a similarity with the shape and character of an oyster which may open and shut at times. But how could this organ be a river? This is a sense-organ having the activity of excreting unnecessary fluid of the body known to be urine and also other fluids at times. The passage through which fluids flow at a regular measure is known to be a rivulet or a stream or a river. So the river Suktimati is found out at last and this river flows near the kings capital, the uterus which is one of the most important organs of a feminine being and which is near the river. Now we are to find out the hill named Kolahala. It is the small erectile part of the female genitals at the anterior part of the vulva. It is a webbed object and its two parts get separated being pressed from outside. As it is highly sensitive, it spreads excitement throughout the organ. The king Uparichara observing it to be the seeker of coition with Suktimati, got angry and kicked heavily upon the head of it, instantly it cleft and through a duct below it, fluid came out forcibly into the passage of the organ. This is the coition of the hill with the organ Suktimati and as a result of this union twin babies were born in the womb of the river – one of them was a he child and the other a she baby. The king appointed the son in his army and took the other child as his wife.

What a mystery is it that a hill can procreate human children in the womb of a river?

Let us try to analyse the symbolical presentation of a universal fact. The King Uparichara is the personified passion. He is able to roam in the sky like a celestial body and his name is also Vasu, of course, none of the Vasus who are celestial ones. But who is Uparichara in our body? This phenomenal world is always perceived by the mind. Things that have a motion, that can change come under the purview of the mind. Any existence having no motion or change is beyond the mind. However, the highest point of this movement in the body is the Chitta (the faculty of thought perception and memory). Upon the field of this Chitta, manas (the mind), buddhi (the intelligence) and ahamkara (the ego) remain active and these four constitute the inner mind. Upon the chitta there appear the traits (vritti) always and the mind under the influence of those traits resolves to enjoy the sense-objects. But to execute the resolution, the mind entrusts buddhi (intelligence) to decide the ways and means. Then buddhi with the help of reasoning decides the means and conveys them to the mind which then with the help of senses and sense-organs executes its resolution and the ego enjoys the savours of those sense-objects. Therefore, to create a body out of another body the mind, intelligence, chitta, ahamkara, the other body and chitta have their distinctive roles. But the role of chitta is the foremost one and that of the mind, senses and sense-objects are secondary.

All the fruits of actions of mankind remain stored in the chitta in form of seeds which become expressive in favourable conditions to incite the mind. Under their influence, to enjoy sense-objects and making the mind resolve to act according to the dharma of the vrittis.

The mental trait that is desirous of enjoying the savours of erotic pleasure is the king Uparichara which has already been said. He is the king of the Chedi Kingdom which is a pleasant one and guarded by the gods. The kingdom is very much fertile provided sufficient rainfall occurs there. In absence of rainfall it is barren. The famine body capable to bear children, is the chedi kingdom. And an able man being inspired to procreate offsprings, nurtures this kingdom to have the benefit. But it needs rainfall to yield crops, otherwise nothing to gain. So rainfall in form of semen is a necessity to have the desired result. The capital of the kingdom is the uterus and the river Suktimati flows nearby. The uterus is the most important organ so far creation is concerned.

The story goes to say, once Girika the queen of Uparichara, after her menstrual period was over and taking a bath herself, invited the king. But on the same day the manes of the king ordered him to go for hunting. After a long hunting of games the king become tired and rested for a while under an Asoka true (Saraca Asoca or Saraca Indica) when thinking of Girika and her invitation suddenly he felt ejaculatory effect of his semen. He thought this semen should not be wasted rather be sent to his wife who invited him on the day. So placing the semen on a leaf he ordered a hawk to carry it to his wife Girika. The hawk started flying and in the mid-air another hawk thinking there should be some food on the leaf started fighting with the first one and during the scuffle the semen fell into the water of the Yamuna. There an apsara being cursed by Brahma, assuming the form of a fish was sporting and when the semen fell she gulped it at once.

Now let us explain the said facts in terms of realities of the human body. The menstruation in case of young females is a universal phenomenon and it takes place once in a lunar month when too much ova are created in the body. But how are they created? The food and drink that we take in regular course are digested with the body heat and the elixir of them turns into blood and the waste is excreted. Now, this blood being conditioned with the body heat turns into flesh which also being conditioned creates bones which again being conditioned in the same process creates marrow which again conditioned in the same way creates semen in case of males and ova in case of females. While semen rests in head after an ambulation through the whole body, the ova rest in the uterus after moving in the same way. Though created in the same manner they are different in nature. Hence they attract each other eternally. Both semen and ovum are food for each and take no time to swallow each other coming in contact but do not survive for a long time, rather die instantly. Yet if any of the ova or sperm survives even after gulping the other then the conception occurs.

Traditionally it is widely permissible to procreate children after the menstrual period is over. Hence the king Uparichara being called for by his wife, Girika, become very eagar to have the association of her. But meanwhile the manes ordered him to go for hunting. He obeyed. Here the game of hunting is but the acceleration of excitement of the famine body in question by kissing, embracing etc. But why did the order came from the manes? It suggests to do the act in the way as did his manes in the past, which is satisfactory enough. The King Uparichara obeyed the order and sat to rest under and Asoka tree (Saraca Indica). What is it that he had to rest in course of his action?

We have already said that semen rests in the head and for the purpose to create another body it had to be attracted therefrom. Being attracted it comes down through the spinal cord and for the time being rests in its sacs known to be the testicles and at the right time comes therefrom for ejaculation. This is the rest of King Uparichara under the Asoka tree. But wherefrom does come the tree and how? The male organ already penetrated into the passage of the female organ has its end near the inflated uterus which is supposed to be the foliage of a tree and the male organ is the trunk and semen is still there at its base. In Sanskrit the 'asoka' means devoid of grief and pining. Having them in mind one cannot do this act; it is for pleasure. When it is in the male organ and not yet ejaculated, the famine organ seeks to have the same but does not have it, then the rhythmic movement of the two bodies has been symbolically described as the struggle of two hawks. But when it is ejaculated, it fell in the water of the river Yamuna. At the time of coition the uterus becomes inflated being a little elongated and full of secretional fluid in which there was a cursed apsara having the form of a fish, Adrika by name who at once gulped the semen that fell into the Yamuna (uterus). But who is an apsara?

It is a myth that apsaras are semi-celestial bodies expert in music and dance with which they cast their spell to fascinate the gods in heaven. Who are those gods whom they enchant in this way? They are our senses. We have already said that the characteristics of semen and ova are diametrically opposite and hence they attract each other. Yet the ova rest in the uterus. It is said that they rest in the uterus being cursed by Brahma, the creator and Indra blessed her to be free from the curse after delivery of a human child from her womb. Brahma is the first of the Hindu Holy Trinity and Indra is the Lord of the celestial world.

Because of the power of attraction of ova, they are regarded as nautch girls and as they live and swim in the natatorium within the uterus they are called apsaras. In Sankrit the term 'ap' means water and 'sara' means to move and hence they are called apsaras. Actually they are ova in the uterus.

Having swallowed the semen of Uparichara, Adrika survived and began to enlarge day by day; meanwhile the passage of the uterus through which the sperm fell into it gets blocked. The ovum that swallowed the sperm begins to cover itself around with a thin and almost transparent membrane. Later on from the navel of the foetus a muscular cord connects it with the inner wall of the uterus through which the foetus gets its sustenance. Gradually the foetus evolves and grows. At the time of delivery the baby comes out of its mother's womb being enclosed in that sac of fine membrane having the umbilical cord attached to it, that seems to be a fish caught in a cast-net and the umbilical cord appears to be the cord of that net. Therefore the fisherman got two human babies cutting open a bigger fish.

The fisherman brought the babies to the king who took the he baby as the future king of his kingdom and offered the she baby to the fisherman who took her to be his own daughter and she is Matsyagandha (fishy smell) Satyavaty. Later on the king's son became the king of the kingdom of Matsya and the daughter of the fisherman became a ferry woman.

Satyavaty is introduced to the readers as a grown up woman in charge of ferrying passengers from one bank of the Yamuna to the other, of course, at the behest of her foster father. Who is Satyavaty in terms of realities (tattva) of human body? Satyavaty is the phenomenal nature. Nature is always fully grown when we come in contact with it, be it phenomenal or otherwise. Now Satyavaty is a young woman working for the welfare of the society. She ferries travellers and passengers. Once the great muni Parasara met with her on board.

We have already said that Satyavaty is the phenomenal nature. She ferries travellers from one bank of the Yamuna to the other. But she does not descend on land from her boat. One bank of the river is the symbol of birth while the other is that of death. The boat symbolizes the human body that is guided by the phenomenal nature. She cannot alight from the boat as in that case the body will lose its guidance. And Parasara meeting with her became so enamoured that he sought her body then and there to enjoy. The young Satyavaty was at once in a fix — she could neither refuse nor ascent. Cleverly she took the middle path saying that she was still a virgin under the guardianship of her father and the openness on board, the event would be visible to the munis, rishis and common people waiting on both the banks, which was not at all desirable. But the muni refuted her objections saying that even after union with him Satyavaty's virginity would remain unimpaired and he would create so dense a mist around them that nobody could visualize the event. Now Satyavaty had to agree to the proposal of the muni. The union then took place and the outcome was the birth of Krishna Dwaipayana who immediately after his birth left his mother for austerity and went away with his father. Vyasa has presented the narrative in such a manner that going through it almost everybody would surmise that Parasara raped the innocent fisherman's girl and victimisid her for ever. But it was not that; we would discuss it later on. Now let us have the identity of Parasara.

The Tale Of Parashara

The vengeful Vishvamitra killed the hundred sons of Vashistha. The grief stricken father resolved to kill himself by drowning in the river Beas, but failed as the river was short of sufficient water. He was returning home with a distracted mind. Suddenly he heard the recitation of Vedic hymns behind him. He looked back and saw his eldest daughter-in-law was following him at a distance. He asked her, "who is reciting the Vedic hymns?" In reply his daughter-in-law, the wife of Shaktri told him, at the time of her husband's death she was carrying and their son was reciting them being within his mother's womb for long twelve years. And this son of Shaktri was Parasara, the grandson of Vashistha.

How could a human child remain in his mother's womb for twelve years and how could he get mastery over the Vedas which required to be taught by an able teacher? Where and how could he get the teacher to train him in the Vedas in his mother's womb? It seems to be a critical enigma. But it is not an enigma at all. Parasara studied the Vedas as other students of his time did and do in present time also. He too studied the Vedas being within the veil of maya as other students did and also do now-a-days. This veil of Maya has metaphorically been said as mother's womb. Maya is also the mother of us all and she protects us as a mother does. It can never be seen and hence her name is Adrisyanti (invisible).

Parasara studied the six-part Vedas. In Sanskit the word 'Vid' means to know and the term 'veda' denotes knowledge; but what kind of knowledge is it? The Vedas contain the knowledge of the phenomenal world that could be acquired through the mind and senses and its range is upto the door step of the Divine knowledge as God or Brahman is beyond the Vedas. One is supposed to study the Vedas to go beyond them. However, Parasara studied them in six parts, viz. 1) Siksha, 2) Kalpa, 3) Vyakarana, 4) Nirukta, 5) Chhanda and 6) Jyotisha.

The first part is siksha which denotes learning. One is to select the subject first and then to decide the way to acquire knowledge on the subject. On the other hand, immediately after birth the human child comes under the purview of Maya the first duty of which is to create illusion regarding Truth and make it oblivious of It. The existence that springs of Truth, becomes forgetful of It. The phenomenal world becomes true to him. He begins to grow up with this conviction and leads the life remaining unaware about the dividing wall between the existence of beings and Truth. Under the influence of Maya beings are after earning money and fame and to get a good footing in life that he may get but this type of education in the world of Maya cannot give him peace. On the other hand, it is to know of his own role amidst immense diversity of creation that he is destined to know. But he is ignorant of it as it is beyond the knowledge he has since acquired and hence the phenomenal world around him appears to be the truth. It is truth indeed, but relative, not absolute. Yet it is the manifestation of the Absolute that has to be realized ultimately, accepting this relative truth and one is to learn the ways and means as to how this mission be fulfilled.

The next one is Kalpa meaning manifestation, rather formal manifestation. The formal manifestation of Absolute Truth is the Kalpa. The immeasurable universe is the existence of the Absolute Being in whom the seeds for creation of this universe were there and even after the creation of it that Absoluteness was by no means disturbed. On the other hand, every human being is destined to realize that Absolute Being and to do that one has to know the universe i.e. to know the Creator through His creation and there is no other way. But life is very much shorter in comparison to that of the universe and also its vastness is incomprehensible. But the elements that made the universe, are there in human body too; it is the microcosm of the macrocosmic universe. Therefore to unravel the mystery of creation one has to follow the course of it in respect of one's own body. The other meaning of the term 'Kalpa' is the principles of sacrifice. As the creation of the universe is a sacrifice so also the creation of this body is a sacrifice. So knowing the principles of creation of human body one may attain the Truth. This is the second part of the Vedas to learn.

The third part of the Vedas is called "Vyakarana" which literally means the grammar that is the science of language. But the term has been used here with a different connotation having a different perspective, nor does it point to the Mughdhavodha or Panini either. It refers to specially ordained action (Vishesa Karana Karma). But what is that? To fulfil the human aspirations one is bound to perform such actions that will lead one to attain the aspired goal. Such actions are the manifestation of man's manhood, the inspiration of which comes from the core of his heart and leads him to a better understanding step by step in his quest to unravel the mystery of creation culminating in realization.

And finally he becomes able to attain his goal. This is the science of action known to be 'Vyakarana'.

The fourth part of the Vedas is the "Nirukta" which means not said or uttered. It has another meaning — the unmanifest. In this immeasurable universe everything is manifest. Then which is the unmanifest that we are to know? As this universe is full of consciousness and it is an accepted fact, likewise it is also full of vitality. The activities of the vital energy are apparently intelligible to us but the principles of that are not. But the activities of five vital breaths manifest the Self within the body. The Self encased in the body is at the root of the performance of the vital breaths. The five vital breaths being active with the energy of the Self keep us alive and active but we are not much conscious of it. Analyzing the activities of the vital breaths in the body separately we may have an idea of the Self and our knowledge in this respect will enrich us regarding the Self. The five breaths being divided into forty-nine act within the body which is totally unknown to most of us. But if we could know the activity of each of these forty-nine breaths (air) we could know much of our body as well as the Self too. To learn this is to learn "Nirukta".

The fifth part is Chhanda meaning rhythm. To make a flow of sound sweet and beautiful, pause and metre are used gracefully. They are the gifts of rhythm. Not only it is used in poetry and music, dance and painting but also in other forms of art to make them pleasant and beautiful. It is said that the creation consists of sixty-four kinds of arts and in each of them rhythm is existent to make it beautiful and pleasant. The aggregate of these sixty-four arts is variously rhythmic and harmonious. The sense of sweetness and measured pause are its main criteria. The science which enlightens you in your ordained actions with sweetness and elegance, is the science of rhythm.

The last part is Jyotisa (astrology). The millions of stars and planets are orbiting larger stars as well as rotating round their axis in the space of which we know very little. Some of them are luminous but others not. They all are floating and those which have no light of their own are lighted by the brighter stars nearby. These heavenly bodies are very much different from what we see around; they are really unknown to us and arouse awe and wonder. The vastness of their appearance, swift speed, large orbit, their radiance and diffusion of heat speak of the littleness of our humble existence here on earth. At the same time they are different from each other. Immense is their significance that seems to be incomprehensible. The knowledge of these unearthly bodies is called that of Jyotisa that teaches an individual to be humble and modest.

All these six branches of the Vedas are there in the human body which require to be learnt within the body as the life is too short to learn them externally. Now let us see how they are existent in the human body. This body is held erect by the spinal cord having three very important arteries viz. Ida, Pingala and Susumna. There are six nerve-centres in it, through which consciousness reveals itself remaining active in them and phenomenal consciousness passing through these nerve-centres becomes finally dissolved into Supreme Consciousness and that is the prime aim of life. And to achieve that goal one has to study the Vedas to learn the significance of life in the perspective of the immeasurable universe. So he asks himself, "who am I?" "why am I?" "where am I to go?" "whom do I belong to?" To get the answers to these questions a man has to undergo training in certain disciplines and hence the learning has been given the first place. In ancient India this learning was divided into four viz. 1) Brahmacharya (pre-marital disciplined way of life), 2) Garhasthya (disciplined family life), 3) Vanaprasatha (in advanced years one should leave one's home and hearth and go to the forest to pass the remaining days of one's life in spiritual meditation), 4) Sannyasa (ascesis).

The revelation of consciousness of the lowest nerve-centre is of four kinds. The body has also four directions, the lower part of the body from the navel is the direction of the south while the upper part of the body is the north, the front side is that of the east and the back side is the west. The direction of the north signifies gradual progress and the south is for waste or loss and downfall. The east signifies knowledge and the west stands for ignorance. In modern times these divisions are not in vogue but the Garhasthya (family life) retains the remaining three in it. The directions of the body have not been changed nor their significance either. However, according to Vedas learning consists of these four subjects — a) Conscience, b) Detachment, (c) Valuable possession viz. 1) Restraint of external senses, 2) Restraint of internal senses, 3) Forbearance, 4) Faith (shraddha), 5) Uparati (Love for the adorable one), 6) solver and (d) urge for liberation.

The second part of learning is the Kalpa (sacrifice). Since the beginning till the dissolution of the universe in Brahman is a sacrifice. It contains the creation, evolution of creation and finally dissolution. We have already said that the human body is also a Kalpa and all the faculties of it are there in human body. These faculties are six viz. a) birth, b) existence,

c) growth, d) change, e) waste or loss, f) death. Firstly, birth — it takes place from another body and having an identity that has a particular time under given circumstances. After birth, the born gradually becomes conscious of its existence (asti). The seeker of knowledge should know of this. The body coming into existence begins to grow and the growth continues for a long period of time and one is required to observe this growth. That which grows, is subject to change and this has also to be observed. Again, that which has growth and change, is sure to waste and the body also faces loss that should be observed. That which is born and has the loss is subject to death. These six aspects of life are to be known by the seeker of knowledge and the second nerve-centre of the spinal cord manifests consciousness in six ways.

The third nerve centre contains Vyakarana (grammar), which manifests consciousness in different ways to different directions and from this centre the phenomenal cognition begins to purify. After being trained in the sacrifice and sacrificial rules the austere person needs to cross over certain steps of knowledge regarding creation. These steps of knowledge are seven and passing over these seven steps if anybody reaches the eighth, his realization enlightens him regarding all this. This process is known to be Viloma Darshna meaning the vision in reverse order. And to achieve this state one has to perform ordained deeds (Vishesa Karma) being inspired by the urge to know the unknown. This lesson is the gift of the third nerve centre of the spinal cord.

Having been enriched with the lesson of the third never-centre when one looks at one's body and sees that the body is full of vitality. Then one tries to find out the source of its vitality, as the manifestation of vital energy could be visualized but the source of its activities within the body remains unknown. On the other hand, the aggregate of the activities of five vital breaths is the manifestation of the Self or Atman. So in quest of finding out the source, an austere person has to analyse the manifestation of the vital energy and in course of doing so he comes to know that the ten senses and six impulses are instrumental for manifestation of the vital energy.

Then he engages himself in analyzing the characters (dharma) of these senses and impulses and when he learns all this he becomes wise of the source. This consciousness is the gift of the fourth nerve-centre. The manifestation of consciousness of this nerve-centre is in sixteen ways.

After acquiring knowledge about learning, sacrifice, ordained deeds and vital energy (nirukta) the austere person observes that his so acquired knowledge is scattered to many a direction and still the source of this knowledge is unknown to him. Meanwhile he has learnt that his body made of twenty-four elements, is actually a conglomerate of sixty-four attributions (Kala) — they are twenty-four elements, twenty-five realities of admixture of five elements (Panchikarana), five energies (tapa) and ten directions. Even after knowing the attributions and their manifestations, their source still remains unknown to him and he is to know that. So, with a view to know that source he endeavours to draw those scattered knowledges to their source knowing it well that the scattered knowledges are actually rhythmic manifestation of the same knowledge expressed in different characters rhythmically. And knowledge about rhythm is the gift of the fifth nerve-centre which manifests consciousness in sixty-four ways.

When one endeavours to put all scattered knowledge to their centre or source one cannot do it at once. There are certain norms to follow and after persistent efforts the austere person can do it drawing all such scattered knowledges to a single point in the sixth nerve-centre and then in the clean mirror of the chitta (faculty of thought perception and memory) he visualizes the divine esses of the Lord, which are synonymous with the luminous celestial bodies in the space. The chitta is the sky and the divine esses are the stars and planets. This is the lesson of jyotish (astrology).

Of course, this knowledge is called Apara Jnana meaning not the knowledge of the Supreme, Yet it is necessary to have it with a purpose of overcoming it for the knowledge of the Supreme, which is beyond mind and intelligence and which cannot be acquired but dawns on human heart. However, Parasara studied the six-part Vedas for twelve years being within his mother's womb. What could be more surprising than this? But it is not at all surprising. Parasara studied the Vedas living in this material world being confined by the influence of Maya (illusion) as did other students too. So long knowledge does not dawn, Maya remains to be the mother of beings. We all are children of Maya and it is a form of Prakriti (Nature) and provides us with sustenance as a mother does. So Parasara studied the Vedas in his mother's womb. And he did it for twelve years. In Sanskrit the term 'varsa' has two meanings — one being a year and the other is the field e.g. Bharatavasa (the land of the Bharatas). On the other hand, knowledge has two sides of it, one is to acquire and the other is to apply. The knowledge that Parasara acquired through his study of the Vedas extraneously, had applied it introspectively and without doing so neither knowledge be purified nor could there any refinement of consciousness of the seeker of knowledge. Hence he studied the Vedas for twelve years and being in the mother's womb i.e. in Maya's womb. Maya can never be seen; hence his mother's name is Adrishyanti (invisible) and his birth from Maya's womb points to the fact that he has overcome Maya on the strength of his realization and became a Muni. His name is Parasara meaning endowed with the para jnana (knowledge of the Supreme) and who could shoot the shafts of that knowledge to blot out the ignorance of others who deserve it.

The story goes to say, the great muni Parasara met with the ferry woman on board a boat on the river Yamuna and at the first sight the muni was so smitten with desire that he at once wanted to enjoy her body. But the woman being a virgin was under the guardianship of her father and was not allowed to do anything without her father's permission.

Added to this, the open ambience around the boat was also a hindrance to the act. Moreover, on both of the banks of the river there were waiting passengers including the munis and rishis who might visualize the event and that would by no means be glorifying. But the resolute muni retorted that he would enshroud the boat with a mist and nothing would be visible from outside and after the union with him the virginity of Satyavaty would not be impaired. Now Satyavaty had no other option but to agree to the proposal of the muni. The union took place and Satyavaty delivered a son in due course on an island of the Yamuna on the advice of Parasara. Owing to his dark complexion the son was named Krishna and being born on an island (dweep) he became Dwaipayana.

Some scholars think that taking advantage of the situation the fisherwoman was raped by a clever Brahmin who was but a muni of the stature of Parasara and it was certainly a blot on his character while the innocent fisherwoman was wronged for ever. But the author of the Mahabharata did not mean that regarding his own birth. The incident that took place on board the boat being enshrouded was but the initiation (diksha) of Satyavaty by her Guru Parasara. It is customary that the act of initiation should not be seen by any third person and hence the mist was required nor did Satyavaty alight from the boat. But why was her initiation so necessary? We have already said that Satyavaty is phenomenal nature and her consciousness was out and out related to physical matter only. The phenomenal nature is synonymous with maya. The consciousness of the phenomenal nature needs sanctitude, otherwise in the future course of creation beings would not be able to progress so far consciousness is concerned. Hence the seed of this progression has got to be imbued into the heart of the phenomenal nature.

The act of initiation takes place in seclusion where the Guru and his would-be disciple would be there. After observing certain formalities the would-be disciple should worship the Guru completed with a pranama (making obeisance by lying prostrate at his feet). Then both of them sit face to face. The Guru puts his right hand upon the disciple's head and pronounces the mantra thrice which the disciple also recites in unison, taking his face near the ear of the disciple and finally whiffs thrice. The significance of this act is the Guru is Purusha (masculine) and the disciple is a female being whoever he or she may be. The passage of the ear of the disciple stands for genital passage, the tongue of the Guru is the male organ and the mantra is the seed (of Brahman) thrown into the womb of the heart (brain) so that the disciple could conceive and the progeny delivered in due course, is the realization of Truth; but in this case the delivery took place in an island in the Yamuna, the symbol of the flow of life and the island is the faith (shraddha).

This fact does not speak of the rape of Satyavaty by the muni nor is he a rapist as perceived by someones.

We can now safely conclude that there took place the union of Satyavaty and Parasara on board the boat and Satyavaty became a mother indeed but the new born son left the Virgin mother with his so called father for austerity. But why? In the world of matter Satyavaty is the phenomenal nature and creation is in its nascent stage. The sequence of creation would have been hampered had the son been associated with his mother. Moreover, the realization of Truth in phenomenal world appears to be incongruous always upholding Truth as it is the sphere of maya. Hence he is said to be dark complexioned. He is the embodiment of attraction, cultivation and detraction corresponding to knowledge, devotion and surrendering respectively culminating into bliss. Bliss can never be attached to the sense-objects in the phenomenal world and hence Krishna Dwaipayana remains away from his mother vis-à-vis the material world. That is why it has been said that he left his mother for austerity. But actual separation did never take place. He was ever alert to serve her at any point of time. The mother remained as she was although by the grace of her Guru she became lotus-smelled woman instead of one with fishy-smell. Once Satyavaty met with the game-hunting King of Hastinapura and both of them fell in love at the first sight.

Ganga, Shantanu & The Vasus

The tale tells us that the truthful king Mahabhisa because of earning a good amount of piety became eligible for heavenly abode. Once Ganga came to see Brahma where among other gods Mahabhisa was also present. Suddenly a waft of wind took away the cover of her body in the front.

The gods present there stooped instantly. But Mahabhisa began to obseve the scene eagerly and that was not overlooked by Brahma. He at once ordered him a human birth and thereafter he would again be eligible for heavenly abode. Thus punished Mahabhisa began to think over as to whom should he take for his father. After a lot of thinking he decided to be fathered by Pratipa. Actually that happened and he became the son of Pratipa and known to be as Shantanu. Pratipa was an austere king who engaged himself in austerity to have a son, along with his wife on the bank of the river Ganga. Later on he became the father of a son and this son is Shantanu.

Once while the king was in deep meditation on the bank of the Ganga, the goddess assuming the form of a beautiful young lady came to him and sat on his right thigh and begged love of him. The king replied that he was initiated to a vow and he was unable to commit such an irreligious act at that state. Ganga said, she was a divine lady. His union with her would not harm his vow. But the king could not assent to her proposal and to strengthen his position he said, to fulfil her desire Ganga selected her seat meant for sons and daughters and hence the bond between them was one of filial affection and not of love. Therefore, the union with her was impossible. Of course, the king took her as his daughter-in-law. When his son would be born, her marriage with him would not be impossible and he would ask the son to take her as his wife and he was confident that his son would obey him. Ganga was satisfied and left the king. Later on, the king became the father of a son and obeying his father the son took Ganga as his wife.

Now here is a new twist. While Ganga was returning from Brahma's she saw the Vasus swooned and crippled on her wayside. She became curious to know of their such deplorable physical state. The Vasus said, they passed by the muni Vashistha without recognizing him and not paying due regards to him and that made the muni wrathful and he cursed them to have human birth.

They did not like to be born of an ordinary woman but preferred a goddess to be their mother. They requested Ganga to be their mother but on the condition that the newborns be abandoned in the river Ganga so that they were not supposed to endure life on earth for a longer time. Ganga accepted the Vasus' proposal but asked them to find out ways and means to save at least one of the sons as her future husband would like to have one. Meanwhile, Ganga had known that Shantanu would be her husband. She came to know that Pratipa's son would be Mahabhisa in other form to be known as Shantanu who would be her husband and would be the progenitor of her eight sons of whom one would be living. Now the plan is complete and Ganga came to meditating Pratipa, sitting on whose right thigh she won his promise to accept her as his daughter-in-law. Ganga's mission was partially successful.

Now, who is Pratipa? He is Viloma Darshana meaning the Vision of journey of human consciousness starting from its ordinary state to attain the Supreme Consciousness. It is the opposite to Anuloma Darshana depicting the Vision of journey of human life through the course of evolution, sprung of the Supreme. While Shantanu is the embodiment of actionless Supreme Consciousness, Ganga is Chaitanya Shakti i.e. the active energy of the Supreme Consciousness. The creation is possible with the union of active energy and Supreme Consciousness. It may be questioned as to why Viloma Darshana i.e. the vision of the journey to Ultimale Reality from ordinary consciousness is referred to as till now the creation of humankind has not taken place. It is correct and it is also correct that Viloma Darshana begins from the end-point of Anuloma Darshana which had not yet been totally manifested. But we should keep it in mind that the source of creation contained not only the seeds of creation of beings, animals, birds and insects only. It also contained the seeds of every esse, thought, trait, impulse including that of knowledge, faith, love, reality, austerity etc. and manifestation of them took place in due course when necessary through the process of evolution and culmination of all of them was in the creation of human life. Only man can realize this truth through Viloma Dorshana. Prior to the creation of human life there was none to question the significance of actionless Supreme Consciousness and the active Energy of that Consciousness nor could there be anybody to realize the both. Hence Viloma Darshana has been designated as the father of actionless Supreme

Consciousness and the father like persona of active Energy of Supreme consciousness.

However, Pratipa became the father of a son named Shantanu who being grown up later on, married Ganga on her condition that he should never raise any objection to any of her deeds or behaviour and if at all that happened, she would leave him. Shantanu agreed, but the condition had no relation to the promise of Pratipa. Ganga needed the union of Mahabhisa in form of Shantanu and the love-sick king accepted the condition inspired by her promise to the Vasus and that was unknown to Shantanu. In her married life Ganga gave birth to seven sons whom she abandoned in the river Ganga, Shantanu could not make out the reasons for such an abnormal behaviour of a mother. He could not hold his patience any further and asked not to abandon the eighth son after his birth. Ganga obeyed but left Shantanu.

The seven sons whom Ganga abandoned just after their birth were all Vasus. Her eighth son was also a Vasu who was saved. The term Vasu literally means the earth. Here the Vasus are the embodiments of serious oaths to overcome the earth like impediments to austerity; the eighth one Devavrata was not an exception. An austere person may establish himself in Truth overcoming the impediments that are nothing but our ignoranance which build an almost invincible wall between Truth and ignorance. And the Vasus in ourselves make us take oath to overcome that impediments step by step finally to succeed at last. The first Vasu is the oath of virtuosity to decide between the virtuous and pleasurable. Ordinary men and women are always eager to satiate their desires being inspired by their impulses and senses under the guidance of their mind and actions do not ensure their peace of mind nor do they enhance their knowledge of the Creator, their final abode. Hence it is required to consider the fruits of actions performed. A spiritual person needs to know of the fruits of actions performed by him and he should have to take oath to perform virtuous actions leaving aside the deeds of enjoyment of sense-objects as far as practicable. This first oath is the first vasu.

Now, the second one. In course of covering a long distance, a traveller needs rest in a tavern and in that case he aims to reach the first tavern to rest and then he starts to reach the second one. Thus the traveller resting in an inn, aims to reach the next one. Here the fact is not otherwise. The first Vasu's oath is his resolution to perform the actions inspired by virtuosity. To overcome the influence of pleasure, one needs to deliberate between pleasurable and virtuous actions but between what is duty and what not. Of course, pleasurable actions are not always despicable. The mode of austerity that springs out of service and bringing up the little ones, is of the knowledge of virtuosity and the beings become conscious of having pleasure by any means and then their consciousness makes them resolve to start for the next stage. The oath of the second Vasu is to accept wisdom as his refuge which is far better than worldly wealth and with the knowledge of this superiority of wisdom to worldly wealth, the austere person reaches the third stage.

The knowledge of superiority of wisdom and to own it are not the same thing. Knowledge of whatever kind it may be, it is about some subject or object. Wisdom means purified knowledge which does not contain that relating to any sense-object or any physical matter. Knowledge acquired through the mind, the senses and the intelligence, does not come under the purview of wisdom. The knowledge that relates to Atman or Supreme Self is the wisdom which cannot be acquired by the mind and intelligence. It dawns upon the human heart (Hridaya). To know the unknown is knowledge and when it is perfect in all respect, it becomes wisdom. And which is the subject of wisdom? It is Atman. To know about the Omnipresent Atman and the way to know of Atman are the two necessary conditions to be wise. Therefore, the oath of the third Vasu is to know Atman and also to know the way to It.

To know of the ways and means for something does not assure attainment of the goal for which they were meant. One is to progress towards the aim covering the distance for the purpose. It needs to have a firm determination and requires spiritual yoga as also performance of ordained deeds resolutely so that one may be gradually established in manhood and analyzing his own actions at a regular measure one comes to know of the results of them and what is beyond all this and then one takes the vow to do only ordained duties that leads one to the next stage of knowledge. This vow is that of the fourth vasu.

Beings act and act incessantly; actions have their fruits also. Generally there is no way to evade the endurance of those fruits of actions. Is there any action the performance of which enables a person to be endowed with the knowledge of Atman? And if there be any, how to perform it? Generally beings become active being inspired by impulses and to satiate desires for enjoyment of sense-objects, for fame and wealth. All these actions ensures fruits of them which the beings endure in pain and pleasure. At the time of enduring the fruits of past actions, beings are to be conscious about not to earn further fruits of actions. But every action has its fruit. Then is there any action that does not ensure endurance of any result? Yes, there is; it is the action performed being dictated by conscience (Vivek) that does not bear any fruit and it is known to be ordained action. The performance of ordained deeds is synonymous with Brahmacharya and that may enable the austere person endowed with the indirect knowledge regarding Atman.

Brahman being the Creator of the immeasurable universe, its destroyer and also the Lord of its existence, is Omnipresent in and out of it, yet he is differentiated from the universe. In the perspective of the universe he is the Absolute Lord of it. Beings armed with material understanding are the lords of their own lives. But those who act being inspired by the conscience, perform ordained acts that are synonymous with brahmacharya which enlightens them with the knowledge of eternal Atman. To know Eternal Atman performing only ordained actions is the oath of the fifth Vasu.

It has already been said that being inseparable from and identical with the universe, Brahman is actually distinct from it. Again, the cognition of eternal Atman denotes that same Brahman has manifested himself as the universe being Omnipresent in it and existing as Eternal Atman in the universe, is responsible for the evolution of the creation and drawing its culmination through changes although He is never subject to any change, having gunas in Him, He is beyond the gunas and having manifested Himself as the universe, and yet He is formless and therein lies the difference between Brahman and the universe. Of course this knowledge of difference is an indirect one and is a mystery.

Until a spiritual aspirant can solve this mystery, he cannot get at the goal. So to solve this mystery the aspirant seeks to have the knowledge of Brahman and the way to attain the aim that seems to be of great necessity and therefore he resolves to be established in the knowledge of Brahman. This is the oath of the sixth Vasu.

The knowledge of Brahman are a few simple words to utter but not so simple to be endowed with it, although it is not impossible either. Brahman is manifested in immumerable forms as the universe and even then Brahman is Absolute. This knowledge cannot be acquired with the help of mind, intelligence and the senses. To be endowed with this knowledge an aspirant should strive to experience the differences of names, forms and qualifications only to be discarded to have the knowledge of oneness which is very much difficult as every physical existence is different from each other. But the aspirant seeks knowledge of oneness overcoming all differences; his aim is the knowledge of oneness. On the other hand, where there is knowledge there should be an object of knowledge. But Brahman is not an object but is the goal to be attained. The knowledge of Brahman is actual knowledge and any other knowledge in this perspective is but ignorance. The seeker of knowledge is the knower, Brahman is knowable. The aspirant of knowledge should know about the difference and similarity as well as relationship between the knower and knowable, the existence and truth. This resolve is the oath of the seventh Vasu.

We have already said that the knowledge of the Absolute dawns upon the field of faith (Vishwasa) spread upon the heart and upon this field also dawn Shraddha (loving admiration) and Bhakti (devotion) and they manifest in the behaviour of the aspirant. With the dawning of knowledge the spiritual aspirant becomes wise of the knowable; in other words, the existence is being wise of truth. Still then the aspirant is aware of the fact that he is knowing the knowable so long unknown to him, by his energy, his austerity and strenuous efforts. At this stage the aspirant is led by the 'I' consciousness and his goal is a separate existence. So long his 'I' inspired him in the quest of that Supreme being but he fails to realize that the Supreme is not beyond his 'I' nor is it excluded from the Supreme — the Total Existence. Hence the 'I' of the aspirant cannot be established in the knowledge of the Supreme. Maintaining the consciousness of 'I' and 'mine' the knowledge of the Supreme is a far cry. Therefore the 'I' consciousness is a barrier between the aspirant and the Supreme at this step of knowledge and hence the eighth Vasu was required to surrender his 'I'-consciousness for which we are to wait and we would know of his oath in future.

Now we should take a plunge into the story again. Here in the royal palace Ganga was abandoning her seven new-borns — all sons, into the stream of river Ganga, one by one. Shantanu remained silent remembering the condition agreed between them. But at the time of birth of the eighth child he grew impatient and expressed his vexation. Ganga did not abandon the eighth son and on the basis of their condition she left her husband.

A spiritual aspirant begins to know the unknown but the knowledge of the Supreme cannot be attained through any endeavour or austerity. Beings are generally extraneous in vision which ensures ignorance. Hence they need introversion consciously and this change over is sadhana (austerity) which creates an internal heat that turns the ignorance into ashes gradually and knowledge dawns on them. The more the ignorance is gone the more knowledge dawns on them. Despite having the potential to have it, all is not endowed with such knowledge.

In their bid for knowing the unknown beings are to be resolute to overcome the impediments on the way with the help of their prowess that is based on their semen and it is the seed. Their manhood and the fruits of actions remain as seeds within it having the possibility to be manifested in favourable conditions. The body made of twenty four elements becomes manifested and his knowledge and ignorance, faith and faithlessness, actions and non-actions, duty and non-duty, the possibility of which remains existent in that seed and they are manifested as and when necessary under the given circumstances. And during his austerity his prowess becomes active to produce heat within to burn the impediments and ignorance. In other words, the semen with the help of its prowess, swallows the ignorance cutting through the knot of the nerve-centre.

The semen runs through the middle artery running through the spinal cord known to be Susumna, is known to be the Ganga and in the water of this river the queen of Shantanu abandoned the seven Vasus one after another. The queen Ganga is the Primordial Energy and the upward flow of semen through the artery (susumna) is the reflexion of that Primordial Energy, is known to be the energy for austerity. Being armed with this energy when an austere person becomes able to cut through the knot of ignorance in that artery then the semen swallows up the ignorance resting on that knot, that remains within the semen as the seed. Ganga abandoned her seven sons in the river Ganga, but in case of the eighth one she could not as she promised to the Vasus earlier. Her eighth son was saved although she left Shantanu as per condition.

We have already said that the 'I'-consciousness i.e. the ego is the eighth Vasu whom Ganga saved and left for heaven. We have also said that the queen of Shantanu is the Primordial Energy pervading the whole universe. In the realm of humanity the role of this energy is as the strength of austerity; again, without its active participation one cannot be endowed with the knowledge of the Supreme Being, the goal of the austere persons.

An austere person with the help of this energy may progress upto the end point of austerity but he cannot undo his 'I'-consciousness i.e. his ego because it is his 'I' that inspires him in his pursuit and his same 'I' that delights in his success, also thinks 'I' am the doer. The 'I'-consciousness remains till the end of austerity when the austere person thinks, 'I' attained this state by my austerity. Therefore, 'I' and 'Mine' remain even after the austere pursuit is over. 'I'-consciousness cannot make 'I' consciousness extinct and on the other hand, so long 'I'-consciousness is there, attainment of Supreme consciousness is but a far away dream. The energy of austerity cannot undo 'I'-consciousness and now its necessity is over. Therefore, Ganga saved the eighth son and she requires not to remain with Shantanu any more. So she had to desert him.

The eighth son of Ganga was given the name, Devavrata and later on owing to his terrible oath he become known to be Bhishma, a disciple of both Brihaspati, the Guru of gods and Sukracharya, the Guru of demons. He was a man of great wisdom and a valiant warrior. He was equally an excellent performer in the theatre of war and at home. He was firm and steadfast in duty, soft in affection; he strides a greater part of the epic like a colossus. In the battlefield of Kurukshetra in the dark night of dancing death he alone kept the flame of life burning. Here we are to narrate a little of his wisdom and valour.

The term 'ego' can easily be uttered but its range of influence is by no means shorter. It dominates the region of Chitta (faculty of thought perception and memory) from end to end. The consciousness of 'I am the doer' is the basis of its existence. The feeling of 'I am the enjoyer' comes then automatically. Again along with the faculties produced by the Chitta the understanding of 'I' and 'mine' become existent as already 'I am the doer' and 'I am the enjoyer' feelings are there. Therefore the ego rules over the thoughts and actions of the beings. Their minds, senses, impulses are subservient to 'me' and 'mine'. Every being is an 'I' and the world is full of 'I's. Of course, in this realm there are immumerable 'I's but one 'I' is different from another. I am different from all other 'I's being the doer and enjoyer. And the source of these two is the esse of 'me' and 'mine' and this is the root of all ignorance. All other steps of ignorance are the associates of the ego. Crossing a step for the next one of ignorance the austere person finally comes to know of the nature of his ego. We have already said the ego is rooted in chitta which is the field of its actions and it is the Swarga (heaven) for the beings. All the Vasus are the residents of this heaven. But they were crippled being cursed by the muni Vashistha and were destined to be born as humans which they apparently detested. But human body is the only medium through which one can have knowledge overcoming his ignorance. The knowledge of ignorance is the remedy that would make them normal and that is possible by human birth. Hence the invocation of curse. It has been mentioned that any austerity cannot undo the 'I'-consciousness, but austere person may have the directions to convert the immature 'I' to mature 'I'.

In the tale we come to know Ganga's son Devarrata is greatly wise and a valiant person.

The efforts of austerity of the beings begin with 'I'-consciousness and it is also in them who are devoid of any spiritual aspirations. In fine, human life is full of 'I'-consciousness in all respects and hence spiritual endeavour starts with "who am I?" The spiritual austerity begins with this question and every effort is made the person's 'I' as the doer. He passes the steps of ignorance one by one and his knowledge develops. Thus his 'I' becomes wiser leaving behind his ignorance. Now, the 'I' of the spiritual aspirant is engaged in the pursuit as also his 'I' is gaining knowledge because of the pursuit and his both 'I's are one and the same, yet they seem to be different in the context. Therefore, the ego which by its energy passing through the stages of ignorance identifies its own self, at least ideally through its efforts, questions cannot be raised regarding its valour. Devavrata is a valiant person indeed and wise too. We have already said that the ego is rooted in the Chitta and its field is his action area. The base of Chitta is on the border-line of the world of mind and hence on the one side of it is the world of matter and on the other the spiritual world. The ego is the lord of the world of matter having a clear idea of the spiritual world too. As the faculties and traits rising out of the Chitta are the inspiration for the activities in the human world, the ego is the over-lord of the life associated with matter and sense-objects. The ego is stationed in the Chitta getting experiences of ignorance of different kinds and he is the able ruler of material life. As it remains on the border-line of the material world, it may hold the reflexions of the intents and esses of the heart. As much as the mirror of the Chitta is free of soil the more it will be lighted with the illumination of the heart. As it can hold the reflexion of the illumination of the heart, it becomes enriched with an indistinct presence of Supreme Consciousness and hence it is called indistinct Consciousness (Abhas chaitanya) although it is not that Consciousness. Even then in the perspective of phenomenal consciousness it is by no means trivial but its importance is praiseworthy. Hence Devavrata (the ego) is wise indeed. No other reality of the body is capable of reflecting the illumination of the heart in such a manner. As in human life and in case of manhood the ego is an important reality and also an insurmountable impediment likewise in the tale of the Mahabharata he is a very important character and a doer of many an intricacy. His life, full of problems and successes, doubts and failures, is colourful as the dusk of the late autumn and also as the full moon night in autumn after a brief spell of rain.

The Sons Of Satyavaty, Shantanu

"I am Ganga, the daughter of the great rishi Jahnu. The rishis always serve me with devotion. I became your wife for some divine mission. Please accept this son as my gift to you and bring him up." This is the farewell address of Ganga to Shantanu and saying this the goodess of heaven returned there, as there was no need any more of her human form. What is the significance of all this? What was due to be created by the union of the Supreme Consciousness and the Energy of the Supreme Consciousness, has been created and thereafter in the perspective of creation the role of the active Energy of the Supreme Consciousness was over and hence she needed no formal existence any further.

Now Shantanu is alone. The Supreme Consciousness cannot create anything unitarily. On the other hand, the fulfillment of the reflection of Consciousness in the form of ego is impossible in association of the Supreme Consciousness; the manifestation of the ego under the shadow of the Supreme Consciousness is bound to be impeded. Hence, the child Devavrata being the prince of Hastinapura remains away from the king who comes to know of his identity at a later time when he is grown up in body and mind and charms his father with his skill in archery. Both father and son come closer to each other, but each remains alone. As the actionless Supreme Consciousness and reflexion of the Consciousness are related to each in other way, no new creation is possible now being associated with each other. On the question of creation none is capable of holding the seeds for creation and hence even though the son is qualified in many respects, becomes a constant source of worry for the father. On the other hand, Shantanu becomes desirous to have sons on seeing Satyavaty during his game hunting, but her father appears to be an unsurmountable obstruction to his marriage to Satyavaty and at the root of all this is Devavrata. The existence that holds the reflections of the Supreme Consciousness and can itself reflect them that existence cannot be denied in course of creation. Shantanu is now on the horns of a dilemma. The solution is not unknown to him but it is very much difficult to go through. It has been mentioned earlier that the position of the ego is at the meeting point of the spiritual world and the physical world. After the creation of spiritual world, the physical world had to be created and for that purpose a neat order was necessary. But Devavrata himself was an obstacle to it as he was not yet entangled in anything physical nor was the Supreme Consciousness either. In the context of the physical world Supreme Consciousness is stationed in the heart beyond the heart but the ego is not. Yet both of them have their important roles to play in creating the physical world. In these circumstances when Devavrata learnt that he himself was the only obstacle to the union of Supreme Consciousness and Phenomenal Nature, he activated himself with his own domineering authority with a sense of duty to help the union of them. But his first effort suffered a setback by the father of Satyavaty by expressing doubt and that was natural. In the event of the union between Supreme Consciousness and Phenomenal Nature, if the authority of Abhas Chaitanya remains domineering on both of them, the sequence of creation was sure to be disturbed and under the circumstances the authority of the ego requires to be circumscribed. The fisherman imposed a condition that Devavrata himself or his successors should not have any claim upon the throne although he was the crown prince. At once the Vasu in Devavrata woke up and took the oath in that regard as desired by the fisherman. The pleased father addressed the prince, "for the well-being of the kingdom your intentions are highly commendable; so you become the lord of the bride and hence you have the sole authority to even make a gift of her." The will or order of the fisherman has to be considered carefully. Mind it, the authority to protect the bride, even to make a gift of her is given to her would-be step son while she is going to be the queen of the kingdom. Satyavaty's husband is the king of the land, but he has no authority over his queen, which has been bestowed upon her step son who has been debarred from ascending his father's throne. But why? Is it not something unwanted? Somebody may say, the clever fisherman foresaw her early widow-hood and in that case Devavrata was the right person to protect her. In fact it happened. But regarding the authority of Devavrata over Satyavaty the truth is otherwise. We have already said, the Supreme Consciousness (Brahman Chitanya) exists in the heart beyond heart and only be realized; the phenomenal cognition can have no idea of Him and hence Devavrata's authority is over phenomenal nature. The ego when related to the Supreme Consciousness is Abhas Chaitanya (reflective agent of the Supreme Consciousness) but when related to phenomenal nature then it is its overlord despite being the reflective agent of the Supreme Consciousness. Hence Shantanu is her husband and Devavrata is her lord. Now the step son accompanied his would-be step mother to Hastinapura for marriage with his father. The marriage ceremony was solemnly accomplished.

The first issue of them was the son Chitrangada. It is said, "He was a man of exceptional forbearance and great might and best known in all subjects." "The second son was Vichitravirya. In his childhood days Shantanu breathed his last. Chitrangada became the king. After some time king Chitrangada became involved in a brawl with a Gandharva of his namesake and both were engaged in a fight for three years. At last, the Gandharva killed the king Chitrangada casting a spell upon him. On the death of Chitrangada Bhishma arranged to enthrone Vichitravirya". The story says, "After the accession to his father's throne Vichitravirya began to rule the kingdom showing his great respect to the wise Bhisma and according to his orders. The great Bhisma also very carefully looked after him." But no such comment regarding his relationship with Chirangada be found in the text nor is it mentioned in the text during the fight between the two Chirangadas at Kurukshetra as to whether skilful warrior Bhisma took any part in favour of his step brother. It may be inferred that he remained inactive. Only after the king was dead the throne became vacant. The gandharva left for heaven without making any claim for the kingdom. Therefore, it may be concluded the feud was a personal one and as no question of kingdom or throne was raised; hence Bhisma did not get himself involved in it. It is to be noted that Bhisma's love and concern for Vichitravirya were greater and he was less concerned with Chitrangada. He had no reason apparently to be partial in expressing love and affection for both, yet his affection to Vichitravirya was greater.

Bhisma cannot be upbraided for his partiality in expression of love and affection to his step brothers. In terms of realities as the result of the union of Supreme Consciousness and phenomenal nature the firstborn was the Great Divine Mahattattva (the aggregate of all pure elements for creation) and the second born was the Great Divine Ahamkara (the divine ego). The first born being the Great Divine Mahattattva itself cannot create and destined to be transformed for the purpose and it was inevitable, Ahamtattva (reality of ego) springs of Mahattattva and all other elements for creation are sprung of this Ahamtattva. While the Great Divine Ahamkara (ego) is incapable of creating anything and for further creation its transformation was necessary although he was transformed form of the Great Divine Mahattatva and it was also of short span of existence.

On the other hand, out of the three brothers born of the Supreme Consciousness only the first-born Abhas Chaitanya (the reflection of Supreme Consciousness) can hold and reflect the Supreme Consciousness and the sphere of his authority and action is so vast that it could not be compared with that of the other two brothers. By the ordination of Satyavaty's father he held the absolute authority over her and that was proclaimed in presence of many; none of them objected to it but approved. The wise Devavrata was very much conscious of the rights and duties of his own and as such he became close to Vichitravirya to serve his own purpose better.

In order to fufil his purpose Bhisma became active for the marriage of Vichitravirya. Meanwhile, news reached the royal palace that the three daughters of the King of Kasi (presently Beneras) would be given by marriage by choosing their grooms themselves from amongst a good number of suitors assembled in the royal court being invited by the father of the brides. The practice is known to be Sayamvara. On hearing the news, the lord of the royal house-hold at Hastinapura became active at once. In consultation with Satyavaty he proceeded to the court of Kasi with the purpose of abducting the princess to get them married to Vichitravirya. Arriving at the court there he addressed a short speech to the present kings and princes on the system of marriage at that time mentioning that marriages by sayamvara were a matter of pride indeed, but marriage by abducting bride was also an act of no lesser pride either. Then he revealed his intention to take the princesses away to Hastinapura to get them married to his brother Vichitravirya. Those present might rescue the princesses by fighting with him or by any other means. Some of them fought but failed. Bhisma started for Hastinapura with three sisters. On the way Salva invited him to fight. Bhisma fought Salva and made him unarmed, killed his charioteer and horses but did not slay him.

Now, the question is why Bhisma abducted the three princesses of Kasi, to get them married to his younger brother? Even defeating Salva why did not Bhisma kill him although he killed the charioteer and horses? We have said earlier the scope and limit of the action of ego was the too vast. Be it Anuloma Darshana (vision of the sequence of creation) or be it Viloma Darshana (vision of the reverse order of creation i.e. the sequence of austerity); in both of them the role of the ego (as abhas chaitanya) is equally important. But how could we know of this importance? We know it as knowledge dawns on mainly in course of the sequence of creation (anuloma darshana) and that be revealed in the sequence of austerity (viloma darshana) meaning thereby on the courses of both the sequences, knowledge reveals itself in two directions. Bhisma's return to Hastinapura with the three princesses denotes the being's honest action performed in course of austerity and Salva is the thorny impediment to that honest performance. Any obstruction to austerity or honest performance cannot be destructed by any austere person but to be defeated to overcome it. Bhisma was right; he did not slay Salva. Now there remains the question of abduction of the sisters. According to tradition then prevalent, Vichitravirya had to present himself in the assembly of kings as a suitor in the court of Kasi. Instead, Bhisma went there to abduct the sisters and did his job. But Bhisma was not the suitor. The wise Bhisma understood well that his action was neither logical nor moral altogether. Hence he needed to harangue over the prevalent procedure of marriage. Again, he understood that there was no certainty of accepting Vichitravirya as the husband by the three sisters, if at all he was present in the court. But Bhisma had the necessity of ascertaining his brother's marriage with them. So, to perform his duty he had to depend upon his physical strength and succeeded. But what was the necessity? In reply, we are to make a mention of the king of Kashi who is the epitome of wisdom (Prajna) in human life. It is held that Lord Shiva, the third of the Hindu Trinity, is the symbol of highest spiritual wisdom and Kasi is supposed to be his own seat; hence the king of Kasi is wisdom. His three daughters — Amba, Ambika and Ambalika are the faculties of destruction, disbelief and certainty respectively. As the wisdom can overcome the faculty of destruction, likewise it can overcome the faculties of disbelief and certainty as then the austere person is established in Truth. Wisdom is neither subjugated to nor influenced by these three faculties. Prior to be wise they remain in the character of the austere person and once he is established in wisdom, they have no influence upon the wise, although he is their father. They remain active in human character until the person becomes wise by austerity. They achieve their adulthood being detached from the austere person's character and to be attached to the character of another person. Hence, the arrangement of their marriage. So long their exclusive existence was not discerned, then it was their childhood; and on the other hand, without their existence in any human character, they are meaningless altogether. So they need to get married. Now, there was no certainty that the three sisters would accept Vichitravirya as their husband had he been present in the assembly of suitors in the court of Kasi. Bhisma understood it very well and he also understood that the transformation of the Great Divine Ego was imminent but that would not be possible in absence of the faculties — the three sisters. Hence Bhisma wanted to unite the faculties with Vichitravirya as their husband as soon as possible. So he had no alternative but to abduct the sisters and that was a fitting attempt by him. After the abduction he challenged the present kings and princes to free the sisters by defeating Bhisma, if they liked so. Some of them fought and failed. But the king of Kasi neither showed any concern nor did fight to free his daughters as a man of wisdom knows well that he should not be concerned about the fate of the faculties which he had already overcome. The wisdom is always calm and unconcerned. On the other hand, Bhisma had the necessity of uniting the sisters with the Great Divine Ego, Vichitravirya who himself was not competent enough for it. He was dependent upon Bhisma. Though

Bhisma had some faint idea of the conclusive effect of this union, neither Satyavaty nor Vichitravirya had an iota of it.

When the royal palace was abuzz with the preparation of marriage the eldest sister Amba disclosed her mind that she was unable to marry Vichitravirya as she was attracted to Salva and he also did not think otherwise in mind. She decided to accept him as her husband and had the sayamvara took place at Kasi she would have offered her bridal garland round his neck. Her father had no objection to it.

The lord of the royal household at Hastinapura become restive listening to Amba. In consultation with the Brahmins Bhisma freed her; Vichitravirya married Ambica and Ambalika. After seven years Vichitravirya died of consumption after sporting with the wives but left no issue. Now one may question of the results of this marriage with the faculties of disbelief and conviction. The king was incapable of procreating offsprings and hence the result of this marriage cannot be visualized with bare eyes. The Great Divine Ego is also ego and has his activities too. It was his duty to install his two wives in each of the seven steps of knowledge and he did it in seven years. From the first step of knowledge an austere person has to experience doubt and overcoming it he attains certainty which inspires him to progress for the next step where also he experiences doubt and then overcome it with conviction. Thus upto the seventh step of knowledge both of them exist and the eighth step of knowledge is beyond all faculties. The story says, "....the king Vichitravirya sporting with his wives continuously for seven years died of consumption in his youth." His life after marriage was ordained to be of seven years." The eighth step of knowledge does not accept any faculty and hence the king waning step by step finally dies in the eight step. It may be questioned why did not the queens die instead of the king?

The answer is, the Great Divine Ego himself is incapable of holding and carrying any seed for creation what his queens are quite able to do. The king died, but his existence remained in what existed.

Satyavaty's two sons are dead now. The elder one died in the battle field and younger one died of consumption. The death of the younger one has been explained but that of the first one has not yet been discussed. He died while fighting with a Gandharva of his namesake. But who is Gandharava Chitrangada? The Gandharvas are celestial entities but not gods; they are expert in music and dance and usually they are regular performers in the court of gods in heaven. They are also well conversant in scriptures as well as in the art of war. They may roam at their will in heaven and earth. They may be friends of men and foes as well. Such a Gandharva killed the king Chitrangada in a fight at Kurukshetra which continued for three years.

Kurukshetra is the human heart and the gandharva is the natural principle of manifestation. Three years' duration of the fight between two Chitrangadas means to activate the manifestation of the aggregate of the elements of creation with the help of three gunas — Sattva, Rajas and Tamas. The principles of nature in respect of manifestation are many. The Great Divine aggregate of elements and these natural principles of creation — both are worthy of being decorative ornaments of the Creation. And for continuous progress of the sequence of creation, transformation of the Divine Aggregate of elements was absolutely necessary. This material world is the transformed existence of the Great Divine aggregate of elements and nature is behind it all.

In the glorious dawn of the Sacrifice of Creation the silent oblation of their own selves by two sons of Satyavaty remains concealed to the vision of ordinary people, but it reveals itself before the vision of the wise.

Vyasa And Devavrata

Two sons of Satyavaty are dead now and two are alive — one born of her and the other her step son. On the line of his father Chitrangada and Vichitravirya were Bhishma's brothers; Vyasa was also his brother having been related to his step mother. It may be assumed that they were not unknown to each other. But it seems to be unnatural that the story of the birth of Rishi Vyasa was unknown to Bhishma; a disciple of Brihaspati and Sukracharya was unaware of the identity of the parents of Vyasa who divided the Vedas. Bhishma was a versatile scholar of his own time but was not in the know of the story of Vyasa's birth, which seems to be improbable and he came to know of that from Satyavaty when they were discussing about getting sons in the fields of Vichitravirya by engagement.

However, these two sons of Satyavaty were very much distinguished in their own spheres. One being incapable of creating anything yet is entangled in the phenomenal nature, does his duty well; and the other being capable of creation remains aloof of the phenomenal nature despite accepting it. He never entangles himself in material affairs and does his duty aiming to the Supreme Consciousness. Therefore the two brothers are poles apart by nature and vision. Hence a good relationship between the two cannot be expected of. One is the epitome of the Energy of Guru and his endeavour is to circumscribe the influence of ego inasmuch as it is possible while the other despite accepting the importance of the energy of Guru, tries to reduce his influence in the phenomenal world. So the relationship between the two is mostly formal.

When Satyavaty sought the permission of Bhisma regarding engagement of Vyasa to procreate sons in the fields of Vichitravirya narrating his birth during her virgin years, Bhishma came to know of the parents of Vyasa and replied that "he who fixing his vision to dharma (faith), artha (wealth) and kama (desire) acts considering the correlation between dharma and its consequences, artha and its consequences and kama and its consequences, he is really intelligent; as you permit, this is religious, good for us all and for our dynasty too. So I fully endorse your selection." If we carefully view this statement of Bhishma, we would see that the deed which he is incapable of performing, Vyasa is the ablest one to do that in his time. To engage an honest Brahmin was his own proposal and now there was neither any scope nor any reason to oppose Satyavaty. He had but to agree. Yet no signs of his satisfaction over the issue were visible and of course that was not to be. The ego never likes to show any weakness of its own rather strives to deny that for which it never runs short of pretexts. Satyavaty requested him firstly to procreate the dynasts in the fields of Vichitravirya, which he refused on the ground of his past oath saying. "....if the sky gives up sound, the moon abandons its cool glow, Indra renounces his prowess, the king of Dharma gives up dharma, I cannot renounce Truth...." Saying this Bhishma expressed his inability to act at the behest of Satyavaty and finally said that "....the breach of an oath of a kshatriya is highly animadverted one and a fallen kshatriya is lost for ever.... So begin the performance of desired action by wise priests who can judiciously decide the course at the given time." It means Bhishma is unable to breach his promise following the dharma of a kshatriya and if he does it, he would be lost. Although to continue the dynasty it was not irreligious then to procreate children by engagement, yet the impediment to do so on the part of Bhishma was the dharma of a kshatriya and hence the dharma of a kshatriya if becomes to be an insurmountable hindrance to observe the dharma of a kshatriya, Bhishma is undone. And this is his argument. It is to see as to whether he was reluctant to act to honour Satyavaty on the ground of breach of his promise or to be upbraided in case of breach of oath. Had the dharma of a kshatriya stands in the way to observe dharma on the part of a kshatriya, then that would have been the prime reason for his reluctance to perform as requested by Satyavaty. But the question of upbraiding for fall from his dharma came from him as the first reason. A man established in his dharma cares two figs for upbraiding in case of his fall from dharma to protect his own dharma. Yet Bhishma was correct to advance his arguments as ego always upholds the I- Consciousness in support of his position. But the I- Consciousness is not all; he is basically the reflector of Supreme Consciousness. He was a man of dichotomous character; one of his characteristics was rightly manifesting, and of course, rightly in relation to phenomenal matters and the other is always hidden from human eye like a subterranean flow. The first one makes him secluded and independent giving him a towering personality and the second one makes of him a religious person. His aloofness, independence and towering ego debar him from procreating dynasts in the fields of Vichitravirya.

Such a self-guided person who is but the ego incarnate can hardly accept and respect Vyasa. So long Bhishma knew that he was the sole philosopher and guide of Satyavaty in her life in Hastinapura and now he came to know from Satyavaty herself that a rishi of Vyasa's stature was her own son who could be the solver to her. At once the thought of his own standing in relation to Satyavaty came into his mind and his sense of independence grew greater being somewhat shocked emotionally; but he had neither an alibi nor earth under his feet to deny universally venerated Vyasa. So with cold courtesy he received Vyasa as well as the proposal of Satyavaty.

Bhishma and Vyasa — both are very important characters in the Mahabharata but their outlook in relation to Satyavaty are different. One is her guardian and protector at the time of need and the other is always eager to solve her problems and finds pleasure in his mother's satisfaction by fulfilling her wishes. In his behaviour Bhishma is always established in his I- Consciousness as 'I am the doer' while Vyasa established in his humility and modesty, is eager to serve his mother to the best of his ability. Bishma is the uncrowned king of Hastinapura and a king maker. Vyasa is an ascetic person since his birth and a realized visionary. Vyasa's existence is based on Truth while that of Bhishma is on his I-Consciousness. Therefore, it was not possible for him to accord due respect to Vyasa who cared very little of that as he knew it was not possible for Bhishma. So there was a great difference between the two. When Bhishma says.... "if he acts considering the consequences then he is intelligent indeed...." He does not speak well of Vyasa who epitomizes the energy of Guru in himself. Because of this regardless attitude to Vyasa, Bhishma utterly fails to recognize him as the Truth incarnate himself and he becomes a dwarf in stature to Vyasa.

The Birth Of Kuru Princes

"Mother, remember me at your time of crisis" — saying these words the child who left his mother in early childhood, has now come to Hastinapura at the call of Satyavaty. She requested him to procreate dynasts in the fields of Vichitravirya. Vyasa agreed and said that the queens should observe a vow as directed by him for a whole year and then he would do the needful; no profaner could touch him. But Satyavaty was impatient and wanted her daughters-in-law were carrying immediately. Being insisted Vyasa agreed.

We said earlier, Satyavaty was the phenomenal nature. She is also the part of Truth. She is the energy of Consciousness being the manifestation of Supreme Consciousness (chaitanya) and on the basis of this reality her marriage with Supreme Consciousness was possible aiming to continue the sequence of creation and hence she was the mother of the Great Divine Ego and the Great Divine Aggregate of Pure Elements. Till now the formal creation was far away. The actual significance of Satyavaty's identity of Phenomenal Nature remained hidden from the eye. On the other hand, the radiance of Supreme Consciousness upon the sanctified surface of the mind, is known to be the part of truth of the mind. And now that part of truth of the mind, even if activated, turns to be filled coming in contact with the material world. So now it is needed to manifest the phenomenal nature first and hence she could not accept the proposal of Vyasa regarding observance of the vow by her two daughters-in-law. Satyavaty herself could not deliver any material form carrying it within her womb, but she needed to manifest that form through the faculties of doubt and conviction that followed the phenomenal nature and the ego with a view to make it possible as the consequence of union with the energy of Guru. So she cannot wait but Vyasa has no haste in this regard. Moreover, any faculty of mind suddenly coming in contact with the energy of Guru, is sure to pervert and apparently the energy of Guru is to resist this perversion and hence Vyasa suggests observance of the vow for a year and thereafter they should meet Vyasa. But in order to keep the flow of creation continuing even if it is perverted is the sole desire of Satyavaty. So, Vyasa opined if her daughters-in-law could endure his repulsive disposition then he would give her untimely dynasts suggesting to the perversion of the faculties. It may be noteworthy here, without the perversion in nature nothing could have been created and the immeasurable universe is the outcome of the perversion of the Primordial Nature. The phenomenal nature that Satyavaty is but the perverted form of the Energy of Supreme Consciousness.

At the time of union with Vyasa, Ambica became the victim of that perversion in body and mind being afraid of his frightful appearance and she closed her eyes till the end. Resultantly, she conceived a blind child. The faculty of doubt cannot look at Truth in full view as in that case she will lose her identity. So Truth is always repulsive to her. Moreso, the faculty of doubt cannot bear Truth under any circumstances. Ambica gave birth to a blind son — the first Kuru prince. The energy of Guru knows it all. When Satyavaty asked Vyasa of the result, he told her that the child would be blind. But a blind prince would not serve her purpose and she requested him to give another child in another womb, who could be a perfect dynast to ascend the throne in future, Vyasa agreed. But Ambalika was also a faculty of mind — conviction. Of course, in comparison with the faculty of doubt, the faculty of conviction is characteristically empowered to visualise the glory of Guru but at the same time considering her own littleness, this faculty also becomes pale in fearfulness owing to perversion and the perverted Ambalika accepts Vyasa. So her union with Vyasa was neither easy nor natural. He informed Ambalika that her son would be pale in complexion and the name would be Pandu (pale). This son of Ambalika was the second prince of the line. Listening to the result of his second union Satyavaty asked Vyasa to give a son in the womb of Ambica, perfect in all respects for the welfare of the kingdom. This time also Vyasa agreed. An anxious Satyavaty entreated Ambica in this respect. Ambica heard her mother-in-law uttering nothing as if she was agreed; but she decided her course of action taking the recourse to deceit as the faculty of doubt does never like to come in contact with the energy of Guru. Doubt precedes deceit that follows doubt. She contrived to engage the maid of the royal house-hold to act in her place. The maid was bedizened in royal clothes and tutored of what she was supposed to do. She was sent to present herself to Vyasa to play the role of Ambica unknowingly. The maid was particularly conscious to comply. But Vyasa was in the know of all this. For the satisfaction of Vyasa the maid offered her services and the complacent Vyasa blessed her saying." You would be free from your bondge of slavery and you will get a son of uncommon understanding and a religious one." This son of the maid is Vidura and his mother is the faculty of virtue (sadvritti). In the perspective of the journey of the faculties of doubt and conviction aiming to the phenomenal matter and their prominence in this regard made the role of the faculty of virtue dimmed to a great extent but finally she gets her prominence.

Owing to Vyasa's direct participation, the royal house of Hastinapura got there princes— Dhritarastra, Pandu and Vidura. The first two were not qualified in all respects and hence birth of the third was possible. But he was regarded as a prince after his mother's bond of slavery was over. We are to note that the three mothers are three faculties of the mind and their life and work are guided by Satyavaty and Bhishma. Satyavaty is the phenomenal nature as well as a fraction of truth and under her guardianship these three princes are born and their aggregate is the human mind. Dhritarastra is the resolution of mind, Pandu is the dissolution of it; Vidura is the bhakti of it. All three of them primarily epitomize the will force of the mind and analyzing their lives and actions we may find that the three express their wishes, of course, to different aims. This difference is due to the dominance of gunas in their characters. The mother of Dhritarastra, Ambica, is the faculty of doubt which testifies to the dominance of tamas and it is evident in the life and actions of Dhritarastra. The mind resolves to enjoy sense-objects being inspired by tamas. Ambalika is the faculty of conviction which comes through deliberation and in course of deliberation there comes the conclusion that helps in dawning of knowledge. The propensity to deliberate is the outcome of rajas that inspires the beings to search for what is there beyond resolution and the result of this search is pure knowledge that is Pandu. The maid of Ambica is the faculty of virtue. The mind has the faculties of virtue and vice as well although the manifestation of the faculty of virtue in human life and deed is but rare indeed. The reason for the faculty of virtue has been said to be the maid-servant is that the esse of service is the most favourable esse in the realm of austerity in relation to Guru or the adorable one.

The Marriage Of Kuru Princes

Although the consciousness (Chetana) in the phenomenal nature is the manifestation of the Supreme Consciousness (Chaitanya), Chetana (consciousness) is incapable of revealing the Supreme Consciousness as it is the manifestation of the Supreme Consciousness and being related to physical matter. It has its own limitations. But in its own sphere it manifests in many ways. That is evident in the birth of three princes who are mind themselves, which means they are consciousness too. Satyavaty is now successful in her efforts to create further but with the active participation of the energy of Guru, who is always impartial in his actions in all respects. Satyavaty is the mainstay and the three brothers are her loving minions. At the same time she is the correlative link among them.

The two opposite forces viz. resolution and dissolution are always in action and reaction, that produces the result of distraction which is the mind's virtue and it is represented by Vidura. His mother is the faculty of virtue of the mind and he is virtue himself epitomized as bhakti. Now we get four parts of the mind — the partial truth, resolution i.e. ignorance, dissolution i.e. knowledge, and bhakti and Satyavaty maintains consistency among them; she never becomes extinct; hence the mind is active ceaselessly on the material plane. Again, being fathered by the same person, brought up in the same environment and educated by the same teachers, the three brothers are different in thought and action. On the other hand, we know nothing of their childhood and adolescence, but they are introduced to us when they are grown up men. The reason is the mind never endures the childhood or adolescence — it is always fully grown up.

In the cognition of beings generally it is held that matters evolve and it is also an accepted fact that the mind does not fully develop in childhood but in the grown up state. What is the nature of the evolution of mind? If we closely observe the nature of evolution of human body, we would see that the so-called evolution of mind is dependent on that of the physical body. We get the proper identity of mind, discerning the growth and development of the physical body and that would be commensurate with the development of body. The relation of mind is bound with the physical body inseparably. Again, the evolution of mind could be discerned only when it comes in contact with sense-objects meaning thereby how the mind acts and reacts coming in contact with them. Of course, only actions and reactions would not determine the growth and evolution of mind; one is to observe as to how much attraction the mind expresses coming in contact with the sense-objects and how it inspires the beings to accept or reject those sense-objects expressed through the body. Therefore, in absence of physical body the actions and reactions of the mind cannot be discerned; hence the physical body is a must. The physical body is always up to enjoy the sense-objects and to do that it requires the senses and sense-organs and to guide them to do so the mind plays a vital role. The body enjoys sense-objects being inspired by the mind only when it is developed to the extent of enjoying them. The growth and development of the mind ensures the education of the mind coming in contact with the sense-objects. On the other hand, the owner of the mind never accepts that his mind is not fully grown up; a child would not accept that his mind is under-developed. The correlation of progressive development of body and mind is the reason for this and the mind becomes fully developed in youth.

So we are introduced to the three princes in their youth. Of course, it becomes known to us that in their childhood arrangements for their education and physical training were made by Bhishma. The role of the ego in this respect be noted. It is the ego that inspires the beings for further progress and in absence of it, the education of beings remains incomplete. It never happens that there are body and mind and no ego. Though the mind is not the off-spring of the ego, yet there is a filial bond between them and the ego is the guardian of it in beings' childhood.

Now let us have a brief identity of the brothers. The eldest Dhritarastra had an exceptionally strong physique, Pandu was an unrivalled archer and the third Vidura was a very pious man. Dhritarastra was blind. It was impossible for him to be an archer but he had a very strong body. Blindness and physical strength were his characteristics. He is the resolution of mind. When the mind resolves to enjoy sense-objects, he does that forcefully without any consideration of the consequences and to translate that resolution he applies his strength; if failed, he applies his full strength to do away with the obstacles to enjoy that sense-objects. Until the resolution is strong enough it is bound to be futile. But resolutions are made not to achieve any results but otherwise. Hence it is natural that Dhritaristra would be a very strong man. Again, when the mind resolves to enjoy some sense-objects, he does it indiscriminately; hence he is blind. Therefore, he is blind and strong as well — they are his main characteristics.

Pandu is an unrivalled archer. An archer is required to strike the target and to do that he needs a strong ocular vision. His success in hitting a distant target for which he does not need the strength of a wrestler but a strong vision, forbearance and skill that are the most required qualities of an archer. It is to note that the qualities that are absent in Dhritarastra are conspicuously present in Pandu. Dhritarastra and Pandu are opposite to each other — in physique, in character, in life and in action as resolution is contrary to dissolution — as ignorance to knowledge.

Two opposite characters are bound to cause impact and one is to attract the other owing to contrariety as chill does the heat. But this contrast is not everything as there is a correlation between the two also and that is the identity of their mothers. Ambica and Ambalika both are sisters and co-wives of king Vichitravirya. But what about Vidura's mother? She is the maid of the royal house-hold. There would certainly be a yawning difference between the princess and the maid of royal house-hold even after she obtained her freedom. So being fathered by the same person Vidura was disqualified for the throne as he was born of a maid; likewise there was a difference between the two elder brothers and Vidura — the third prince.

It is natural that on completion of their education and training and also attaining adulthood they would get married and in this regard also Bhishma was the guardian. Considering the dignity and nobility of the dynasty the guardian entered into a marital alliance to select Gandhari, the daughter of King Subala of Gandhara, as the bride for Dhritarastra and the daughter of the King of Madra, Madree for Pandu and on the pretext of discussing the matter with him Bhishma got Vidura's endorsement. Now here is a question, why Bhishma sought the approval of Vidura, the youngest brother? We have already discussed that since their birth the three brothers were brought up under the guardianship of Bhishma and his role in this regard was very important. In relation to the human body the manas, buddhi, chitta and ahamkara constitute the inner mind and the ahamkara based on this composite mind enjoys the sense objects for which the mind acts and reacts to fulfil its desires and the result of that actions and reactions is enjoyed by the ahamkara and hence to make the marital alliances Bhishma emphaises upon the nobility and dignity of the brides' dynasties. But why Vidura was required to approve of the marriages of his two elder brothers?

We have already said that Vidura is Bhakti. It is a thing that enables beings to realize Truth while it can have a clear idea of Eternal Truth. Hence Vidura is a part of Truth. We have also said that Satyavaty also is a part of Truth. Now we get two parts of Truth; one in form of Satyavaty who being phenomenal nature is a part of Truth of mind whose vision is directed to further creation while Vidura is a part of Truth Eternal, whose vision is directed to the Absolute Reality. So there is a difference between the two.

The wise Bhishma knew well that denying the part of mind that has the capability to comprehend the Eternal Truth, neither the resolution of mind nor its dissolution could be activated at all and they could not manifest themselves in the realm of material world. Hence he sought for Vidura's approval as a necessary one which was accorded to by Vidura. If so necessitates, the part of Eternal Truth of mind may co-operate with the ego, but he has no compulsion to comply with the ego's orders or dictates always and this truth was not unknown to Bhisma as well. As he was at a distance from Dhritarastra and Pandu, Vidura maintained a distance from Bhishma too. Though for the time being Bhishma is silent on the issue of Vidura's marriage yet that takes place under his guardianship at a later date.

However, the marriage of Dhritarastra and Gandhari was solemnized. But the newly married Gandhari though was of clear ocular vision blindfolded herself in compassion. Meanwhile, news reached the palace that Kunti, the adopted daughter of the King Kuntibhoja, would choose her groom in an assembly of suitors at her father's court. On the advice of Bhishma, Pandu presented himself there and the princess Kunti offered her bridal garland around the neck of Pandu.

Madree too became his wife a short time later. Of course, we did not come across any detailed description of Vidura's marriage with Parashavi. Now we get four wives to three brothers.

As there are truth in falsehood and in the inspiration of Creation in destruction, likewise there remains a longing for knowledge in ignorance, detachment in attachment but that existence is very subtle and cannot be easily discerned, and its exposure is very rare. This truth is not unknown to attachment, yet she has to sacrifice consciously this cognition to become the wife of blind resolution otherwise she would fail in her dharma. So Gandhari having clear vision willfully blindfolds herself so that not a single ray of light of knowledge can reach the realm of ignorance.

The second princess came from the north. The Himavant standing in the north as a guard has made India a fertile land in absence of which the dry wind from Central Asia could have made it a desert. The Himalayan mountain ranges with their incomparable natural beauty attract the men and women since time immemorial. The way to the Himalayas is the path to renunciation and realization. It is necessary to have the aim fixed, strong conviction and transparent vision to tread the paths to that. The second princess, Kunti as an inspiration directs to those paths. She is nivritti that never means the absence of faculties, rather it means the getting answers to all the questions that baffles the ordinary consciousness and the encourage one to find out the right way to lead the life in an ordained way without succumbing to avarice and not to fall from dharma. Her conviction is based on truth and her vision to her aim is unwavered.

The third princess is from Madra which is her birth-place and her father's kingdom. The kingdom of Madra is to the south of Hastinapura and the direction of south is meant for decay and loss. If you look at the Indian Peninsula you will see that the width of the land-mass gradually decaying is getting the shape of a spear-head and finally jutted into the Indian Ocean. The whole of the southern part of the country, contrary to the northern part, is but a promontory and Madri is from one of the kingdoms of this decaying land. Hence the third princess of Hastinapura is the symbol of decay and loss — and she is Anuvritti. But what is Anuvritti? It is the faculty of mind that leads the beings from attachment to detachment, from dishonesty to honesty, from material to spiritual is called the faculty of Anuvritti — the bridge between attachment and detachment and it is regarded as the shadow of nivritti. But when the mind expresses this faculty it remains pervaded by attachment to material objects, yet it becomes conscious regarding this attachment only to overcome it and this effort is inspired by Anuvritti and its span of life is very short. With the beginning of progress of the faculty, anuvritti dissolves in nivritti; hence she is short-lived.

We have three directions that provided three wives. Now one direction and one wife are yet to be discussed. As without four quarters of the compass it is not complete, likewise without the fourth wife our discussion would not be complete. So it is necessary to have the identity of the wife of Vidura, Parashavi. But we have no information regarding her place of birth or the identity of her parents in the story. Not only that her presence in the story is very scant. She remains hidden from our view. As the moon-beams sometimes come to the earth through the fissures of the thick clouds, she appears in the story very rarely.

Earlier we said, she came from the east which is the direction of the rising sun; it is the direction of light i.e. knowledge opposed to ignorance. On the other hand, wisdom is revealed through virtuous practices; a man of wisdom cannot be otherwise. Therefore, the east is the direction of virtuous practices and Parashavi symbolizes that coming from the east. But the story does not provide us with any evidence to this effect.

One may question the prudence for discussing the directions from which came the princesses. But it is necessary as we have already said that it is a study of the realties of human body as it is the mainstay on the way to self-knowledge and one sets off the journey through austerity to achieve one's goal depending upon one's physical knowledge. With the progress in his efforts an austere person comes to know the realities of the body and his comprehension becomes stronger that the body is material but Atman is consciousness and in the mirror of this physical body Atman cannot be fully reflected. For this cognition the realities of the body are to be known. Secondly, the body cannot be activated in absence of mind. The mind is the conductor of the physical body. It is also obligatory to know the actions and fields of actions of such energies of the mind.

The lower part of the body from the navel is the direction of the south and the upper part of it is that of the north while the anterior is the direction of the east and the posterior is that of the west. It is to note that the upper and lower parts of the body are opposite to each other but interrelated. So is the case of anterior and posterior of the body. In characteristics and manifestations of those characteristics, howsoever, they might be contradictory but they are interdependent to some extent. Hence, Gandhari and Parashavi being contrary to each other are not far away; they identify each other. On the other hand, Kunti and Madri are closely related. The meeting point of the anterior and posterior cannot be clearly defined in the body and the relation between Gandhari and Parashavi is not so close.

The inspirational energy of the four quarters manifests the actions and reactions of the mind. Each one of them attracts the mind to pull on to it and hence the activities of the mind are scattered to all directions. Austerity begins with this scattered mind to make it introvert knowing the four quarters in order to be endowed with Self-knowledge.

Pandu's Conquest, Forest Life, Despondency, Getting Of Sons And Death

The eldest prince was blind and the youngest was born of a maid and hence both were not qualified to ascend the throne. Only Pandu was eligible for ascending the throne of Hastinapura and he did so. Meanwhile, he married Madri and in no time Kunti and Madri were in friendly terms. The king began to pass his time in extreme happiness enjoying the company of his two young queens. "Thus enjoying the company of his two queens for thirteen nights he got out of the palace with the view to conquer the world....". The young king enjoyed the company in extreme happiness sporting with his two queens for thirteen nights only and then all was over. The period of extreme happiness was for thirteen nights and not days. This appears to be somewhat puzzling.

But we are to keep in mind that Pandu was not only the husband of his two wives but he was also the king of a flourishing kingdom. He was due to perform the duties of a Kshatriya and that of a king as well. The passing of time for his own pleasure in fun and frolic and sporting with his queens, would have made him a fallen man. But why was the duration of his happiness for thirteen nights?

It has already been said that Pandu was pure knowledge and Kunti was detachment (nivritti) while Madri was Kunti's shadow-like bridge between attachment and detachment (anuvritti). As they both are inspirational energies, so also is the pure knowledge too and the aggregate of these three energies makes a complete mind and this mind is the king of Hastinapuna. Now let us have the identity of these three energies. The Pure knowledge is the state of dissolution of mind. Be it resolution of mind or dissolution of it — it is the mind that expresses itself in two ways i.e. resolution and dissolution and both have their existence according to their pre-eminence. This existence is Asti (existence) and that which has its existence (Asti) has its manifestation being aided by the inspirational energy of detachment, in other words, detachment is its lustre (bhati) and the result of this manifestation is bliss (priya or ananda) which is always dependent upon detachment and hence anuvritti is the shadow of detachment. Now existence (Asti) manifestation (bhati) and priya (bliss) constitute a complete mind. This completion of three energies comes through natural process that needs imbalance as without imbalance of forces nature cannot be activated and here in this regard that imbalance is caused owing to the predominance of asti (Pandu). The inner chambers of the palace are also under the administrative control of the king and hence the frolic and sport with the queens take place for thirteen nights. The circle of the mind containing asti, bhati and priya (existence, manifestation and bliss respectively) though complete yet the field of its activities is not wide enough. But it strives to have a wider area of activity and with a view to get a greater perspective, it becomes active in thirteen realities, they are five subtle sense-objects (tanmatra) and eight bondages (asta pasa). The seeds of realities of the body and the doctrine of the identity of body and soul and also of faculties remain deposited in

Nature prior to creation of the body and they become active at a proper time and under conducive conditions. The dissolution of mind or pure knowledge expresses itself in the domain of Maya and in the perspective of phenomenal matters and that material world is yet to be created, but it is necessary. Therefore, the world of matter has to be created and for that purpose subtle sense-objects were created. Had it not been done the great elements (Maha Bhutas) would not have been created and the creation of the material world have remained a dream only. At the same time the insensate nature of matter also was made to be possible, otherwise the insensate nature would not be manifested. The eight bondages are helpful in expression of insensate energy of matter. Added to this, as the darkness evaluates the radiance of light, similarly the manifestation of pure knowledge becomes splendent in the perspective of insensate nature of matter. So this insensate nature of matter is necessary in the realm of maya and the bond of maya is necessary in the sacrifice of creation and hence the pure knowledge steps in. Sound, touch, form, savour and smell are known to be the five subtle sense-objects but beyond the realm of phenomenal maya these five are the source of the Great Elements and in the perspective of material maya, these five are the sense objects — the source of immumerable sense-objects. The Sense-objects and bondages are closely related in the field of matter and to make this relationship ever inseparable, the subtle sense-objects (tanmatra) require transformation to sense-objects. On the other hand, sense-objects and bondages both ensue ignorance and hence thirteen nights have been referred to in respect of Pandu's enjoyment of sporting with his two queens.

It is also important to note that king Pandu set out for conquering the four directions and collected a good mass of wealth defeating all leading kings of that time. What does it mean? There are the mind, the subtle sense-objects and eight bondages too; but the closeness among them is conspicuously absent. If the mind so desires, it may enjoy sense-objects and the bondages are very much helpful in this regard but it can never enjoy sense-objects itself and it requires the assistance of senses and sense organs for the purpose. The senses carry the sense objects to the mind to fulfil its desires and hence the attachment between the mind and the senses is absolutely necessary, otherwise the senses cannot be activated. Therefore to sow the seeds to activate the senses is necessary and Pandu's conquest of the directions is but the effort to establish the authority of the mind throughout the body although the creation of the physical body is still long way far.

But such a purified mind is full of knowledge and not of resolution. So its manifestation would be different from that of resolution. Be it full of resolution or dissolution, the movement of the mind remains in the domain of maya although their vision would be contrary to each other. If the mind of resolution looks downwards, that of dissolution will look upwards. Hence, Pandu decided to wander in the forest with his two queens and after due preparation he left the capital and reached the foot-hills of the Himalayas and resumed his game-hunting. The necessary provisions were used to be carried by the servants of Dhritarastra. But why did a conqueror of the directions of the world decided to live in the forest? The pure knowledge can never be satisfied with enjoying sense-objects only. Alternative arrangements are necessary to remain beyond the circumference of enjoyment of sense-objects and hence such a decision. Of course, this wandering of Pandu in the forest was necessary to weave the fabric of the argument of the story. But there were many such dense forests elsewhere also. Why was the foot-hills of the Himalayas chosen? Pure knowledge can never be propitiated with sense objects — we have said it earlier. Its quest is to find out what there is beyond the limit of sense-objects and their enjoyment. Hence Pandu selected the forest at the foothills of the Himalayas as the North is the direction of self-knowledge that renders the answer to the question, who am I? The self-knowledge is a precondition to the knowledge of Brahman. The snow capped Himalayas is the symbol of Hridaya bhumi (field of the heart) and the forest at its foot-hills is that of chitta bhumi (land of the chitta) while the trees there are the symbols of the faculties. Away from the hustle-bustle of the capital, there are chances to identify every tree, every flower and every fruit in loneliness that may smoothen his way to cross the forest and finally to reach the Himalayas some day. In this effort, his two queens are his inspirations. This is the significance of Pandu's dwelling in the forest.

Pandu's life in the forest with his two queens was going on undisturbed. But a Kshatriya king cannot pass his time idly being oblivious of the dharma of a Kshatriya being a forest-dweller. So, Pandu did never abstain himself from game hunting in the forest. One day during his sporting course of hunting he shot five arrows targeting a deer engaged in coition with a doe. The wounded deer said to Pandu that he was the son of a muni and both he and his wife assumed the forms of a deer and a doe and while he was engaged in coitus, hitting him with the arrows Pandu had committed a crime. So the deer cursed Pandu would die while performing the same with his wife who also would follow the suit.

Several questions may arise now. Even if the munis and rishis be forest dwellers, they have some huts or cottages to live in. What inspired the son of a muni and his wife to assume the form of a beast? Why was the muni engaged in the act with his wife in broad day light despite being forbidden in the scriptures? What were the reasons for their assumption of the form of a four-footed beast? Why did the king being well-versed in scriptures shot the deer in that state? Why did he need five arrows to kill a deer that was not fleeing?

Pandu, the epitome of pure knowledge is but the mind and the mind exposes the energy of volition and this exposure establishes its existence; without this exposure its identity cannot be revealed. It cannot be stunned for a long time. On the other hand, ignorance is there on the mental plane to counter pure knowledge. Therefore, pure knowledge will be in quest of what there is beyond this ignorance and this quest is man's austerity. Pandu's wandering in the forest is a step to this direction. But the king is a Kshatriya and his dharma is to wage war. There are hints to this in his life in the forest. The conflict is between knowledge and ignorance which is but the first step to austerity. The hints become expressive of the fact that the provisions for Pandu are carried to the forest by the servants of Dhritarastra; he is the king of Hastinapura and has not renounced the kingdom. He is not apathetic to worldly interests but his vision is fixed to what is there beyond this material world. Now, he has two visions fixed to the pleasurable (preya) and to virtuous (shreya). These two are in conflict in him and he strives to be free of the pleasurable which is still unattained and hence the conflict.

Despite this conflict he aspires for virtuousness, yet he is happy in game-hunting.

The Chitta is a field as well as the firmament. As there are luminous stars and planets in the sky, similarly the faculties are abuzz in the firmament of the Chitta; as the sky holds the sun, the Moon and other stars and planets, the Chitta also holds the seeds of the fruits of actions that are exposed as faculties at times. As the clouds overcast the sky, likewise, the Chitta becomes smudged with the origination of faculties. Moreover, the mind, the intelligence and the ego exist in the Chitta and the mind, the intelligence, the ego and the Chitta constitute the inner mind (Antahkarana). On the other hand, the Hridaya (the heart, not the physical heart) is also a firmament and a field too as the Chitta is. In the firmament of the Hridaya, the divine esses are also moving like the radiant sun, the glowing moon and the twinkling stars that make it beautiful. The Primordial Nature extended herself in the field of the Hridaya as faith; there originate Shraddha (adorable admiration), Bhakti (devotion) and Nirbharata (complete self-surrender) upon that field and these are the four splendours of the Hridaya, as the mind, the intelligence, the ego and the Chitta are the mainstay of the inner mind.

Now, what is the difference between the two skies? In outer nature, so far the atmosphere is stretched forth that far we may see the sky from the surface of the earth and there is also the space beyond that sky which cannot be seen with bare eyes. But that void is also sky. Likewise, in the vision of an austere person the firmament beyond the atmospheric sky containing the stars, planets suns and moon, is the Hridaya with faith, admirable adoration, bhakti and surrendering being its four feet and in the same manner its lower sky containing the mind, the intelligence, the ego and the Chitta — the inner mind — is a four footed existence. As the various esses paint the Hridaya, likewise innumerable faculties paint the Chitta too. They are united and they are the deer and doe engaged in intercourse. It is a deft metaphor — a symbolical presentation of a bare fact.

Therefore, the Hridaya is the deer and the Chitta is the doe. The contact between the two is their coition in the story. Even then there remains a question as to why the young muni engaged himself in such an act in day time and in the forest leaving behind their home! Of course, the muni has advanced an explanation and that is fear of public disgrace. But to have close company of one's wife is never a subject to public disgrace; more so, if it happens in a room, there remains no question of public upbraiding and had that been so he should not have married. On the other hand, the king, well-versed in scriptures, shot five shafts to hit a static target. But why?

Generally, one cannot discern that there is another sky beyond this visible one, called the space and both are connected despite being different in character. But we know there is space beyond this sky. Similarly the sky of Chitta and that of the Hridaya are connected with the other; while the space beyond the Chitta is not visible to us till the Chitta remains smeared with faculties. But when the Chitta becomes transparent being free from faculties, one may visualize the unending splendour of the Hridaya. But the task is not so easy to cleanse the Chitta. Yet it is possible. An aspirant for spiritual life begins his austerity with the smeared Chitta and his aim is first to cleanse the Chitta. In his efforts as much slough is cleansed that much clear the Chitta would be but that is not all. However, sometimes the austere person gets the idea of the splendours of the Hridaya although till then he is subjugated to his mind. Then being in the realm of mind he seeks to have the right to the realm of Hridaya notwithstanding the fact that he is to forsake the wealth of the mind that he enjoyed so long. But that needs fixed aim and a single minded pursuit. The symbol of the like austere person that Pandu is, that the shafts aiming the deer engaged in coition, who was the symbol of Hridaya and the doe was that of the Chitta. So long the austere person remains extrovert in vision, such intercourse takes place hideaway and it takes place in the forest to be visible to the human eye; but this intercourse is unending.

Why the author used the imagery of coition to speak of the union of the sky and the space?

It is true that the inspiration, consent, pleasure and the blissful experience of both the partners in coition remains equal otherwise such an act cannot be a happy one. In the feeling of pleasure, consent and action itself the role of the mind, the intelligence, the ego and the Chitta is foremost although the inspiration for ananda (bliss) comes from the heart (hridaya) and that remains unknown to the active partners. On the other hand, as the source of inspiration for blissful experience (ananda) is the Hridaya (heart), likewise this bliss is the demanding leitmotif of it, which the Hridaya enjoys. Sprung of Hridaya the inspiration for this bliss energises the inner mind (antahkarana) which, in turn, having it, offers this bliss (ananda) to Hridaya. But this reciprocal action of Hridaya and Antahkarana remains unknown to the ordinary men and women. In the outer world also apart from the rays of the sun, that of many stars which are not generally visible, reach the earth to make it fertile, helping creation of life and its sustenance. And the creation on earth thankfully sings paeans aiming that light. The interaction of these firmaments is going on uninterruptedly and in a greater sense it is the universal coition and hence Vyasa's use of this symbol is extremely an apt one.

Pandu has hit the deer engaged in intercourse with five arrows shot one after another. A man conversant with scriptures and the science of war had to spend five shafts to kill a static deer. But why? We should keep in mind that every being is a target of these five arrows and is bewildered in pain. So to become perfectly composed one is to find out such an antidote that may give him peace and equilibrium bestowing peace of mind doing away with the restlessness. That antidote is the bliss and the field of Hridaya is the place of bliss. So it is needed to give up these five shafts in search of unturbid ananda (bliss) so that nothing can make one restless any more; in other words, it is to surrender oneself before the alter of Ananda going over to the temple of Ananda (Hridaya). These five arrows are of dharma (faith) artha (riches), Kama (desire) and moksha (emancipation) along with that of Shanti (peace). Until a person is established in his own dharma he cannot find out the true significance of his own existence; but he who knows of this, knows well that his desire is of bliss and which way to proceed. When it proceeds towards its actual goal, his aspiration and restlessness of mind will go away. But prior to this achievement his restlessness of mind persists and he searches for bliss and try to proceed towards that goal. In such a state of mind pure knowledge Pandu shot those five shafts remaining on the plane of Chitta i.e. finding the trace of bliss after an arduous search for it, he submits to bliss. But the deer was not yet dead. He said, he was a son of a muni assuming the form of a deer and in future

Pandu would die in course of similar action. Thus after cursing Pandu the deer died.

The arrows shot by Pandu killed the deer only and not the doe. She remained unhurt though embraced death along with her companion. The wounded deer disclosed that he was the son of a muni which means he also was a muni — the seer of Truth. But why? The Hridaya is the plane of bliss. Here in bliss one realizes Atman. To realize Atman or Brahman one has to give up those five arrows with the aim to have the realization full of bliss. Pandu shot the shafts to attain that goal. But he could not be successful squarely as there was a difference between the hunter and the hunted as a result of which he failed to advance to nurse the wounded dear; rather, he entangled himself in a web of reasoning with the deer to prove his innocence. All this happened because Pandu had the subtle desire for enjoyment of sense objects in his sport of game-hunting. As a result he was cursed by the deer that he also would die while in coition with his wife and she would also court death following him. The curse was actually a boon to Pandu.

Firstly, when the austere person reaches the Hridaya, the coition between Hridaya and the Chitta ends as the necessity of it is over by then. It was necessary to inspire the beings to be in quest of bliss. Then upon the plane of bliss the individual self becomes engaged in coition with the Supreme Self and no other coition is at all necessary; but it is possible only when the austere person attains the mental state beyond all desires to enjoy sense objects and that is his/her mental death which ultimately ensures coition with the Supreme Self. Such a death of both partners ensures bliss in coition — this is the significance of the curse by the dying deer which Pandu failed to realize.

Sorrowful Pandu became repentant and thought to erode away the fruits of his actions by enduring them. Being specially influenced by the aversion to worldly pleasures and enjoyment of sense-objects he resolved to give up familial bond and strive for emancipation henceforth and also decided "......to adopt strict austerity......giving up everything good or evil I would pass my days either in an empty room or under a tree making the body gray with dust. I shall take pain and pleasure alike without accepting blessings or obeisance from anybody regarding praise and upbraiding equally. I shall ever remain content without being cruel to one either mobile or immobile. I shall care for every being with filial affection. I shall beg for my livelihood...." It is to be noted that these resolutions of Pandu are that of a sannyasin. The reasons for his apathy to worldly pleasures is due to the curse of the dying deer. He asked his queens to return to the capital, but they could not be acquiescent to the king's proposal. They argued that apart from the order of sannyasa, there were many other orders and embracing any one of them one may be an austere person. So the king should accompany them and they three would observe austerity to attain the highest goal. Unable to desist them the king began to observe austerity maintaining abstinence and wandering at different places. He became free from the sins since incurred.

We are to note that the king being cursed by the deer became an austere person with a view to be emancipated. But where is the certainty that emancipation will assure him the union with the Supreme? It is also to be noted that the inspiration for his strict adherence to austerity was despite his having strength and capability of having sex with his queens, Pandu is debarred from doing so owing to the fear of courting death. Therefore, there are two sides of his austerity; (1) the king, fearful of death, remains away from coition and (2) he likes to be oblivious of this fact notwithstanding being capable of that. So, his apathy to worldly pleasures and so called renunciation were imposed and not sprung of the core of his heart; hence it is an austerity for desires. From the spiritual point of view, it is his utter failure although this failure is the harbinger of success.

The fabric of the tale has been woven taking materials from the life of ordinary beings, but the ascertainable goal is none of the material objects. The ordinary beings are always engaged in enjoying sense-objects and hence the world around them is beautiful and on the other hand, to the enlightened seers, the world around is beautiful being the manifestation of splendid magnificence of the Creator and they feel the urge to be united with Him. Just see the difference of vision and approach of the seers and that of Pandu which denotes the difference between the seers and Pandu who become an austerer indeed, but he could not keep away from the attachment to sense-objects and further progress of the story will approve of this.

One day Pandu saw that the Siddhas were going somewhere. On enquiry he could know that they were going to meet with Brahma in a synod of gods, rishis and the manes in the realm of Brahma beyond heaven. Listening to this Pandu at once decided to go there and accompanied them with his two queens. Seeing Pandu following them, the Siddhas told him that the road was a very difficult one and it was almost impossible for the queens to get access to the destination and they advised Pandu to desist from the journey. Pandu rightly understood the beckoning of this advice. He realized that although he had repaid the debt to the gods, to the rishis and to the humans, he utterly failed to repay the debt to the manes as even being worthy and capable of procreating progenies he could not be a father. Until and unless one is free from all debts, one cannot have the access to Brahmaloka only by dint of the results of one's austerity. Disappointed Pandu became sorry and sought to know as to whether by any means he could have progenies in his own fields. In reply the Siddhas told him that they were visualizing with their divine eyes that Pandu would have offsprings of infinite virtues in his own fields; so he should have to be active to have sons.

We have said it earlier that Pandu's apathy for worldly objects was imposed and not natural. Hence his austerity was full of desires. One's austere pursuits are for going beyond the mind and austerity is of mental plane and any austerity practised with the help of mind is sure to be full of desires. On other hand, real apathy to anything worldly ensures entitlement to Hridaya but the mind can never have it. The cleansing of the Chitta may not ensure that title.

So long the austere person is under the tutelage of the mind his Chitta is not transparent. Pandu too suffered from his failure. However strong his austerity might be that could not ensure his attainment of Hridaya and this was the significance of what the Siddhas told him. They said also that the path leading to Brahmaloka was too difficult to traverse and even the birds cannot go there, not to speak of other beings and beasts; only air and the Siddhas can go there. This opinion of the Siddhas testifies to the fact that Pandu's austerity could not empower him or his queens to reach

Brahmaloka. He was not free also from all bondages and until that happened he could not reach there. Pandu is the mind even if he is pure knowledge. It was not possible for him to reach the Hridaya and the reason for it has symbolically been expressed that as yet he could not repay his debt to the manes. This bears two beckonings; one, to continue the course of creation. Every being is required to procreate offspring with his own seed as he came into being by his father. God Himself has created this universe with His own seed. But Pandu is unable to follow the instance. The incapability of creating offspring makes a man incomplete in many respects.

Secondly, though he is pure intelligence or knowledge Pandu is the mind. Resolution and dissolution of it are but two sides of the same coin. The immeasurable universe is the manifestation of the Creator's resolution and opposite to it is the Creator Himself. Yet there is dissolution in it, otherwise, being in the domain of resolution how does the quest of humankind search for God? Again, there was resolution in the Creater, otherwise how was the creation possible? Therefore, both resolution and dissolution are two manifestations of the mind only. Sometimes, one of them becomes prominent but the mind is mind and it is unable to realize the Supreme Reality. Austerity needs the help of the mind; it never does perform austerity nor can it do it.

The Great Mental sacrifice of the Supreme is the sacrifice of Creation which has three stages viz. firstly, the causal world; secondly, the subtle world and thirdly the physical world which are created one after another as per the sequence. The part of the tale under discussion is of the early stage of the subtle creation and a lot of which is yet to be created. Pure knowledge is the lord of subtle world and the mind of resolution is that of the physical world. But as a good lot of the subtle world is yet to be created and the creation of the physical world is much far away, the pure knowledge, failing to augment its area of influence in its own sphere, rushes towards that of causality. It seeks to establish itself in the causal world and it is his hunting of the deer and to be cursed by it. His progress to the causal world was needed to be halted, otherwise further creation was sure to be stalled invoking chaos. This is antagonistic to the Divine Will altogether. Secondly, where beasts and birds cannot go but the Siddhas and air only can the mind cannot go there. The existence of beings (jiva satta) is allowed to go there. But no beings have yet been created, hence there is no question of going of the existence of beings. In the story this existence of beings has been termed as Siddhas and air. Apart from this, the existence of beings cannot go there of their own but pulled by the energy of Bliss of Guru. Hence the Siddhas advised Pandu to carefully perform his ordained duty.

The existence of the beings referred to above would be available only when the human beings are created which has not yet been done. So the incapable Pandu approached Kunti to procreate a son by a man of his clan or any superior one. Kunti refused both of them and argued for some time. Later on, Kunti agreed to it finally. She narrated to him how she got a mantra from the great rishi Durvasha during her virgin years and told Pandu that on getting his permission she might carry his desired son in her womb. Pandu said at once, "....Dharma is the greatest of all, he is really an adorable one being full of piety, please invoke him." Kunti did so incanting the mantra. Dharma appeared and gave Kunti a son who was very religious, valiant, truthful and an observer of vows. The son is the first Pandava, Yudhisthira. After some time Pandu told Kunti that a man of strength in the Kshatriya clan was more praise-worthy; hence now you please give birth to a son who would be immensely strong in physique. Obeying Pandu Kunti invoked Vayu to give her "a son having great powers, of a great physique and who could humble one's vanity easily." This second son was Bhima. Even after having two sons Pandu's craving for having more sons had not been gratified. Now he desires to have a son who would be the greatest among all the realms. He thought of Indra, the king of gods in heaven was the greatest among gods having immense strength and prowess. I would satisfy him by my austere endeavour to this end and pray to give me a son of immense prowess. He consulted with the great rishis disclosing his resolve to them and asked Kunti to observe vows for a year and he himself became engaged in austere endeavour. The gratified Indra appearing before Pandu, promised to give him a son as he liked. A gladdened Pandu asked Kunti to invoke Indra. Kunti did so and had a son by Indra. This third son is Arjuna. But Pandu's desire for having more sons was not satiated and like a femine-striken hungry person he wanted to have more sons.

Meanwhile, seeing that Kunti was giving birth to sons again and again Madri become envious of her. Once she opened her mind to Pandu. He, then, knowing the lack of effort on the part of Kunti, asked her to help Madri getting sons as the mantra to invoke the desired god was known to her and without her help Madri could not be a mother. Kunti agreed. Being helped by Kunti, Madri invoked the divine apothecaries, the twin Ashvins and ultimately she became the mother of twin sons — Nakula and Sahadeva. Kunti grew to be envious of Madri as she became the mother of two sons at an instance and promised not to help her in future for getting more sons. Pandu was happy now with five sons.

The inspiration for having sons to Pandu was to attain Brahmaloka as he would be free from the debt to the manes being a father and it would not be impossible. But he could have been freed from that debt had he been the father of a single son. Then why was he so eager to have sons one after another? We have said it earlier that in order to firmly seize the manifestation of Self, human body is necessary and it is an outcome of the evolutionary sequence. Without a body the individual self cannot manifest itself. So the body is necessary and it is a step forward to the process of evolution and this is Pandu's desire for sons. The five Pandavas are five Great Pure Elements (Mahabhutas) that are necessary for creation of human body and they are the progenies of pure knowledge, so to say; but they are divine, Being a Kshatriya Pandu is reluctant to rule his kingdom and eager to attain Brahmaloka. But why?

We should keep in mind, this immeasurable universe is the creation of Brahman and it is also true that its culmination is the human form — no better form has yet been created. The humans only can realize Brahman by their earnest efforts for which all the elements are there in human body. But it needs a determined resolution and earnest efforts to have the desired results. And in that efforts the state of dissolution of mind attracts him to that way. Pandu is the dissolution of mind that is reluctant to rule the kingdom and his vision is fixed to Brahmaloka. But why is it so? What has been created step by step in this universe, in every granule of each of them Brahman is existent. Ordinary Consciousness is a creation of Supreme Consciousness; both are Vodha (consciousness) but differ in manifestation — the limitations of ordinary consciousness are not there in Supreme Consciousness and the whole of creation is natant upon the ocean of Consciousness and the beings, in due course, established in that consciousness create a circle while, of course, in doing so they need firstly to fix their vision to the centrifugal movement. Then passing through certain stages the same vision be fixed to the centripetal movement. The change of vision is occurred by the dissolution of mind and hence Pandu's vision is fixed to Brahmaloka and not to the kingdom.

On the other hand, until the human body is created, the culmination of the sequence of evolution would have remained elusive, Again, in absence of physical body austere pursuits are impossible, and the circle floating on the surface of the ocean of consciousness would not be complete without austere pursuits. So the elements were necessary for creation of the physical body.

The five sons of Pandu are the five pure elements having their particular qualities and characteristics in each of them. The first Pandava is the first element of ether or space for the physical body. He is born of nivritti (detachment) fathered by Dharma. In the perspective of energy nivritti is the energy of action who got the seed of Dharma. Dharma bears the existence and also manifests it. Dharma has no specific form and hence different beings and objects have different dharmas. As the dharma bears the existence, similarly the space or ether bears the creation and hence the reality of space is the first step towards creation. This first step was created by the seed of Dharma which is the reality of space or ether Yudhisthira, the first Pandava who himself used to be called later on as Dharma also. Dharma is the greatest; Dharma is Yudhisthira and he is the reality of space that helps manifest other realities holding them near the heart.

The second Pandava is Bhima who is exceptionally strong in physique. Vayu is his father and Bhima, the son of Vayu is also Vayu (air). It keeps the body animated being divided into five vital breaths and holds the body erect remaining around it. It helps manifestation of energy and keeps the universal body lively and livening. So Vayu in the form of Bhima is full of energy and prowess undoubtedly.

The third Pandava is Arjuna. There is a little variegation in the history of his birth. To have a son the greatest in all the worlds, Pandu began austere pursuit to satisfy Indra, the greatest of the gods and had a promise from him to this effect and following Pandu's dictates Kunti also observed a vow for the same purpose. Thereafter she invoked Indra incanting the mantra and having the seed of the king of gods she became the mother of Arjuna. This third Pandava is the reality of Tejas (fire). The fire is there at the root of creation, evolution and its culmination too. In absence of fire the whole of universe is but a seed.

The fourth and fifth Pandavas, Nakula and Sahadeva are the realities of water and earth respectively. It is to note that five Pandava brothers have five fathers but two mothers. But why? The father of the first Pandava is Dharma and he himself is also dharma. Dharma is the quintessence of all existence. The dharma of man is manhood. Again, human body has its own dharma which, in turn, is instrumental for manifestation of manhood. Hence dharma is the foundation of all existence. The vital breaths are essential in observance of one's own dharma. A body devoid of vital breaths cannot observe the dharma of a man. So to activate the vital breaths the fatherhood of Vayu (air) was necessary and he was invoked. The role of the vital breaths was not sufficient to observe one's own dharma. One is to know of one's own dharma and how to observe it for which the knowledge of ways and means is also essential; in other words, it is to realize the nature and manifestation of Dharma and to adopt the right course to observe it. Every austere person knows it well that the task is not so easy. It needs firm determination, fixed aim and the urge to be victorious by defeating the antagonistic forces of life. So the energy of tejas is necessary and hence the god of gods, the presiding deity of thunder is invoked after satisfying him by austere practices to bestow fatherhood upon the third Pandava.

After Dharma, Vayu and Indra the twin Ashvins became the fathers of twin brothers — Nakula and Sahadeva. It may be noted that the last two elements are visible and be touched but the first three are not so but perceptible. The first two viz. ether and air and the last two viz. water and earth are coordinated by Tejas like a grand pillar between the sides. To highlight this distinction of his character, his procreator was the god of gods, the deity of thunder, Indra. On the other hand, the twin Ashvins were the fathers of water and earth. The Ashvins were the divine apothecaries. But why were the apothecaries needed? The realities of the body wear away and to replenish them similar realities are to be taken from nature by means of food and drink for nourishment and to maintain equilibrium, otherwise the body may be sick and weak. And in that case, medicines may be required to take to bring back the equilibrium of realities of the body. The sources of medicine are three only — minerals. vegetation and poison. The water and earth are needed for these sources.

For nourishment and equilibrium of realities of the body, the role of these two elements is equally important and hence their fatherhood has been given to twin Ashvins.

The significance of five fathers to five Pandava brothers is shortly discussed. They are born of two mothers and why not of one? Kunti is the mother of first three brothers and Madri is that of the last two although there is an indirect role of Kunti in their birth. But why? Kunti is nivritti (detachment) that does not denote the absence of faculties but to accept that necessary for ordained actions. Madri is anuvrittee who having her vision fixed to detachment, accepts the faculties of both detachment and attachment. An austere person embraces detachment being inspired by dharma, by activities of vital breaths and with the prowess of tejas. There is no other way. The way of detachment is the way of order and discipline. Detachment and order are almost synonymous but detachment is the inspiration for order and the real nature of detachment is revealed in the perspective of attachment. But the inspiration for freedom from unbridled enjoyment and the culmination of it comes from anuvrittee and it bridges the gap between pravritti and nivritti although its span of life is not long enough. The Ap (water) and Kshiti (earth) are born of it. On the other hand, beings inspired by ignorance run after happiness that comes from the enjoyment of sense-objects that draws them more and more to ignorance and the attraction comes from these two realities (water and earth) that follow both pravritti and nivritti (attachment and detachment) also, of course, if trained in this regard. Secondly, organs are generally dependent on the reality of earth and water. Therefore, it is quite logical that the realities which follow attachment and detachment at times, would be born of anuvritti (Madri). To point out these characteristics Vyasa has given their motherhood to Madri. Thirdly, the primary inspiration for enjoyment of sense-objects comes from the quest of happiness, which is but the shadow of bliss and hence Madri, the energy of that bliss is the mother of these two realities.

Now Pandava brothers are five and Pandu is happy; so also his two wives. They three were passing their days in the forest without any hazards. After some time came the season of spring and Pandu set out for wandering in the forest. Madri followed him. The season was spring and the forest was full of blossoms. The shaft of Cupid pierced the king's heart despite Madri's interdictions being swayed by amour fou Pandu passionately embraced her. Death kissed the king as cursed by the deer earlier. Being attracted by the loud cry of Madri, Kunti hastily proceeded towards her with five sons. Lying under the chest of the dead, Madri forbade the sons to come and asked Kunti to come alone. She did so, coming nearer Kunti did not fail to rebuke Madri; even she threw her sarcastic envy aiming her. "O the princess of Madra! You are blessed indeed as you have seen the complacent face of the king."

When Pandu died the Pandava brothers were very young in age. Meanwhile, Madri too died following her husband. The responsibility to bring up the five brothers fell upon Kunti. What is the significance of all this? In the pleasure of creation the role of the energy of will is most important; and that energy of will is active in Pandu. But it alone cannot create anything. It needs the energy of action. Without the active participation of energy of action, the mission of the energy of will is not to fructify. Hence the role of Kunti is so prominent in relation to the birth of Pandava brothers. But the energy of will and that of action cannot make a full circle of energies. Hence the energy of bliss is necessary to complete the circle. The energy of bliss is also Pandava mother but short-lived. Whatever may be the role of the energy of will in the context of creation, the energy of bliss plays a vital and foremost role. When the act of creation is over, the bliss exhausts and the will too. In other words, the bliss that activates the will that also exhausts in bliss itself. Hence, Pandu is dead as also Madri.

Pure knowledge loses its purity coming in contact with sense-objects having the selfish intent.

Karna — The Son Of Virgin Kunti

Shurasena was the king of the Yadavas. Kuntibhoja was the king of the Bhoja kingdom. They both were related by blood and close friends. Shurasena promised to give his first born to Kuntibhoja to adopt and bring up as Kuntibhoja had no issue. So king Shurasena gave his first-born, a daughter to Kuntibhoja. Her name was Pritha. But in the kingdom of Bhoja she was given the name of Kunti after her foster father's name. There she grew up having a good education. Once when she was young, Rishi Durvasha happened to be the guest in the palace for a fortnight. The responsibility to look after the rishi was given to the young princess who was gentle-natured and had the heart full of devotion. At the time of leaving the palace the rishi complacent of the service rendered by the princess, gave her a boon in form of a mantra saying that intoning it she could invoke any of the gods who, so invoked coming to her in person, would give her a son each. What a peculiar gift to his virgin devotee by a powerful rishi!

Curiosity is a universal phenomenon among the beings especially the feminine ones. It has also an element of doubt underlying in it. So once Kunti out of curiosity sought to test the authenticity of the mantra and what the rishi said to her, invoked the sun-god incanting the mantra. In no time the god appeared in his brilliant radiance. The embarrassment of the virgin princes knew no bound. The god ignoring the fearful and perplexed princess's all resistance, gave a son into her womb. To become a mother during virginity goes against the social order and it is a matter of shame too. So social upbraiding got the better of the mother's affection and the young mother decided to abandon the new-born. Putting the child who was fully armoured, in a chest she left it to float upon the river stream. Later on, the carpenter, finding the chest rescued the baby and gave it to his wife, Radha to bring the baby up. The baby having the identity of being the son of the carpenter couple, began to grow up. This baby, the son of virgin Kunti, is Karna.

We have said earlier that Gandhari is pravritti (attachment), Kunti is nivritti (detachment), Madri is anuvritti (the bridge between the former two), and Parashavi is behavioural virtuousness. Actually, they are the faculties of mind and the author according to the need of the story, presented them as feminine characters ascribing the necessary human qualities and characteristics to them so that they may appear to be real ones of flesh and blood. But these faculties are the inspirations of the mind vis-à-vis the energy for expressing its actions and reactions. The energy (Shakti) is identified by its manifestations; and its state of equilibrium of its forces is generally beyond our comprehension. Its manifestation is of two kinds; the first one is the manifestation in formal identity separated from the origin and the second one is the manifestation of formal dissolution of the created i.e. the return to the source or origin. So there is motion there in both ways and where there is motion there is a vision of aim. Hence, we may safely conclude that the faculties too have two visions — the extrovert and the introvert. Gandhari of the story is pravritti (attachment) and hence she is the inspirational energy for enjoyment of sense-objects. An extravert vision is necessary for enjoying sense-objects and Gandhari represents this extravert vision. But the faculty of detachment does not do so; she is the energy for order and discipline. She keeps herself away from sense-objects and she is prone to deliberate and hence her vision is introvert. But anuvritti (the bridge) has two visions equally and she can discern the actual character of extravert vision and able to consciously change the direction of vision. So Madri has a good relation with both Gandhari and Kunti, but the relation with Gandhari is an outward one and it is otherwise with Kunti because of her conscious consideration.

However, we are concerned with Kunti (detachment). Her father was Shurasena and foster father was Kuntibhoja and at his place the virgin daughter became a mother. The sequence of events is no less confusing. Her father was Shurasena and her foster father was Kuntibhoja. The daughter had to lose her father's protective shelter when she was a mere child, but had the protection and shelter of her foster father, her both fathers were related by blood and close friends. Now let us see, who was Shurasena and who was Kuntibhoja in terms of the realities of human body? Faculties are of the mental plane and originate in the field of the Chitta. But earlier we have said that nivritti (detachment) is a faculty of discipline and order. More so, it is also true that under the influence of the faculty that follows order and consideration, despite having sense-objects for enjoyment as and when necessary may some day act to help the chitta being free of faculties manifesting itself as an aiding agent, and then it will turn to be the non-existence of faculty being an energy itself and then it is not nivritti but a guiding principle or force. While its field of action is the chitta, it did not arise of it. Its action then will be powerful enough so that other faculties of the chitta would be defunct and ultimately the chitta would be as clear as crystal.

On the other hand, the Hridaya (heart, not the physical organ) is the realm of esses (bhavas); there they play incessantly to attract and inspire austerers aspiring spiritual uplift and a single esse has the power to undo all the wants of life making it meaningful with enlightenment. So each of the esses is a great warrior and the aggregate of them constitute a great army and the lord of this army is Shurasena. He is the father of Nivritti. Shurasena, the king of the great warriors, is also the king of introversion of vision, while the faculties that arise in the Chitta, are actually agents for enjoyment and they take away the transparency of the Chitta making it smudged with the urge for enjoyment of sense-objects. The faculties that smear the Chitta, are not its treasures but impediments and they are not born of Chitta but manifest themselves taking refuge in the Chitta; they are the seeds of the fruits of actions of earlier births having the intent of enjoying sense-objects. Hence the realm is of enjoyment of sense-objects spurred by the fruits of actions of previous births. These seeds of actions of previous births remain deposited in the chitta and become active in a conducive ambience at a proper time. Hence the chitta is the foster father of the faculties. It is unable to procreate. On the other hand, Hridaya (heart) is capable to procreate the esse. Nivritti has the energy of transport one from non-existence of bliss to the realm of bliss but its field of activity is the plane of Chitta and hence the daughter of Shurasenna is the foster daughter of Kuntibhoja, having extrovert vision.

Rishi Durvasha, the guest in the palace of king Kuntibhoja, being satisfied with the service rendered by the princess, granted a boon to her in form of a mantra incanting which she might invoke a god who, in turn, would give her a son in her womb. On one side, the kingdom was of enjoyment of sense-objects, on the other, the princess was young and beautiful. Hence to be curious was natural. Once when she was alone Kunti invoked the sun-god intoning the mantra and the god appeared. Ignoring her vocal resistance the god gave her an armoured son into her womb.

What an amazing fact is it! The royal guest, a great rishi being satisfied with the service rendered to him, gave a boon to a princess by the influence of which a chosen god appearing in person would give her a child. Curiosity of the faminial beings is proverbial. Had the rishi been oblivious of the fact? No, it is but otherwise. He was well aware that the princess would soon be curious to test the effectiveness of the mantra and having this conviction he gave his boon to her. But why?

We should keep in mind that though she was away from her father's home, the influence of the environment was very much in her mind. But in the kingdom of her foster father she had to pass her days in a newer ambience abiding by the morality, custom etc. until she would be given by marriage to someone. Her stay in the kingdom of enjoyment of sense-objects was bound to be led by the prevailing norms there. Despite her birth in Hridaya her field of activity was Chitta the influence of which was bound to regulate her life and action there. But howsoever strong the influence of the faculties of the Chitta be, she was constant in order and discipline and not fallen off. Even her invocation of the sun God and having a son by him were not acts of indiscipline and disorder.

The existence of Guru, the spiritual incarnation of the Supreme Consciousness is far away from the understanding of ordinary beings whose minds are smudged with superstitions, traditions etc. and of course, this distance is in the concept of beings, but not in the vision of Guru. And to undo this distance, one has to progress spiritually and ultimately by realizing the importance of Guru. At the same time, the key to this progression is the mantra given by Guru though the effectiveness of the mantra depends upon the faith of the recipient. Faith is the corner stone of dharma and its manifestation too.

In the story Durvasa is Kunti's Guru. He gave the mantra to his disciple being satisfied with her service to him. Had she been honest enough to take it with deep faith, the would have been blessed with newer understandings, being free from illusion and ignorance. Each of the arisen understandings is a son to the recipient being born of the womb of Hridaya of the recipient. But Kunti was not free from the influence of the environment around her and hence she could not squarely rely on what her Guru told her to be absolutely true. For the lack of confidence Kunti became curious and wanted to test the truthfulness of what her Guru said. Whatever night be the influence of the surroundings, that of her own existence was even stronger nonetheless and she invoked the sun-god and none other. The result of this curiosity is Karna, the gift of the sun-god. But Kunti had no way out as in the understanding of ordinary beings absolute belief is not possible.

The good understanding inherited by birth impelled Kunti to invoke the sun-god. The sun is the symbol of knowledge. As the darkness hides itself with rising of the sun similarly, ignorance becomes non-existent as knowledge dawns on human heart and bliss prevails due to the destruction of ignorance. Therefore, what is created by the union of nivritti and knowledge being inspired by curiosity upon the field of doubt, is required to be kept secret. Otherwise, if it be made public, along with it the doubt and curiosity would also be public that the beings do never like; rather, they want to wrap up their non-fulfillment, their weakness before the public eye. On the other hand, the revelation of radiance of knowledge makes doubt and curiosity non-existent in the bliss. If that is revealed, Kunti's doubt and curiosity would also be revealed. So she had the necessity to keep the incident of child-birth a secret.

Now let us see who is this son? Despite being the faculty of order and discipline, detachment is not free from the influence of enjoyment of sense-objects and hence it is possible to be confused and doubtful. The kingdom of Bhoja is the realm of ignorance and therefore it is not unnatural that the princess be doubtful. On the other hand, one is not supposed to test the qualities of one's Guru after one's initiation; rather one may do that prior to initiation. Hence, the tradition in vogue is to associate with the Guru before initiation, but not to test him after that. This tradition is meant for undoing one's doubts and confusions prior to initiation. But Kunti failed to make a successful use of that chance while her Guru remained a guest at the palace and that was her fault, though she failed owing to the conditions prevailing around her.

Curiosity grows of confusion which is the product of ignorance. Kunti was the princess of the kingdom of ignorance, being the adopted daughter of Kuntibhoja. By birth she was established in order and discipline. Her curiosity is the outcome of the conflict between these two forces and the culmination of which is doubt. Yet to refute this conflict, on her part, she took the refuge of knowledge and invoked the sun-god being the epitome of knowledge and neither Indra, nor Chandra, the moon-god nor any other. Came the god and Kunti, bathing in the radiance of the sun, became shy and reluctant as it is obvious that ignorance is bound to shrink observing its own reflection in the mirror of knowledge. Howsoever reluctant one may be, dawning of knowledge is imperative that one must have to accept. So the sun-god did what was due to be done and the virgin mother got her son.

Ignorance attracts knowledge. If a dark cave becomes illumined suddenly, the people outside may not know of it, an indistinct presence of light may or may not be visible. Likewise, when one's realm of mind becomes illuminated by the arisen knowledge at heart, people around may not know of it which means that remains a secret. Hence the union between Kunti and the sun-god remained a secret and on the same analogy the result of that union namely, the son also required to remain a secret. So the baby was kept in a chest and abandoned to drift down the stream of a river. The chest being found by Adhiratha, a carpenter, the baby got the refuge of a mother in Radha, the carpenter's wife. The son of Kunti became the son of Radha.

The seed of Brahman given by Guru to his disciple becomes fruitful if the disciple acts on the advices of Guru following the order to do so. The resultant delight following this fruitfulness, spreads through his body and mind giving him an experience that was quite unknown as yet. This experience is short-lived but its effect enhances the faith of the austerer and makes it more durable and he expects to have such experiences more and more although he cannot share it with others while it pervades his whole existence. This expectation in form of greed in an austerer's life, is the son of Kunti — a gift of the sun-god.

Seeing the baby in the chest Adhiratha took him to be his own son and handed over the baby to his wife Radha. Now, who is Adhiratha? He is beings' belief in the identity of the body is the soul or the materialistic view of life of beings and the smudged nature of the existence is Radha. The ordinary beings cannot lead the life without the materialistic view of it and remaining within the nature of beings greed makes them attached to sense-objects. He is born in the kingdom of enjoyment of sense-objects while detachment to sense-objects is his mother and the epitome of knowledge, the sun-god is his father; yet the inspiration for his birth is doubt in the advices of Guru which are regarded as the dictates of Brahman. Inspite of his place of birth being the realm of enjoyment, he is a valiant warrior owing to the energy of the sun-god and a dutiful person as also a liberal giver under the influence of detachment. But he is away from his mother since his birth notwithstanding the mother's confusion and doubt were done away with his birth. Yet he is left off. Ignorance is the pre-condition to enjoy sense-objects and without such enjoyment existence of beings becomes meaningless. So it was imperative to abandon him so that he may remain away from the influence of detachment as well as knowledge. Therefore he was put in a chest that floated down the river stream. The veins that carry the flow of blood through them in the body, are the rivers in it and each of the corpuscles of blood is a chest that carries the baby who is greed personified. Greed-carrying blood corpuscles were seen by the materialistic view of beings noticing it at once accepted it to be his own and handed over to the smeared nature of beings to bring him up. Being caged in the corpuscles of blood greed remains hidden in the existence of beings spreading its influence within the body and mind of beings. Generally its actual identity is not clearly revealed to the beings, but when it gets a favourable ambience for enjoyment of sense-objects, beings may know of its prowess.

Karna is one of the main characters of the tale on whom lady luck did not smile.

The Birth Of A Hundred Sons And A Daughter Of Gandhari

Once Vyasa appeared in Dhritarastra's palace being struck with hunger and thirst. Receiving him cordially Gandhari entertained Vyasa earnestly. A complacent Vyasa wanted to grant her a boon for the service she had rendered to him. In reply Gandhari said, "if you are so pleased, then allow me to be the mother of a hundred sons as strong as my husband having the qualities equal to him." Forthwith saying, "that is done" — Vyasa departed.

After some time Gandhari became carrying. But even after a lapse of two years she could not deliver. One day she heard that Kunti had become a mother of a son as handsome at the rising sun; this son was Yudhisthira. Gandhari grew to be envious and angrily caused an abortion without the knowledge of her husband. To her utter dismay she discovered that a lump of flesh harder than iron was born in her womb. Struck with anger and sorrow crestfallen Gandhari when arranging for throwing away the lump, came there Vyasa. Seeing the lump he asked, "What have you done, Soubaleyi?" Gandhari replied, On hearing the birth of Kunti's son prior to her own she had caused an abortion of her pregnancy. Then she asked Vyasa to produce a hundred sons from this lump as he gave her the boon to that effect. Vyasa then advised her to keep the lump of flesh keeping there one hundred pitchers full of clarified butter and also to sprinkle water on the lump, and that was done. Meanwhile Gandhari was thinking that it would have been better had there been a daughter too. In course of sprinkling of water the lump was fragmented into one hundred and one pieces. Then following the advices of Vyasa, each of the hundred pieces was kept in one hundred pitchers and the rest one was done with the same way bringing yet another pitcher. All the pitchers were filled with clarified butter and kept hidden. Showing the last pitcher Vyasa said to Gandhari that a daughter would be produced of that pitcher and to keep them all as they were; after two years one hundred sons and a daughter would be produced of them.

After two years Duryodhana was born and on the same day Bhima also was born. Then after one month ninety-nine brothers and a sister were born. Now we are to consider the perspectives of birth of Pandu's and Dhritarastra's sons and daughter. It was the inspiration of Pandu for the birth of Pandavas while it was that of Gandhari for the birth of Kauravas. Pandu desired for sons unequalled in the world full of divine qualities, whereas Gandhari desired for sons as strong as her husband having also the qualities of their father. Pure knowledge personified as Pandu had the desire to repay the debt to the manes at the root of the inspiration for having sons while attachment personified as Gandhari had the inspiration for having sons was for enjoyment of sense-objects and this became evident in her confession that she caused abortion of her pregnancy getting the news of Yudhisthira's birth. Though Dhritarastra was on the throne of Hastinapura, he was not the king but a regent only despite the fact that he was the eldest brother. Had his son been born earlier, at least on that plea, the right to the throne could have been claimed. But that hope was dashed off. So infuriated and envious

Gandhari aborted her pregnancy and saw a hard lump of flesh was there in her womb. She grew angrier and the end in view was her father-in-law, Vyasa.

In dire disregard she decided to throw it away. The growing of a lump in the womb is not unnatural but what the unnatural was that the boon of Vyasa did not fructify. After carrying for two years if a woman sees that a hard lump of flesh instead of any son or daughter is produced in her womb, she is sure to be crestfallen. Boundless disappointment makes Gandhari afflicted so much so that she sarcastically asked Vyasa to create a hundred sons of that lump. Unperturbed Vyasa made known the procedure to have the anticipated result and left Hastinapura. After two years it was evident that Vyasa's boon was not ineffective.

The mind of resolution is blind and owing to its blindness, it desires to enjoy sense-objects; and for the same reason it goes beyond righteousness knowing well of its scope and limit and becomes unbridled for enjoyment of sense-objects. Even if truth, dharma, conscience may influence this mind, but for an insignificant period of time and that influence cannot leave a durable impression upon it. This blindness of mind enables it to enjoy many a kind of sense-objects both possible and impossible. On one side, this mind is the father and on the other, attachment personified in Gandhari is the mother who wanted to have the sons equal to her husband in strength and qualities. So, it may easily be inferred the nature of their sons who took four years for gestation to come to proper shapes, two years in the womb and two years in pitchers. Apart from all this, they were not delivered in normal course; an abortion was necessary. Of course, it was not an easy task to deliver one hundred sons and a daughter at one go. Unnaturally delivered an unnatural object, a stiff lump of flesh and this is the ignorance of beings that has no specific shape but its strength is no less at all. Hence the lump was as hard as an iron-ball. The role of ignorance is in the realm of maya. Practically ignorance invokes maya which waters at the root of ignorance; so their relationship is very close and fast. Ignorance is the fruit of the tree of desire planted by both the blind mind and attachment guided by tamas. It has more than a hundred faculties. After sprinkling water upon it, the lump was fragmented into one hundred and one pieces which were kept in equal number of pitchers full of clarified butter from which after two years the first born was Duryodhana who remains undefeated in any fight with the beings; but he may be won over being blessed by Guru. In every step of the life of beings Kama (desire) is evident conspicuously. His brothers are the faculties of mind while the sister Duhshala is the evil counsel of beings. She too maintains a good relation with ignorance. Both Dhritarastra and Gandhari are happy now.

But why had the children to remain within the womb for two years and within the pitchers for another two years? What does the fact signify? The earth takes a year to circumambulate the sun along its orbit; in other words, this movement completes in a span of one year. Similarly all movements of beings are meant for orbiting the circumference created by their desires that are four is number. They are dharma (faith), artha (wealth), Kama (desire) and moksha (emancipation). Apart from these four they have nothing more to desire. The beings under the influence of ignorance, crave for sense-objects to enjoy and then artha (wealth) and Kama (desire) play a very important role in their lives for a particular span of time. Then they think to earn money to satiate the thirst for sense-objects, is their dharma and amidst these enjoyment of sense-objects they would attain their emancipation. The beings' endeavour in this regard points two kinds of movement for the different spans of time that denote the period of time the lump of flesh remained in the womb. During these two spans of movement the beings cannot properly identify the impulses and faculties that drag them to deeper ignorance separately as such and therefore, the time taken of their life in the womb is to be of two years. Secondly, even being under the influence of ignorance, some of the beings may seek self-knowledge which is quite natural. But the impulses and faculties of the mind then become antagonistic and try to attract such seekers to retract their course from their spiritual quest playing a more vigorous role. Irrespective of failure or success, this movement of the impulses and faculties is of a square one i.e. a span of one year. But a determined aspirant may overcome the activities of those impulses and faculties to deter him and makes progress in the realm of spirituality to become enlightened. When the impulses and faculties observe that the aspirant is not paying any heed to them, they transform themselves to become the agents for help to him. Any spiritually enlightened person may testify to this remembering his/her earlier days of spiritual life. Therefore, in this case also there are two movements of the impulses and faculties. These two movements of them are of square ones of two spans. And now, during these two spans of life of the impulses and faculties indicate their life in pitchers full of clarified butter. But how and where?

If you look at someone's head it may seem to you that a pitcher is fixed to the shoulder upside down. Actually the head is the pitcher full of clarified batter containing millions of other pitchers filled in similar way; they are the neurons of the brain that transmit nerve impulses, consisting of grey matter. We should keep in mind that ignorance as well as impulses and faculties are the creation of Guru (in the instant case Vyasa), the lump of flesh born of attachment could not be particularly identified but the impulses and faculties could be identified after being sprinkled water upon the lump and kept in the pitchers, after it got fragmented, to testify the tenacious efforts of the humans. At the same time, the impulses and faculties be established in their respective dharma so that they may manifest themselves in their respective fields to fulfill the mission of Guru, be it in the sphere of enjoyment of sense-objects or in that of spiritual enlightenment. In both respects they remain established in their dharma, of course, due to transformation their action becomes commensurable by the demand of circumstances.

So, Gandhari's sons and daughter could not go beyond this rule.

The Application Of Poison To Bhima

After the death Pandu and Madri, time ripened to get the identity of the energies of attachment and detachment in the perspective of each other. On the ground of bringing up her children in their own place Kunti came to Hastinapura with the young Pandava brothers. In the royal palace the Kauravas and the Pandavas began to grow up together. The Kauravas gradually became envious of the Pandavas because of their mental, physical and behavioural excellence especially the prowess of Bhima became to be an object of grave concern for them. In plays and games being utterly humbled by Bhima again and again in their mind grew a violent enmity, especially in the mind of Duryodhana who even resolved to kill Bhima. So to get rid of Bhima, Duryodhana began to find out a chance and that came in no time. The crooked Duryodhana invited the Pandava brothers to take part in a water sport on the river Ganga on a certain day plotting a plan to kill Bhima. Yudhisthira accepted the invitation. On the appointed day arrangements for food and drink were made in the tents on the river bank. Duryodhana feigning his love for the Pandavas began to distribute sweet meats to them and what he offered to Bhima was poisoned. Failing to understand the evil design of Duryodhana, Bhima swallowed them all and then they all became engaged in water sports. Owing to physical exertion and also to the influence of poison he became tired in a short while and feeling drowsy he came to the edge of the water and fell fast asleep. Then came Duryodhana, bound him tightly and threw him in the water of the Ganga. Unconscious Bhima, in such a state fell upon the snake-princes of the kingdom of snakes in Patala. This audacious behaviour on the part of a human, made them furiously angry and they began to bite him vehemently. With the snake-bites the poison in Bhima's body was eaten away and he regained consciousness. He saw that the snakes had bitten him so much so that his body was full of morbific sores. Bhima grew angry and began to beat the snakes and a good number of them died; of course, a few of them fled away from the spot and went straight to their king, Vasuki and narrating before him the incident they requested him to know the identity of the new-comer boy of human origin. Vasuki came and saw that the newcomer was none other than the grandson of king Kuntibhoja who happened to be his friend. So the boy deserved to be regarded as his grandson also and Vasuki took him to his place with due affection and cordiality. There the assembly of snakes requested Vasuki to permit him to drink nectar (amrita). Vasuki permitted and Bhima drank eight vessels of nectar and stayed in the kingdom of snakes for eight days and thereafter the snakes led him to a forest and he came back to Hastinapura.

We have said earlier that impulses and faculties are created by the blind mind and attachment while the pure elements are created by the pure mind and detachment. Yudhisthira is the reality of ether and Bhima is the reality of air. The air remaining in the body, keeps it animated and its absence in the body makes it a lifeless matter only; but it does not own this energy of animation nor is it its own creation. The vital energy of air is the gift of Atman or Supreme Consciousness. The association of Atman with the element of air within the body makes the air endowed with vital energy which is manifested as vital breaths, the vigour of which enlivens the beings. In every action of beings the role of the air as vital energy is imperative. At the same time the role of the energy of vital breaths is very much important in the activities of impulses, realities and senses too. This truth was not unknown to Duryodhana, but Kama (desire) was not so liberal to accept the truth. He likes to be the suzerain of every aspect of life and to some extent he succeeds too. He cannot put up with anybody stronger than him and hence he seeks the death of Bhima. At the same time, he failed to comprehend that he himself would be rendered inactive if Bhima dies. The reason for this failure was that the physical body has not yet been created; and also the extent of influence of desire and its actions upon the body was beyond his understanding. Therefore, he resolved to kill Bhima to got rid of him. To execute his design, malicious and hypocrite Duryadhana did not face any difficulty and it was easy for him to drown unconscious Bhima. But air cannot be undone so easily.

Bound with creepers unconscious Bhima was thrown into the water of Ganga to die by drowning. But actually he was sent through the Susumna artery known to be the Ganga. Air as pure element cannot act as vital breaths as the vital energy of Atman has not yet imbued with it, hence he was sent to nether world i.e. the lowest nerve centre of the spinal column as the imbuing of that energy was of paramount importance for creation of human body. Atman or Brahman is actionless, immutable. What we know to be the action of Brahman or Atman is actually the action of the Energy of Brahman (Brahma-Shakti) and being existent in the Muladhara nerve-centre, performs the actions of Brahman in the body. And it is said that this energy of Brahman, assuming the form of a snake, is existent in this nerve centre being encircled in three and a half coils. As this energy happens to encircle itself in coils, is imagined as a snake, but it is the formal rendition of AUM, the primeval sound of that Great Explosion which is known as Big Bang. This energy is Vasuki, the king of snakes in the nether world; it is AUM and also the Primordial Nature of Brahman, that performs on behalf of Brahman. To her poison or the effect of it is absolutely insignificant. The application of poison to Bhima has been used for the plot symbolically although it is suggestive of the fact that Kama (desire) overpowers the element of air so that the prowess of it in form of vital breaths cannot be established. In fine, the infusion of vital energy into the pure element of air, is a dire necessity and it is evident in the cordial reception given by Vasuki. And lastly Bhima was allowed to drink nectar (amrita) to the quantity of eight vessels that approves of his right to journey upto the eighth step of knowledge which enables mankind to be established in manhood.

The inhalation and exhalation of vital breaths by the beings get on through the Ida and Pingata arteries. Although these two arteries are connected to the Maladhara nerve-centre yet the air inhaled and exhaled passing through these two arteries do not reach or return to and from Muladhara nerve-centre but the inhaled air goes upto the navel wherefrom it goes to the Muldhara through the Susumna artery and being aided by the energy of Consciousness it spreads throughout the body to keep it animated and thereafter exhalation makes its journey in reverse order. The close relation between Muladhara and Manipura nerve-centres has been emphasized to highlight the perspective of the application of poison to Bhima. Prior to it, that was the childhood of Bhima. Secondly, on the question of enjoyment of sense-objects being allured by desire, the pleasure of taste-buds takes the first place in case of men and women. So the poisoned sweetmeats come to the fore.

The tale tells us that unconscious Bhima was bound with creepers and then thrown into the water. The creepers are the symbol of the veins, nerves and arteries through which the inhaled breath moves in the body to keep it animated providing vital energy to it.

It is said that Bhima was allowed to drink nectar in the kingdom of Vasuki. It makes one immortal. But Bhima did not become immortal; rather he died. That which is created, is subject to die and Bhima was not an exception. Then why was he given to drink eight vessels of nectar? What does it signify? To attain eternal divine bliss beyond death, one has to make a journey to the eighth step of knowledge and also to attain manhood with the active energy of the element of air in the body and this Divine Bliss is the Amrita (nectar).

One may question as to why were the element of space, Yudhisthira, a universally respected person and that of the element of fire having unparalleled prowess not considered to bestow the energy of vitality which was but given to the element of air? The space is universally existent but it has no motion; it is static. The fire is also universally existent and it has its motion that needs the aid of air. The other elements also have their motion which is basically dependant upon air. On the other hand, nature (dharma) of air is motion and it is swift. No element can move throughout the body swifter than air and hence it has been endowed with vitality relegating other elements.

The Birth Of Kripa, Kripee And Drona

The great rishi Gotama had a son named Gautama who had a son named Saradvana. It is said that he was born of a reed and hence he used to be called Saradvana; observing brahmacharaya (premarital abstinence) he gained many a weapon and became skilled in their use so much so that even Indra became frightened lest his dignified seat be lost to him. Therefore, he sent an apsara Janapadi by name to create some impediment to disturb his austerity by alluring him and to make a fallen man of him. As ordered the apsara came to his hermitage and began to show gestures in front of the meditating Brahmin and finally she succeeded. Saradvana became smitten with desire very much yet he, owing to his austerity, remained restraint. But inspite of all that his semen was ejaculated and while he was leaving the place, his semen fell upon a reed being divided into two wherefrom two babies were born, a son and a daughter. These two babies were found by the soldiers of king Shantanu who was then in the forest for game-hunting sports and the soldiers followed him. The soldiers brought the babies to the king who then took the responsibility to bring them up. Thus brought up by the grace of the king, they became known as Kripa and Kripee. After a long time Saradvana came to know that from his fallen semen a son and a daughter were born. He came to the palace at Hastinapura, saw the son and daughter and let them know of their identity as well as the lineage and imparting some training to them, he returned to his hermitage. After some time Kripa became a worthy teacher of archery and was appointed as the teacher of the Kuru boys.

No human child can be born of a reed and this would not be accepted by any person of minimum common sense even. The transformation of a sperm into an embryo and then at last a human baby, is an evolutionary process that needs certain conducive conditions which are absolutely absent in a reed. But the author has written it and we are reading that with awe for aeons of time. But what happened actually? Saradvana and his offsprings were born in the same method in which other human offsprings are born in the womb of their mothers. Vyasa did not suppress the truth but used a metaphorical imagery owing to certain considerations. Either of a pair of tubes known as fallopian tubes along which eggs travel from the overies to the uterus has been presented to the readers in the symbol of a reed as a metaphorical imagery. These tubes are essential for the birth of human children in a womb. But the author did not say that, what he has said is truth indeed but with a coating of allegorical symbolism. The whole of the epic is an allegory and full of symbolism; hence the use of them is reasonable. Had it been said that a rishi got his children by an apsara while he was engaged in austerity and lost his restraint being allured by her, the ordinary readers and listeners would have been shocked to learn that there was no difference between the rishi and them in similar situations and this could have led them to be hesitant to honour the rishi with due respect. And such statements are not rare that despite his all-out restraint ejaculation of semen took place as if common weaknesses were not there in rishis or munis. Does it happen otherwise in cases of ordinary men? The answer is an emphatic no.

It is said that Indra being afraid of losing his seat of dignity owing to the vigour of Saradvana's austerity sent an apsara to detract him from his projected aim, by alluring him. Now the question is, a Brahmin is observing his austerity why should Indra be afraid of his austerity? But Indra had the reason to be fearful. Every kind of austerity is meant for integrating variously scattered visions around to a single vision directed to a single aim; otherwise, the prime cause of austerity be defeated, which means to transform the vision into an introvert one. The body is guided by the mind and until manhood is attained, life of beings is guided by the mind and nothing else. The vision of mind is all over the four quarters around and it is necessary to reduce it to the centre and when it is so done, the mind loses its suzerainty over the human affairs. On the other hand, the mind is called the eleventh sense and it is the overlord of the senses. This mind is Indra. With the introversion of vision the mind loses its seat of dignity. So it sends an apsara to create a hindrance to austerity with a view to defeat the purpose of austerity; this is but a regular feature of austerity. But why? At the initial state of self-discipline a special kind of heat being created in the body makes it restless in excitement which is so much disturbing that the body cannot endure it easily and resultantly excites the passion for sex enhancing the possibility of appearance of the apsaras. We have discussed about the apsaras with reference to Satyavaty. In this particular case, the name of the apsara is Janapadi meaning one who moves only in human habitation having a distinct boundary. What has happened to Saradvana may happen to other aspirants also. But as the inspiration for austerity is stronger than that of enjoyment of sense-objects, it cannot persist for a long time in the life of a spiritual aspirant and hence Saradvana becomes able to leave the apsara and again absorbs himself in his austere pursuits. No other apsaras appear there to disturb him, at least, no such information is with us.

Now the tale of Drona. Rishi Bharadvaja of the line of rishi Amgira was engaged in austere pursuits in the Himalayas for some time. Once in the morning on completion of his bath in the river coming to the river-bank he saw that apsara Ghritachi was present there after bath. Suddenly a strong waft of wind took away the cloth covering of her body and the youghful charm of the apsara infatuated so much so that his semen ejected instantly. He then put the semen in a pitcher (drona) and got a son of that pitcher. The son was named Drona. Had it been possible to have sons by keeping semen in a pitcher, then the existence as well as the necessity for women in the society would have rendered superfluous. The description of the incident upto the enthrallment of the rishi is true to the fact, but thereafter there is the use of symbols. Not only the rishi was fascinated but he placed his semen into the uterus of the apsara also. This organ becomes inflated to the shape of a pitcher during coitus. In the early morning after taking a bath in the river the beauty of the apsara made him so passionate that the rishi failed to restrain himself but had to enjoy that body as semen cannot be wasted away ineffectively which is almost a sacrilege. Although it was not at all glorifying on the part of a rishi to enjoy the body of an apsara in the morning being charmed with her beauty, losing his restraint. But it is also true that the impulses and senses of a rishi even remain vibrantly active as they are in common man. Therefore, to keep the rishi on the safe side suggestions and symbols have been used.

The apsara who was the real inspiration for Drona's birth was Ghritachi. The semen as well as ova look like clarified butter. The ova remain in the feminine body that accepts semen for child birth and the organ itself may be called a vessel for clarified butter. It may be surmised that when the waft of the strong wind took away the cover from the apsara's body Bharadvaja for a little while saw the pelvis region as a result of which he became so impassioned that he could not avoid coition. It is a fact that among many persons one becomes vexed with such a scene and turns the look, but in a lonely place the reaction turns to be otherwise as one becomes passionate. Hence the time is early morning and the venue is the river-bank.

Still now the creation is in its early subtle stage. The great elements have since been created and their evolution is in progress. But as their Panchikarana (admixture of the pure elements) has since not been completed and the creation of life is far away. A good number of realities needed for the evolution of life has not yet been created. But the process is on. Prior to creation of beings it is necessary to create some realities, impulses and propensities needed in life and in this case imagination is created and the son of Saradvana, Kripa is that imagination. He and his twin sister, Kripee were saved and brought up by the grace of Shantanu and both of them did not ever forget that. On the other hand, prior to creation of life necessary elements and realities to sustain life on earth and its evolution were created by the Creator. But generally we are not aware of it. Yet it is an undeniable fact. He who knows it with the help of his imagination becomes humble before the Lord in gratitude. Imagination acts so splendidly.

Both Saradvana and Bhardvaja were rishis, both lost their restraint on seeing apsaras suddenly and both of them got their offsprings of apsaras. Both of them are symbols of the energy of Guru. In every stage of creation the energy of Guru plays a vital role in various ways. Now Drona is the rationality of tradition and custom. Both of them play very important roles in human life and both of them are important realities of life. Both in the material and spiritual worlds, they have an undeniable role so far human life is concerned. Both of them obtained various weapons which were actually directives of Truth and got from their Guru. Again, the twin sister of Kripa is the wife of Drona. Beings learn to imagine by birth and likewise they get the intelligence born of tradition. Secondly, the understanding born of imagination becomes a helpful agent of beings in their spiritual pursuits. Similarly traditional reasoning too helps them in that field. In fact, the beings step into the spiritual world according to their tradition they inherit and take up particular way of austerity to fulfill their aspirations in this regard and such efforts both imagination and traditional understanding help them in many a way. They both are interrelated and the correlation between them is Kripee, the wife of Drona and she is the energy of traditional intelligence which is deeply rooted in the existence of beings though cannot be indentified easily.

Drona, The Military Teacher

Drona, the intelligence born of tradition, broke his mind to the Kuru boys before he started training to them saying. "Boys, please promise to do some favour to me on completion of your training and I would impart good quality of lessons indeed." Listening to him all the boys remained silent only Arjuna spoke, "what you will ask us to do we will do that, no doubt." Courage is the prime quality of tejas and it is the manifestation of tejas. It has the immeasurable quest for knowing the unknown and knows it by dint of its courageousness. Apart from this, without the assistance of tejas traditional understanding cannot manifest itself. Hence he did maintain a close relationship with tejas and he needed this promise eagerly. Owing to this Drona used to pay a special attention to Tejas. The training was going on. The teacher had to assess the progress of his students regarding the lesson imparted to them. Therefore, arrangements were made to assess the excellence of the students who did agree to the proposal of Drona in this regard. This test had two sides of it; one, to observe the standard of skill in using the arms in conventional way and secondly, to ascertain the characteristic excellence in using the arms in an uncommon way. After assessing the skills of the students a novel test conceived to assess the skill of the contenders in the art and science of using the arms. An earthen bird was placed on a branch of a tree high above the ground and the contestant is to sever its head by shooting a shaft. Many a contender came but their words revealed that they were incapable of hitting the bull's eye. Lastly, Arjuna was called for and on his appearance he was made understand what he was to do. Thereafter he was asked as to what he was seeing, he said. "I can't see the rest of the bird's body except its head." "Then hit your mark", ordered Drona and he came out successfully. To succeed in life one needs singularity of vision to the aim, otherwise, success eludes one, be it material or spiritual, singularity of vision is essential. It is now evident that only Arjuna had this singularity of vision which other kuru boys were devoid of.

Then began the testing of individual skills of the boys and Arjuna was profusely praised showing his skill. Then suddenly Karna appeared there and challenged Arjuna in a duel. Arjuna at once agreed. But Kripacharya intervened and asked for the parental identity of Karna and said, "The princes do not fight with one who is not a prince." Listening to him Karna became ashamed. Seeing Karna's dilemma Duryodhana at once installed him to the throne of the kingdom of Amga (the human body). Next to it during the acrimonious altercation between Bhima and Duryodhana the sun set down and the duel was not fought.

Why did Karna appear on the scene of the skill testing of the princes and why did he challenge Arjuna to fight a duel? It was a test for the students of Drona and he was not a student of him. Secondly the citizens of Hastinapura knew that it was a test of skill of the princes only and it cannot be assumed that Karna was unaware of it. He knew that he was the son of a carpenter, why then did he challenge the best skilled prince? In terms of the realities of the body Karna is simultaneously covetousness as well as discernment of duty. The source of origination of the both is pride. As covetousness aspires to acquire the seat of dignity likewise the sense of duty does so by performing duty. Being driven by his vanity to achieve greatness Karna appears to challenge Arjuna though he is the son of a carpenter and not a prince; yet he challenged Arjuna to propitiate his arrogance. Again, covetousness and the sense of duty do not like to respect the discernment of tradition but ultimately become compelled to do so if the true character of his arrogance is held up to them, and that is done by Kripacharya, the reality of imagination who is able to restrain covetousness as well as impetuousness. Avidity and discernment of duty are two important realities of life but they need to be used being disciplined and in an ordered way. In this respect order and discipline were scaled down and hence imagination put him to the right track by asking him of his parental identity. Karna became ashamed. He could have amended himself had there been no hurdle.

But that did not take place as Duryodhana forthwith installed ashamed Karna as the king of Amgarajya (Kingdom of body). Duryodhana is desire which is at the root of human existence which is also inspiration of leading life on earth. The terribly mischievous Kama (desire) did so being deluded to be more powerful in association with avidity and to find a friend in him to remain ever unconquered. The desire of beings pertains to the body that sings paeans to it. Now covetousness is made the king of the whole body to be subservient to desire and in exchange, covetousness promised to exert all his efforts in favour of desire. Inspite of all this the duel did not take place.

Karna's actual father was the sun-god and he was born being fully armured. This fact was unknown to others and to him also and he used to be known as the carpenter's son. Yet he sprang up to challenge Arjuna owing to his self-conceit at the root of which there was an immeasurable pride as he was aware of certain divine grace existent behind his birth being armoured and he had an idea that this grace would make him invincible and unconquered in life. This awareness made him proud and self-conceited. But he did never share this thought with any second person. This is the character of avarice and this consciousness is reflected in his self and at the same time he was a liberal giver and also dutiful. Between these two forces there are consistency and antagonism as well and as a result of which Karma despite being a colourful character, becomes pale losing his colours at the end.

Drona And Drupada

On successful completion of training and assessment of excellence of skill of the Kaurava and Pandava boys Drupada asked for the fee payable to the Guru saying. "Please bring captive Drupada to me from the battle field and that would be as good as the fee payable to me." On hearing the order of Drona the princes along with Drona set out for a battle against Drupada. Excepting the Pandava brothers the enthusiastic Kauravas began to brag as to who would start the fighting relegating others behind while advancing towards the capital of Panchala kingdom. On seeing them progressing towards the capital, Drupada equipped himself for a battle and began to wait for them. On their arrival Drupada faced them with his superior military skill and utterly discomfited them. Seeing the humiliation of the Kauravas, Arjuna along with Bhima joined them and fought valiantly. Ultimately Drupada was defeated to the joint prowess of Bhima and Arjuna and they brought him to Drona who assured him of his life and said, "In the past you told me, he who is not a king can't be a king's friend. Hence I offer you the half of the kingdom. Now on you are to rule the southern part of it beyond the Bhagirathi and I am to rule the northern bank of the river. If you like it, make friends with me." Drupada replied, "I am pleased with you sir" and accepted the proposal. But he clearly understood that his prowess was no match for Drona. So, he began to move about the earth to have a son empowered with the miraculously divine prowess.

We have already said that Drona is the intelligence bound by stock notions and Drupada is the arterial energy expressed through the flow of blood, in the body. The arterial energy is there in the whole body and to establish itself all over the body; the traditional intelligence needs the help of arterial energy. Hence Drona keeps his eyes over the kingdom of Drupada. Secondly, the movement of blood through the veins and arteries depends upon tejas and air. So tejas personified as Arjuna and vital breath personified as Bhima are very much needed by Drona. They both are his disciples and are eager to pay the fee payable to him. So the traditional intelligence brought the arterial energy under control with the help of tejas and vital breath only for self-aggrandizement. On the other hand, without being bound by stock notions beings cannot be materialistic in vision nor is their existence manifested. The arterial energy being governed by tejas and vital breath cannot defeat them in fight. The defeat of Drupada was certain but owing to this defeat he got the identity of that invisible power that provides him for required energy. Again Drona could not forget the insult to him by Drupada and to pay Drupada in his own coin he proposed to captive Drupada to bifurcate his kingdom and offered him to rule the southern part of it while the authority of kingship over the northern part would remain with him to which Drupada agreed. By this arrangement Drona became a king and there remained no hurdle to be the friend of Drupada, of course, he had no need to be the friend of Drona. But Drona had the necessity to get the friendship of Drupada and the reason has been explained earlier. On the question of dividing the Panchala kingdom

Drona proved his political maturity; it was divided by north and south and not by east and west and the common border between the parts was the river Bhagirathi. The area of activity of the arterial energy is the whole body and the upper part of it controls that of the lower part also. The whole body is the kingdom of Drupada and Drona is but an invader and victorious too. Drupada had to comply with the decision of the victor. Of course, on being a king Drona did never ruled the kingdom living in the capital, rather he left the Panchala with his disciples for Hastinapura and lived there. It may be assumed that his part of kingdom used to be ruled by Drupada. Drona made it possible to extend the area of his influence throughout the body with the help of arterial energy to guide the beings, influencing every corpuscle of blood by defeating Drupada who did not fail to understand the design of Drona; but he was undone as he had nothing to do then and there.

Yet he decided to do what was to be done by him against Drona. He clearly understood that it was impossible for him to win over Drona in a battle. On the other hand, owing to the crushing defeat and stinging insult being unbearable to him he became resolute to have a son "of miraculously divine prowess" to teach Drona a befitting lesson and "began to ambulate the earth." Had the trotting of the globe been a criterion for having a son "of miraculously divine prowess" then all such persons should have had the like sons; but the human history does not say so. Then why did Drupada decided to do so? We should keep in mind that Drupada is arterial energy personified which is existent in the whole body which, in turn, is the world itself and to have a son "of miraculously divine prowess" the arterial energy has to travel the world. Drupada did nothing new. In the body the necessary substance of food and drink transforms into blood that transforms into flesh which again in the same process turns to be bone that in the same manner becomes marrow and again in the same method semen is created out of marrow. This semen is the seed for creation and to have a progeny semen is essential. The whole process is activated by the arterial energy and it is at the root of all these movements. Drupada's globe-trotting denotes to have pure semen that could produce a sturdy baby which is also approved of divinity; hence the son is "of miraculously divine prowess."

The Burning Of The House Of Lac

The mind especially the mind full of resolution is by no means impartial; its only party is its own self. Moreover it is subjugated by the senses and impulses, nor can it resolve timely and independently. So it needs the counsel of others for the purpose of action. When gradually the Pandava brothers are establishing themselves, their dharma is being manifested, their cognition is being evolved as wisdom, the mercury of Dhritarastra's anxiety is gaining impetus to rise high. He thought, if the sons of the late king, Pandu, claim the right to throne, he would have no earth under his feet to ignore it nor could he deny their claim altogether by any standard of logic or morality. Therefore to draw a conclusive decision immediately in order to get rid of them he needed some counsels and called for his minister, Konika, the epitome of shrewd intelligence to confer with. Kanika's counsel was liked much by Dhritarastra but he was not so courageous to translate it into action. On the other hand, his eldest son became extremely distressed as to how to make the course to the throne could be free of all hurdles. He thought of Bhishma and concluded that he was impartial and expected to be less dangerous; hence he was not to be afraid of. Then there was the less possibility of Kripacharya's hostility owing to his relationship with Drona and Aswathama. Only Vidura then is left out; but what could Vidura alone do? So the Pandavas had to go in exile to Varanavata. The necessary arrangements were made so that they could be sent there as early as possible. Once Dhritarasta asked Pandava brothers to go to Varanavata to stay there for some time and they had but to accept the proposal. Yudhisthira along with his brothers took the leave of the royal officers to go there.

Meanwhile, Duryodhana was not idle altogether. He called for his trusted counsellor, Purochana and ordered him to build a house for the Pandavas of combustible materials so that they could be burnt alive inside. As ordered Purochana began to build a house made of wood, bamboo, hemp, resin and lac etc. and completed early. But Vidura could know of the evil design of Duryodhana and warned Yudhisthira about the plot in a code language at the time of their departure from Hastinapura. On their arrival at Varanavata, they were warmly welcomed by Purochana and stayed with him for ten days at his house. Then they reached the house intended for their stay. Reaching there they were confirmed beyond doubt of the combustibility of the materials used to build the house. In the meantime, Vidura sent an earth digger to Yudhisthira with a message. The digger delivered the message and said that in order to ascertain their safety he would dig up a tunnel stretching upto the Bhagirathi. It was decided that the princes would be engaged in game hunting during the day and at night they would sleep in the tunnel dug by the digger. They could learn from him that the house of lac would be ignited on the fourteenth night of the coming dark fortnight. On that day Kunti invited some Brahmins and guests for a lunch at her on a certain celebratory occasion. In the afternoon a huntswoman along with her five sons appeared as Kunti's guests. She served them food and drink liberally which they took contentedly. But owing to heavy drinking they feel asleep on the spot. Bhima ignited the house of lac that night; of course, prior to that he caused to burn Purochana's house to make his death a certainty. Leaving the house of lac in flames the five brothers with their mother trudged along the tunnel to reach the river bank. There they found a helmsman with his boat sent by Vidura, was waiting for them. Boarding the boat they crossed the river and fled away in the forest. For the time being they were saved from the fury of Duryodhana.

The physical body has not yet been created; even the admixture of pure elements (Panchikarana) has not taken place yet. All this is the narrative of the subtle state of elements. But the immediate aim is to create the physical body and the subtle elements are being evolved to that direction. Of course, the creation of physical body is not all, its comprehensive activity in all circumstances must have to be ensured. And also to activate the body certain systems have to be evolved so that its nature be manifest to that direction. Therefore, these systems are necessary prior to creation of the physical body. But there is Duryodhana (desire) — the king of impulses. He wants to establish his authority over everything as far as his vision could survey. Daryodhana, the desire personified is but the demonic energy and he always desires to destruct the divine energies to serve his purpose. The Pandava brothers are five pure elements and their mother Kunti is detachment. They are the divine energies, the extermination of whom is eagerly desired by Duryodhana. But in the unsuccessful efforts of Duryodhana to get the Pandavas ruined we get an eternal system of physical activity.

The physical body is made of twenty four elements. All the realities have not yet been created but they need to be so. On the other hand, owing to the activities of the conscious body the realities wear away that require to be replenished with similar realities taken from the nature and in case of the beings this replenishment occurs by taking food and drink through digestive system. But the humans do never take any kind of food until it is wholesome and acceptable. Therefore, on the question of taking food by humankind appetite is a pre-condition and this appetite is the trusted minion of Duryodhana, Purochana. He was asked to build a house of combustible materials at Varanavata which is away from Hastinapura. Varanavata is the human stomach in the middle part of the body which is at a considerable distance from the capital Hastinapura i.e. the head. The materials used for making the house, such as wood, bamboo, hemp, resin, lac etc. were all inflammable materials that stand for food taken by beings. What we take for food gets digested by the heat of the navel and the substance necessary for the body is taken by it while the rest being unnecessary for it is excreted as waste. In the world of matters everything is created of five elements and the food we take is not an exception nor is the waste too. The difference between the two is our food contains that vital energy which is needed by the body while the waste is devoid of it although both are created of five elements. The house of lac with Kunti and her five sons, is but the vital energy gained by taking food into the stomach by the humans and the burnt huntswoman and her five sons are but the waste of food excreted.

Before leaving the house of lac Bhima ignited it and fled away trudging along with tunnel. In course of digestion of food, its movement in the stomach is performed by air. He also put the house of Purochana beforehand to flames confirming his death. Then they fled away. After digestion the substance in liquid-form goes to the liver through a tubular passage and it goes through the body as blood along the veins and arteries. This is the journey of the Pandavas in the forest and that tubular passage is the river they crossed and all these actions are performed by the element of air and hence Bhima had the prime role in fleeing.

It may be observed that on the last day of their stay in the house of lac Kunti invited some guests to treat them to a sumptuous lunch on a celebratory occasion and in the afternoon a huntswoman with her five sons reached there uninvited on the expectation of being treated by Kunti who served them enough food and drink. But owing to excessive drinking they fell asleep there and finally were burnt.

In this incident Kunti had an indirect part to play in their being charred. Kunti is detachment that does not admit of any unsavoury element in the body. It is the duty of detachment to keep the body hale and hearty keeping it away from all such elements that are not congenial to it.

So, Kunti is by no means responsible for the death of the huntswoman and her five sons in the ultimate consideration.

Meanwhile news reached Hastinapura that the Pandavas along with Kunti died at Varanavata. The charred bodies of the huntswoman and her five sons were taken for that of Kunti and her sons being an irrefutable evidence. Hypocrite Dhritarastra feigned pining for the loss of lives of the Pandavas and their mother endorsing their post death rituals.

This conduct of the mind denotes its imprisonment by eight bondages (Astapasha).

The Tale Of Bhima & Hidimba

During their journey through the forest Kunti became very thirsty. Bhima went in search of drinking water. Of course, before leaving them he asked his mother and brothers to remain there till he returned to them. But Kunti and her other sons were so way-wearied that they fell asleep. Returning with the drinking water Bhima saw all of them were fast asleep; he did not rouse them rather waited for their waking up. The forest was dominated by a rakshasa being known to be Hidimbo. It is generally held that a rakshasa is a member of a non-Aryan anthropophagous race of India. He used to be associated with his younger sister Hidimba. Hidimbo feeling the presence of humans in the forest by way of smelling, ordered the sister to bring them to him after killing them. The sister coming to the location saw a very handsome young man was guarding a lady and four other young men all in deep sleep. She became fascinated with the handsomeness of the man awake to guard the others and at once she fell in love and decided to open her mind to him. But she was well aware that a man would surely reject the love of a rakshasi. So she at once transformed herself into a beautiful young lady amorously desiring the love of Bhima and narrated to him how and why she had come here and seeing Bhima she fell in love with him. She also disclosed that her elder brother was a very strong rakshasa and very fond of human flesh. Neither Bhima nor his five companions could escape his grip. Of course, if Bhima agreed to her proposal she could save all of them from his rage. Listening to all these. Bhima almost reached his patience edge. He boastfully said that it would not be difficult for him to kill a rakshasa howsoever strong he might be. Hidimba, on her part could not rely upon his words at all. Meanwhile, as the sister was late to carry out his order, the brother reached the spot and became astonished to see his sister's physical beauty and immediately understood the reasons for such a transformation which made him more angry with Bhima and resultantly a terrible fight began between the two. Meanwhile Kunti woke up and wondered to see a beautiful young woman as graceful as a goddess in such a dense forest. She asked for her identity in reply to which Hidimba told her everything. After the fight was over Bhima married Hidimba on the directive given by Kunti.

Hidimba desired to have a son fathered by Bhima. So it was agreed between Bhima and Hidimba that they would be separated after their son's birth and thereafter there would be no obligation on either side. At the same time Yudhisthira advised that Bhima would pass his nights with his mother and brothers sporting with Hidimba at daytime. She agreed to this proposal also. After some time a son was born to them and now came the time for separation. The son Ghatotkacha remained under the charge of his mother. Again began the travail of the secret travel on foot in the forest.

The universe is the manifestation of energy and in that manifestation there are creation, preservation and destruction — the same energy manifests itself in these three forms. We can identify the manifestation but not the energy. Emerging out of its source the energy moves aiming to the circumference to manifest itself in various forms including creation, preservation and destruction which is evident universally and particularly. We have discussed it earlier that the substance of food we take, in liquid form goes to the liver to be transformed into blood that runs through the veins and arteries in the body. But this movement of blood is not all. Being conditioned by body heat it transforms into flesh and following the process the flesh transforms into bone, bone into marrow which again transforms in semen. In every step the act of movement is performed by the air. The blood moves in the body through the veins and arteries which have in them acuminate tubular passage, which have very fine muscles in them and their contraction and expansion cause the flow of blood and air is the agent for these actions of the muscles in veins and arteries.

On the other hand, the unruly mind being unbridled by desire enjoys the sense-objects for pleasure is symbolically termed as rakshasa. But as the body has not yet been created let alone the beings, — who then could be the rakshasa Hidimbo? We should keep in mind that although the physical body has not yet been created but the methods to accomplish its activities require to be created prior to the creation of physical body, otherwise the body, after its creation will fail to act. Again neither the body nor the discernment born of the body does know how long it will stay on earth. At any time it may die. It remains alive so long with the help of air the blood flows through the veins providing vitality to it and at any time this flow may stop if the air becomes wanting. And Hidimbo is the repellent agent to stop the flow of blood in veins and arteries. But how does he do it? The blood being conditioned by body heat transforms into flesh; but it takes place after purification of blood and there remains some impurities that need to be excreted. But if the body cannot excrete the impurities that may block the passage, being deposited in the channel as chemical deposit even causing death ultimately. This deposit of impurity is Hidimbo.

Hidimba is also a rakshsha and having the same purpose she is the follower of her elder brother. It is expected to be so and it was. But the handsome physique of Bhima made her fall in love with him at the first sight. She was honest enough to disclose her mind to him and at the same time the thought of his safety almost bewildered her; she even promised to take him away to a safe haven beyond the domination of Hidimbo. Of course, meanwhile she has transformed herself into a beautiful lass. Bhima on his part, did care very little for her assurances regarding his safety. He said that to accept the challenge of any rakshasa howsoever strong he might be, was a matter of play to him. Still Hidimba could not do away with her worries.

Meanwhile, Bhima and Hidimbo locked horns and a severe fight followed ending with the death of the rakshasa. Despite her brother's death Hidimba's resolution did not change. On the permission of Kunti and Yudhistrira, the marriage of Bhima and Hidimba took place instantly according to the Gandharva order i.e. by exchanging garlands only without observing any Vedic rituals. Then Yudhisthira opined that Bhima would sport with Hidimba at daytime and pass the nights with his mother and brothers. Hidimba agreed to this proposal too. Bhima then proposed that she should desert him after the birth of their son. Hidimba agreed. After some time she gave birth to a son and Hidimba realized that the alliance was over; bidding adieu to the Pandavas and their mother she left with her son.

The air provides vital energy to the body. The flow of blood through the veins and arteries is one of the manifestations of this energy. In different perspectives and at different times the same energy acts differently. The blood flowing in the veins and arteries, has many an aims to achieve other than the flow itself. It tends to be meticulously purified and then to be transformed into flesh that nourishes the body. That which is transformed within the body being conditioned by the body heat obviously leaves some wastes requiring excretion; and had that not been excreted, the body is sure to be sick. But in all such activities the order has to be maintained although they take place naturally. The fight of Bhima and Hidimbo and his subsequent death are but the purification of blood and excretion of waste caused by purification of blood. The purified blood transforms into flesh that finds its place under the skin and the flesh so transformed from blood, again transforms into bone. The process of transformation of flesh from blood to be transformed into bones, is Hidimba and newly created bone is Ghatotkacha, that awaits transformation in future.

In the text both Hidimbo and Hidimba have been described as nocturnal beings having greed for human blood living in the deep forest. The innumerable veins and arteries within the body constitute a forest that has been symbolically presented by the author. The brother and sister have been depicted as they are fond of human blood. Though their activities relate to human blood and flesh thereafter, they are said to be cannibals which they actually are not but the symbolical presentation of a particular system to keep the body resilient. As their activities can not be seen with bare eyes, they have been termed as nocturnal beings. In fact, they are neither nocturnal nor are they antagonistic to the humans but a skilled symbolical depiction of a universal law and not by any means they are anthropophagi.

The Sacrifice Of Drupada For A Son

Being utterly defeated by Drona and losing half of his kingdom to him, an aggrieved Drupada became restless to find out a way to mete out a condign punishment to Drona and which ones that came into his mind, were none to his heart. Then he decided to have a heroic son by performing a sacrifice for the purpose and began to search travelling the world for an able priest who could perform the sacrifice for him. At last he reached an ashrama (hermitage) where he met with two rishis; they were Yaja and Upayaja. The king served Yaja for some time and then he opened his mind to the rishi who told him that he was unable to agree to the King's proposal and told him that his elder brother was desirous of success; if he could be approached, he might be initiated to the sacrifice for a son for the king. As advised, Drupada then revealed his desire to Upayaja who accepting his proposal asked him to arrange for the sacrifice. The sacrifice started. At the time of offering the concluding oblation Upayaja asked the queen. "Come, you will have a son and a daughter too." The queen replied, "Please, wait a little. My face is smudged and my body is spreading divine fragrance. I cannot come to you in such a state to have a son. For my sake, please wait awhile." In reply Upayaja said, "No matter whether you come or go the oblation given by Yaja and sanctified by Upayaja with the mantra will never be ineffective. It must accomplish the cherished results;"— saying this the priest offered the final oblation to the flaming fire of sacrifice. Then the burning fire produced a son glowing like a fire-flame intended to kill Drona. Again, the same sacrificial fire produced a daughter of celestial beauty, who could have fascinated everybody at the first sight. Because of her dark complexion she became known to be Krishna and as the son was born of flaming fire he was known to be Dhristadyumna.

At last Drupada was fortunate enough to have a desired son and along with him a daughter too. Drupada had to ambulate the world and served two rishis at their hermitage for a long time. But if we look around us we would surely find that nobody had to labour so much for having a son nor had to overcome so many hazards as Drupada did. But why did all that happened to Drupada? We have learnt it earlier that Drupada is the arterial energy that is responsible for maintaining the flow of blood throughout the body, which being conditioned by the body-heat transforms into flesh, then flesh into bones, bones into marrow and finally marrow transform into semen in case of males and ova in case of females. Moving throughout the body the semen rests in the head and ova rest in the uterus. Both semen and ova desire each other; while semen is energetic and forceful, ovum is calm and placid in nature. These characteristics of them cause attraction to each other. The mutually opposite characters of them play the vital role in this regard.

The successive transformation of the substance of food and drink to blood, flesh, bone, marrow and finally semen and ova and their movement in the body, are performed by the arterial energy and the world is the human body that Drupada travelled. Not only did he travel the world but also served a rishi at his hermitage and then on his advice served another rishi, his elder brother, Upayaja, while the other one was Yaja. Both of them attained Brahman.

Drupada concluding his wandering of the world, reached a hermitage of two rishis in search of a priest for his sacrifice to get a son and engaged himself in service of one of them named Yaja and then of another named Upayaja, the elder brother who presided over his sacrifice. If we could learn the identity of these two brothers in terms of the realities of human body, many a problem with be solved. We have already said that semen moving throughout the body rests in head in case of men; similarly the moving ova rest in the uterus in case of women. The semen resting in the head requires to be attracted as and when needed and so attracted semen then rests in the sac connected to the male organ at the root, which, during intercourse, goes upto uterus being bourne and ejaculated by the male organ. All these actions are dependent upon the functions of arterial energy.

It is also a fact that to have an offspring, a man and a woman have to undergo different states in life and preparation too which may be termed as sacrifice—the sacrifice of creation ordained by the Supreme Lord. Since the male and female beings have the most important role to play in this sacrifice, at the time of offering final oblation the priest, Yaja asked the queen to come to him. In reply the queen told him, "My face is smeared and spreading divine fragrance. In such a state I cannot come to you. Please wait a while for my sake." Immediately Yaja retorted. "No matter, you come or go, the oblation given by Yaja and sanctified with the mantra by Upayaja shall never be ineffective...."

But who is the queen? She is the female organ which becomes smeared with froth during the act and from its opening is spread a sweet smelling aroma during that action. This smell is a gift of Nature; hence it is called divine smell. The queen's request to wait for a while denotes to prolong the intercourse as far as possible. But ejaculation is not to wait, And "the oblation given by Yaja and sanctified by Upayaja" is the semen which going into the uterus produces a foetus in the womb.

What a spleendid presentation of a universal truth, indeed!

The Pandavas' Journey To Panchala

"Listening to the narrative the sons of Kunti felt a pricking pain at heart and as if they were sunk in a sea of sorrow". The narrative related to the birth of Dhristadyumna and that of his sister, Draupadi as well. There should not be any reason to be sorry if somebody becomes a father miraculously getting a son and a daughter having divine ordination. In not very distant past they inflicted a crushing defeat upon Drupada and in the meantime, how did Drupada become the father of two divinely ordained children miraculously? The son would kill Drona and the daughter would perform many a divine duty destructing the Kshatriyas. The Kauravas and Srinjayas are not closely related as yet. But after the divinely ordained son and daughter become more powerful being brought up to that direction Drupada would be more powerful. Then if the Kauravas coming closer to him and include Drupada to their clan, they would be powerful to a greater extent.

Once Kunti told Yudhisthira that she did not like to stay in Ekachakra and the quantity of alms was getting meagre. "If you all like it, let us go to the Panchala kingdom." It was decided to go to Panchala. Meanwhile, suddenly Vyasa appeared there. After an exchange of the state of well being he began to explain the earlier birth of Draupadi. It may be mentioned here, even if, the Pandavas were curious about her, that remained a secret only. Knowing this will, Vyasa made it known to them that Drupada's daughter Krishna would be their wife and for this cause alone they should go to Panchala. Wishing them well graciously he departed and Pandavas started their journey northwards. On the way once at night on the bank of the Ganga a dispute arose between them and a Gandharva named Amgarparna and after its settlement he became a friend of the Pandavas and from him they became aware of the necessity of having a family priest. Arjuna wanted to know of him as to who was that eligible person to become their priest; in reply the Gandharva told him that in the holy place named Utkocha there was man named Debala engaged in austere pursuits. His younger brother Dhoumya was the eligible person to be their family priest. They went there and received Dhoumya respectfully as their family priest. Now Dhoumya was happy and so were the Pandavas.

Again they started their journey to Panchala. On the way they met with a good number of Brahmins who also were proceeding toward Panchala with the purpose of visualizing the grand ceremony of marriage of the princess there and to accept gifts if be available at all. The Brahmins requested them to accompany them and the Pandavas agreed gladly. Coming to Panchala they took the shelter of a potter. They were disguised as Brahmins and their profession was mendicancy.

Listening to the tale that caused "pin-prick" feeling at heart of the Pandavas was related to the birth of Dhristadyumna and Krishna and they were submerged in the sea of sorrow. But why this sorrow? They were destined to establish themselves along with detachment their mother in the realm of the Self and it was right that they did not know when and how that would be possible for them although there was no flaccidity on their part in performing their duties as directed by Vyasa. The role of resolution is the most important one inasmuch as in material and spiritual endeavours to establish one's own right defeating the antagonistic forces.

However, to pay the fee to their Guru the Pandavas defeated Drupada and owing to that defeat he lost half of his Kingdom. Now Drupada was so much blessed that he had two offsprings miraculously. What qualities had he to be so fortunate? Still then the Pandavas were unaware as to what awaited those progenies in future. Only the miracle of their birth kept them at worry. On the other hand, notwithstanding their natural birth, it was narrated allegorically to be miraculous and the reason for all this was to keep the Pandavas worried and thoughtful of the brother and sister so that the Pandavas could not get rid of the thought of them. It was necessary. In support of this necessity Vyasa came to Ekachakra and after a short discourse on Dharma he began to tell a story to the Pandavas, which related to the "divine woman" Drupadi's austere pursuit to have a husband in her earlier birth, at the end of which she got the boon of having five husbands; and Vyasa's intention was to make the legend known to the Pandavas. "She will be your wife," he said adding, "you will be happy indeed to have her as your wife." Then he departed saying that they should stay at Panchala arriving there. Vyasa left the Pandavas disclosing the result of Draupadi's Svayambara (selection of the groom by the bride from among many suitors assembled in an open court) but did not say anything as to how that would be possible. It has been said earlier that the role of Vyasa was that of the Guru. He guided them the way which was beneficial to them and inspired them to do what augured the best for them.

Being blessed by Vyasa Pandavas set out for Panchala and on the way on the bank of the Ganga a hazard halted them for a while. Arjuna was leading the Pandavas and on reaching the bank of the Ganga, a Gandharva objected to their presence there after sun-set and challenged him to a fight as a result of which he himself was defeated to Arjuna and on the mediation of Yudhisthira his life was saved. Finally the Gandharva became a friend of Arjuna. In the perspective of this friendship Amgarparna, the Gandharva suggested to have a family priest with them and it was a necessity. He also informed that Dhaumaya, the younger brother of Debala, was the fittest one. Accepting his suggestion the Pandavas received Dhaunnya as their priest and again started their journey.

In olden days it was a custom to preserve fire in the families of well-beings, apart from the royal houses and hermitages. In the marriage ceremonies, in performing sacrifices, even in death the funeral pyres used to be lighted taking fire from this family fire preserved by the family priest. Noticing that the Pandavas has no family priest nor was there any family fire with them, Amgarpana suggested to appoint a family priest. The family fire and a family priest were the symbols of social standing. All this is a social custom only. The suggestion of Amgarparna was commensurate with prevailing social custom. Kunti and the Pandavas accepted the logic and appointed Dhaumya as their family priest.

The mind is full of resolution and dissolution too. Yet in the material world it is full of resolution and never thinking of dissolution. The resolution is the manifestation of wish; but this wish is not impartial. The mind resolves at the behest of the faculties arisen in the Chitta, which are the seeds of the fruits of actions performed in earlier births and the inspirations of these seeds of the fruits of actions of earlier births are the Gandharvas who are of ethereal existence moving in the sky, so to say and not to be seen at day time but in the dark which means to the wise they are non-existent but very much existent to the ignorant. They follow the established tradition and they inspire others to follow that. Amgarparna was such an inspiration. Now, the conflict between tejas is obvious. So at the first sight he became angry with Arjuna on the alibi that Arjuna disturbed his nocturnal water-sports and challenged him to a fight. The fight took place and the defeated Gandhava's life was saved by the generosity of Yudhisthira and lastly he became a friend of Arjuna.

The gandharvas are the denizens of darkness and in light they are devoid of their existence which means so long the Chitta is smudged they arise there to influence the thought and action of the ignorant. But as the chitta becomes clear and transparent they disappear. On the other hand, beings cannot visualize the chitta, hence arising out of it when they appear before the mind the beings know of them. Ignorance is darkness and wisdom is light. Therefore, the gandharvas are non-existent to the wise. Tejas is the inspiration and energy as well for wisdom which does not cohere with traditional custom, hence the conflict. But even then tejas accepts his suggestion as tejas itself is not wisdom but its inspiration and energy. Therefore, as Amgarparna reminded Arjuna of a social custom i.e. the necessity of appointment of a family priest, he as well as his mother and brothers accepted the suggestion and acted accordingly.

Arjuna was then engrossed in the fire of thoughts of Dhristadyumna and Krishna, ignited by Vyasa. They were going to attend the nuptials of the princess of Panchala at the royal court of Drupada but in the disguise of Brahmins. So they needed a family priest. This is a social custom and the priest is appointed on the advice of Amgarparna. In terms of realities of the human body Dhaumya, the priest is the ardent obedience to traditional custom.

Draupadi's Marriage

At last the Pandavas reached Panchala and found shelter at a potter's house in the guise of Brahmins and their occupation was to solicit alms. On the way they met with their grand father Vyasa and their aim was to remain present in the royal court of Drupada to observe the marriage of the princess Draupadi.

On the other hand, Drupada had the latent ambition to give his daughter to Arjuna by marriage. But Drupada had no information as to whether the Pandavas were alive or dead at Varanavata in course of burning of the house of lac there. Yet by analyzing the sequence of events, it may be conjectured that he had no information at all was not correct. Witnessing the prowess and valour of Bhima and Arjuna in the battle-field, he was convinced that it was not so easy to kill the Pandavas helplessly by burning them. Secondly, it was not impossible for Drupada to make an idea collecting information regarding the rumour of their death, from his own spies; otherwise how a father could have decided to give his daughter to a dead man by marriage? None of the sort and of course not a king. Again, he imposed such a condition to test the mettle of the suitors that was very much uncommon and to his estimation none of the suitors would come out successfully except Arjuna and he did it only for Arjuna. There were a good number of valiant and heroic kings and princes in the assembly. Lest Draupadi being influenced by listening the heroic exploits of anyone other than Arjuna did accept him as her future husband, knowing well that he also would not object to accept the greatest of them and it was at the root of his idea to test the suitors.

But Drupada did not divulge his thoughts to a second one; he wore such a look that he arranged the test only to be sure of the capability of his future son-in-law. But what was the condition? It was that a target to be fixed high above and below it a wheel would be rotating speedily; the aspirant was to hit the target shooting arrows through the hole of the rotating wheel looking at the reflection of the target and that of the spinning wheel below in the water contained in a pot below. The shooter was allowed to shoot five arrows only to hit the target. Drupada declared in the assembly, "The person who would succeed to hit the target shooting his arrows through the whirling wheel after putting bow-string to the bow. I shall give him my daughter by marriage."

However, after the priests of Chandra Dynasty offering oblation to the sacrificial fire and prayed peace for all, Dhristadyumna ushered in his sister well-bedecked and bejeweled Draupadi and introduced her to the present kings and princes and said, "Listen sister, you should offer your bridal garland to him who will be capable of hitting the target." The aspiring kings beholding Draupadi in her bridal attire became so much deluded that thinking "Draupadi would be mine", they stood upon their feet leaving their seats. All of them became engrossed in the thought of "Draupadi is mine", and no other thought appeared in their mind. They were so absorbed in their own thought that could not be conscious enough of those present in the court. But it was otherwise in case of Krishna among the Vrishnis; looking around the court. He could identify Arjuna among the

Brahmin spectators and showed him to Balarama also. Then both of them were glad to know that the Pandavas were alive.

Now began the act of hitting the target. The aspirant kings came one by one, took up the bow and tried to hit the target but failed miserably. Then came Karna, strung the bow and ready to hit the target thinking that he would be the owner of the rare gem that Draupadi was, being successful in his efforts. But the undaunted and proud daughter of Drupada put him through his bid saying, "I am not to marry a carpenter's son." Thus Karna was desisted from his bid being heckled and insulted in an open court. Then came Shishupala, Jarasandha, Salya and other kings and failed; someones were wounded too. Then from the Brahmin audience rose Arjuna and proceeded towards the bow. Seeing Arjuna getting a move on toward the bow the Brahmin audience began to make a loud clamour. Someones even said while the established heroes proved to be incapable of shooting the target, his attempt was nothing but to make the Brahmin society contemptible to the eyes of others. Some others said, the man having a lustrous appearance was fit for the act. Listening to all this, Arjuna came to the bow, circumambulated around it and invoking silently his adorable one strung the bow, took up five arrows and hit that difficult target that fell on earth being struck. The Brahmins became jubilant. Drupada was gratified; he surmised that it was Arjuna who had hit the target. On the other hand, a gladdened Draupadi put her bridal garland around the neck of Arjuna.

But the sequence of the event appeared to be insulting to the kings and princes who argued that with a purpose to damage their reputation Drupada invited them and gave away his daughter to a Brahmin; marriage by selection of a suitor from among many assembled in a royal court was meant for Kshatriyas only and not for the Brahmins. Therefore, they decided to teach a condign lesson to Drupada by killing him; they rose in arms against him concertedly. In this distress of Drupada Arjuna came forward to save him and Bhima was with him. Karna and Salya were the leaders of the hostile group. Karna began to fight against Arjuna and Salya against Bhima. In no time Bhima lifting up Salya threw him on earth but did not kill him. Karna praised a lot for Arjuna's dexterity in fight and compared him with Rama, Surya (the sun god) or Vishnu; in reply Arjuna told, "Following the advices of Brahmins and Guru I have become an expert in the use Brahmic and Paurandara weapons and today I am present here to defeat you." Listening to this, Karna refrained from fighting accepting his Brahmic prowess. Amidst the discussions on the conversation between the two great warriors among the kings, Krishna appeared there and opined that Brahmins had won Draupadi and there was no further scope for fighting. The kings accepted his opinion.

Drupada had the desire that Arjuna should be his daughter's husband. Drupada is the arterial energy and Arjuna is Tejas (fire). It is natural that the arterial energy should accord due importance to Tejas. In absence of tejas arterial energy loses its activity, while in absence of arterial energy tejas remains active as before. On this count tejas is a greater hero than arterial energy which was relative to tejas. A great hero is honoured by everybody. But what was contrived by Drupada to honour the greatest hero in the court before the aspiring suitors was an unprecedented one. In a machine placed high above in which a wheel was spinning and above that machine was the target fixed. The archer was to hit the target shooting his arrow through a hole of that spinning wheel. The wheel that is rotating in the machine symbolizes the six nerve- centre of the body and the target that is above the machine is the symbol of the seventh never-centre of it also known as Hridaya granthi (the heart). The consciousness of an austere person may pierce through these six nerve-centres by one's austerity but cannot do that in case of the seventh one by austerity alone; that needs also the grace of Guru. Yet everybody should strive it as every human being has the capability of doing this. However, in this test a special bow has been referred to, which is the spinal cord of the body in which the six nerve-centres exist and the bow string is the Susumna artery through which the consciousness being gradually purified moves upward and finally bestows the identity of the austere person upon him and also helps him be established in his own nature that is manhood. It has been said there were five shafts to hit the hanging target. These five shafts are — Simplicity, Modesty. Forbeance, Nobility and Expansion. These five are termed as five 'heats' that originate from the elements of the earth, the water, the fire, the air and the ether in the body respectively. But they do not originate from the elements automatically. One is to follow sincerely the dictates of one's Guru, leading a disciplined life and performing ordained actions to get them dawned upon one's heart that would be reflected in one's behaviour. The reality of tejas with its power of consistency synthesizing the five heats can reveal and apply them when necessary. So only tejas can hit such a target. When tejas exerts its self omnifariously no other reality can be equal to tejas. All the kings present in the court were the realities of the body and they were incapable of hitting the target nor could they defeat tejas fighting even unitedly.

Tejas is the greatest hero and the ablest husband of the daughter of Drupada.

The marriage by selection is over. But something is to be spoken about the bride. The beings of the phenomenal world think that their mettle is of their own. All their activities are the expression of their own vigour at the root of which there is their own will. But the being does not know, who he is, wherefrom he has come and why, nor does he know the significance of his life. Being ignorant of his identity he becomes the lord of other beings; he becomes the 'doer' and 'enjoyer'. As he does not know of his origin, likewise he does not know the source of his vigour. Such a behaviour of the beings is termed as ignorance that does not reveal his own self. Again, he has the capability to overcome this ignorance but in an expedient ambience. Beyond this existence of the being, if man is established in his manhood, he becomes aware of his vigour as well as its source too. Consciousness encased in the body as Atman being actionless remains as Immutable and a mere witness of beings' good and evil deeds, but its energy existing in the body reveals beings' existence as well as their manhood. So long the existence of the beings is there, this energy remains beyond the vision of the beings behind the screen and after attainment of manhood when knowledge dawns upon them, this energy reveals its identity to them. This energy is the individual self who is none but the daughter of Drupada, Krishna. Drupada is the arterial energy without the help of which she cannot manifest herself as Individual Self (Jivatma) and hence Drupada is her father and she is his daughter.

Arjuna's Abstinence & Self-Imposed Exile

There was no bond of love and friendship between the Kauravas of Hastinapura and the Srinjayas of Panchala; so when Vidura declared in the court of Dhritarastra that the "Kauravas are victorious." Dhritarastra took it for granted that Draupadi had taken Duryodhana as her husband.

A joyous Dritarastra at once exclaimed, "What a good fortune! What a good fortune!" Vidura was able to read the mind of Dhritarastra and with a view to correct it he instantly said, "The sons of Kunti have gained Draupadi." Hiding his pain under his chest and expressing a deceitful joy Dhritarasta said, the Pandavas were also as good as his sons. Hence their success had made him joyful. On the other hand, the defeated Duryodhana being restless in disgrace and in the thought of destroying the Pandavas sought for the permission of Dhritarastra. But Dhritarastra, on his part, decided to have the opinions of his ministers as to what should be done in respect of the Pandavas and at first he requested Bhishma to suggest.

Bhishma said, "I do not like to fight against the Pandavas. To me Dhritarastra and Pandu both are equal." Adding something more to it, he finally said, "Oh, the Kuru prince, so long the Pandavas are alive even lord Indra cannot dislodge them from their rightful inheritance." Then Dronacharya was asked to spell out his opinion in this respect; he too opined in favour of giving the Pandavas half of the kingdom. But Karna could not put up with the suggestions of Bhisma and Drona; he rather suggested to destroy the Pandavas from their root. Karna's opinion appeared to be so pleasing to the ears of Dhritarastra as if it was a honeyed one. But hiding his glee Dhritarastra had to listen to what Vidura had to say. He also said to divide the kingdom between the Pandavas and Dhritarastra's sons. Listening to Vidura Dhritarastra appointed him in embassy sending to Panchala to bring back Kunti and Draupadi along with the Pandava brothers with due honour and respect.

Vidura went to Panchala. Drupada also agreed to bid farewell to the Pandavas; they set out for Hastinapura being accompanied by Vidura and Krishna. They were warmly welcomed by Bhishma and Dhritarastra and the citizens of Hastinapura. Dhritarastra asked Yudhisthira to accept the half of the kingdom at Khandavaprastha to live and reign there and in that case nobody could harm them any more. Yudhisthira accepted the proposal and went to Khandavaprastha. Vasudeva and Balarama were with them.

The days in Khandavaprastha were happy ones for the Pandavas; but suddenly a disturbing instance took place. Once when Yudhisthira was there with Draupadi in the armoury, a Brahmin solicited Arjuna's help to retrieve his stolen away cows. Arjuna promised to help him but he needed required weapons to track down the thieves and recover the cows but Yudhisthira was in the armoury with Draupadi. Finding no way out Arjuna entered the armoury and without obtaining Yudhisthira's permission, collected the necessary weapons and retrieved the Brahmin's cows.

After finishing his job Arjuna said to Yudhisthira that he had done an unjust deed by entering the armoury without permission and as a penance for impropriety he would go in exile for twelve years maintaining total abstinence (brahmacharya). Yudhisthira, on his part, could not accord consent to his proposal; but yet Arjuna went in exile.

Travelling many places Arjuna came to Gangadvara. Here once taking his bath in the river Ganga when he was coming back to the river bank, the daughter of the Naga king, Ulupi pulling him led to the palace of the Naga king in Patala (nether world) and after finishing his diurnal ritualistic worship there Arjuna asked for her identity and wanted to know as to why he had been brought here. In reply Ulupi said, "There is a Naga in the Airavata dynasty and I am his daughter, Ulupi is my name.....Seeing you washing in the Ganga I became smitten with passion; now offering yourself to me please fulfil my desire." Arjuna at once replied that although he was not averse to her proposal, he was now maintaining abstinence and hence a middle course had got to be taken. Ulupi said, in turn, that she knew the reasons for his abstinence and also that for his exile. But if he did gratify her desire, he would not be fallen from his dharma and even if a little bit of it is caused, then he would gain a better part of dharma providing life to her. After such a conversation the desirous Arjuna spent the night with Ulupi and came back to Gangadvara next morning with her. At the moment of bidding adieu to Arjuna Ulupi offered him a boon, — "you will win over all marine creatures" and she departed.

Coming back to his own men at Gangadvara Arjuna narrated the chain of events that occurred to him to the accompanying Brahmins and went northwards to visit some places of pilgrimage there and then started his journey eastwards. Paying a visit to Gaya and many other places of pilgrimage in Anga, Vanga and Kalinga etc. he arrived Manipura on the coast of the ocean. There seeing the princess of Manipura he fell in love and wanted to marry her. On being approached by him the king of Manipura spoke about a condition that her son would be the king's descendant and had Arjuna been agreeable to the condition, he could marry Chitrangada. Arjuna agreed to marry her. After the marriage he left Manipura for Southern Sea.

In course of his journey towards the South Sea he enquired about the places of pilgrimage with a view to visit them and could know that five celebrated places of pilgrimage viz. Agastya, Soubhadra, Pauloma, Karandhama and Bharadvaja were deserted by the ascetics as in each of them there was a crocodile in the water bodies there as a result of which those water-bodies were unfit for bathing. So they had abandoned them. Despite this interdiction, Arjuna reached Saubhadra among those five places and went down in the water for washing. Suddenly a crocodile seized a leg of him with its teeth. He then forcibly dragged it from water and instantly it transformed into a beautiful damsel. Arjuna in his amazement wanted to know of the sin she had committed in the past. She replied that she was an apsara. Once with her four companions she was returning from the residence of Indra through a forest wherein seeing a meditating ascetic, they all five decided to disturb him in a frolicking mood and the Brahmin being disturbed cursed them to be crocodiles for a hundred years. The cursed apsaras then begged of his forgiveness. The appeased ascetic told them, when they would seize one's leg in the water being transformed into crocodiles, if somebody rescues them from water they would regain their forms. He also told them in which place of pilgrimage they would live in, that would be a sacred place of pilgrimage for the women.

Taking leave of the Brahmin when they were very much anxious for their future freedom, they met with Narada on the way. They saluted him and stood before him wearing a shameful look. He wanted to know why they were sorry. The apsaras told him in detail. Then Narada told them that near the south sea there was a very sacred and pleasant place named by Panchatirtha. You should go there to live in. Within a short time Arjuna would be coming there to deliver you, — saying this the apsara requested Arjuna to free the other four apsaras and Arjuna did it.

With a view to be united with Chitrangada he came to Manipura and producing a son in her womb he set out for the pilgrimage centre, Gokarna and proceeded towards Prabhasa. There he met with Krishna; He wanted to know why Arjuna was travelling in holy places from one to another. In reply Arjuna recounted the events that led him to travel; on hearing of which Krishna said "well done". After a few days of his arrival there, a great celebration began on the Raivataka hill. The high government officers and the ladies of the palace adorned in their best joined in that celebration. There amidst the festivities he saw bejeweled and beautiful Subhadra and on seeing her his mind became desirous. Noticing Arjuna, Krishna passed the comment, "Being a traveller in the forests, you are smitten with passion! How is it! She is the daughter of Vasudeva....and my sister; her name is Subhadra. My friend, if your mind is really attracted to her, say, I'll talk to my father." Listening to Krishna Arjuna became very much encouraged and extremely eager to have her as his wife and requested him to find out ways and means. In reply Krishna said, selection of a groom by the bride was the ruling principle for the Kshatriyas. Yet nothing could be said of the feminine inclinations. "Forceful carry-off is also praise-worthy for the Kshatriyas." Krishna's advice appeared to be honey-showering to Arjuna. He at once informed Yudhisthira and received his approval.

On the other hand, after the worshipping and other rituals were over, the Yadavas were returning to Dvaraka; on the way Arjuna caught hold of Subhadra and carried her off forcibly to his chariot and directed it to move towards Indraprastha. On hearing the news the Yadava soldiers felt insulted and unitedly they decided to rescue Subhadra defeating Arjuna following his chariot. At this time Balarama told them to know of the opinion of Krishna in this regard. Then Krishna was asked to opine on their plan to rescue Subhadra. He said, it was not praiseworthy for a Kshatriya to marry on the consent of his parents. So Arjuna had done the just deed by abducting Subhadra and nobody had been insulted. On his advice the Yadavas being desisted from the recourse to rescue Subhadra, rather arranged for their marriage. After the marriage was over, Arjuna remained in Dvaraka for a year on the request of Krishna and then went to Puskara where they stayed for eleven years. Then they returned to Khandavaprastha.

Dhritarastra was highly expectant that Duryodhana would have won Draupadi. The expectation of the mind engrossed in desire is limitless. The material mind knows to expect only. As Dhritarastra's hopes were dashed and as the thorn of failure pricked the heart of Duryodhana, both of them were eager to destroy the Pandavas. But Dhritarastra was the king;

he was much more deceitful than the desire that was Duryodhana. Hence he had to wear a mask of justice and propriety at least. So, at first he sought to know the mind of his ministers as to what should be his duty towards the Pandavas. He asked Bhishma and then Drona and even after him Vidura to reveal their minds on the issue. All of them opined for the division of the kingdom between the Pandavas and Kauravas. If the Pandavas were deceived, that would not only be unjust but something more than that. The opinion of Duryodhana and Karna was much more pleasurable to Dhritarastra, yet he was to honour the mask and compelled to bifurcate the kingdom. The mind that is a slave to desire (kama) feigns to hide its sinister design with a view to establish its feigning to be a truth and in that act it advances many an argument. Hence Dhritarastra needed the advices of ministers. However, Vidura was appointed to embassy to the Pandavas at Panchala, to bring them back. It should be kept in mind that the steps taken by Dhritarastra were highly antagonistic to that of Duryodhana and Karna who till then were unaware of the sinister design of the king. Had the Pandavas been gaining strength at Panchala with a view to retrieve their right to Hastinapura and if any war became inevitable, Dhritarastra with his sons would lose the kingdom and be compelled to live under the Pandavas which was not at all desirable. There was neither friendship nor enmity between the Srinjayas and Kauravas and hence Dhritarastra was unaware of the strength of the Srinjayas. Therefore, the advices of the ministers were required and on their advices Vidura was sent to Panchala to bring back the Pandavas to have the right to their paternal property. The mind of attachment at times driving away the impediments to the enjoyment of sense-objects and taking the help of truthful faculties honestly feigns to smoothen the means to enjoy sense-objects. In this case also no exception was there.

Returning to Hastinapura the Pandavas got half of the kingdom, of course, not in Hastinapura. Leaving the refuge of the arterial energy the five elements with detachment and the Self (Jivatma) became the residents of Hastinapura but not in the palace there. They were given a tract of arid and barren land where they were to establish their capital to reign and live. Although there is no mention of the exact geographical position of the place in the text, it may be assumed that Khandavaprastha was to the north of Hastinapura. Earlier we have said that Hastinapura stands for the Chitta. As the chitta is the repository of faculties and realities, likewise the heart is also that but containing magnificent esses. The both are interconnected and hence in the clear and transparent chitta the magnificence of the heart is reflected and then there remains no difference between the two. But until the chitta becomes clear and transparent being devoid of faculties and traits of the mind, they remain two different existences and any communication between the two remains beyond the vision of beings. Then the duty of the beings is to strive for cleansing the Chitta and in this respect the role of the Guru is essential as His grace is the inspiration for the effort. This action has been initiated by the event of the Pandavas' getting of the kingdom at Khandavaprastha.

Now the Pandavas have a new kingdom to rule, a new capital to reside and a new wife to enjoy the company with. They are to start everything anew. But five brothers have a single wife. Instances of strifes and disputes over the right to a lady causing estrangement including bloodshed even among the friends and relatives are not rare in the human history. Therefore, it was decided that Draupadi would accept her wifehood for one year to a brother and then the other brothers should behave with her according to social norms paying due respect to her. Again, when she would be with her husband in a room no brother could enter it without due permission. What could be more reasonable than this one? But what would that be in case of a human body? In case of the human body Jivatma (the self) manifests itself through a single element at a time and then the role of the other elements remains non-functional. It may also be noted that the Sanskrit term 'Varsa' denotes one year as well as a place too. So in terms of the body the word means a place or station for action in terms of character and the same term denotes a year. When the Jivatma (the self) remains stationed in a particular nerve-centre (chakra) then that nerve-centre becomes active manifesting the propriety of that chakra meaning thereby that of the particular element while the other never-centres remain inactive. This is a divine rule for the creation and this is the order adopted by the Pandavas for enjoying the company of Draupadi, although the terms of penance for infringement of this order has been adopted in the interest of the progress of the argument.

One day the act of transgression took place. Arjuna needed his arms to retrieve the stolen cows of a Brahmin; but Yudhisthira was there in the armoury with Draupadi. Arjuna in a haste infringed the rule to enter into the armoury without obtaining Yudhistrira's permission. He collected the arms and retrieved the cows of the Brahmin.

Now the question arises that were the Pandavas so short of space that the king had to accommodate himself in the armoury to enjoy the company of his wife and at day time? At any point of time arms might be needed for exigency. Had Yudhisthira been oblivious of it? How to explain all this? The fifth nerve-centre in the spinal cord is the home of Yudhisthira (the element of ether). This is called the Visuddha Chakra (immaculate nerve-centre) and this is his room for living and also the armoury. When the Self (Jivatma) remains in this charka the austere person becomes enriched with sacred devotion and pure knowledge and being illumined by them he becomes capable of performing actions observing the sermons and dictates of Guru perfectly and also applies them in his life and inspires others to do so. These sermons and directives of Guru are the weapons of the beings. Until tejas is awakened these weapons cannot be applied perfectly. On the other hand, the Brahmin of the story is the symbol of a being of lost manhood. His riches have been stolen away by the impulses (ripu) bondages (pasha) and the attendants of maya such as hosts of superstitions and lots of ignorance. Being oppressed by the trials and tribulations, beings some day realize that all their magnificence of manhood have been stolen away that required to be recovered. But that recovery depends upon the awakening of tejas and without its help it is not possible. So the Brahmin of the tale needed the help of Arjuna to whom he prayed for the recovery of his wealth of manhood.

Then a new chapter begins. Successfully completing his mission Arjuna came back to Yudhisthira and told him that in order to collect the arms in haste by entering the armoury without obtaining Yudhisthera's consent, he had violated the accepted order and decided to atone for this infringement, would go in exile for twelve years maintaining abstinence. Yudhisthira could not agree with him. But the determined

Arjuna was firm in his resolve and set out for exile despite Yudhisthisa's non-approval of it. Is it not an instance of disobedience to Yudhisthira or is it to prove his honest intentions? We are to keep in mind that till now physical creation had not started although to fulfil the Leela of the Lord it was absolutely necessary. But prior to that a congenial ambience for the life to be created, was necessary and at the same time the distinctly detailed outline for the life to be led by the beings so created was a need too. Arjuna is the reality of tejas and only he can establish the norms as to how the beings would lead the life on earth; and he can make them capable of attaining the Supreme Self by crossing over the mesh of maya and also establishing them in manhood. The world of the beings is the realm of action and the actions of beings bear the fruits of their actions. Again, while enduring the fruits of the past actions, they accumulate that of their current actions and hence they are required to act judiciously so that their present actions do not attract fruits for further endurance and at the same time by performing ordained actions to wane away the fruits of their past actions, all of which comes under the purview of tejas. Hence the primal intents of life that is to come into existence have been given a form by the role of tejas.

Arjuna's exile was for twelve years and during that period he remained an abstinent. Twelve years make a yuga (aeon). The life of beings on earth since birth to death is but their exile here for a yuga (aeon) irrespective of the exact span of life. Sprung of the source of Eternal Bliss (Ananda) the beings live a life here being entangled in the mesh of the delusion of maya and is it not their exile? Therefore, Arjuna decided to maintain Brahmancharya (abstinence) otherwise, his exile was sure to be futile; but tejas cannot allow his exile to be so.

His other motive was to atone for his misdemeanour shown to Yudhisthira while without obtaining his consent Arjuna entered the armoury to collect the arms. After retrieving the cows of the Brahmin, Arjuna having observed the utility and identity of the weapons, realized that the time was ripe for leaving Khandavaprastha with a view to accord due importance to Guru in the grand perspective of the life of beings on earth. At the same time it was necessary for revealing the essential intents of the life of beings and to do that he had to wander along the path of the existence of beings which was far away from the realm of the chitta. So on the part of Arjuna, it was imperative to leave Khandavaprastha and it was ordained by the Almighty; neither Yudhisthira nor Arjuna could ignore it.

The brahmachary Arjuna began his journey northwards from Khandavaprastha and after some days of travelling he reached Gangadvara. Here once while he was returning to the river bank after his ablutions in the river, he was caught up and led to the palace of the Nagas in Patala (nether world) by a young woman. Being surprised of the suddenness of the incident Arjuna came to know by questioning that she was a princess of the Airavata dynasty. Her name was Ulupi; being smitten with love she had brought him to patala. But who is Ulupi?

It is said that Atman is actionless in the body. He is a mere witness. Yet as Atman is encased in the body it is conscious, active and lively. Notwithstanding the actionlessness of Atman in the body, Its energy is manifest as the countless creations. All his actions are not performed by him but by his energy. The Supreme Self and His Energy are one and the same; but to the ordinary understanding they appear to be discriminative. To the wise they are not so, but one and with the help of this Energy one can realize Him whose Energy she is. On the other hand, Arjuna till now is not a being (Jiva) and hence the comprehensive appearance and the existence of beings are unknown to him. Yet the Divine Will led him to the nether world for union with Ulupi. Nothing is unknown to the Supreme Consciousness that pervades the creation and beyond that. The events that happened in the Pandava palace were neither unknown to the Supreme Consciousness nor His Energy as they are one and the same.

Ulupi is the Energy of the Supreme Consciousness and stationed in the nether world and her location is at Muladhara Chakra (never-centre) in the lower part of the spinal cord. As the lower part of the body from the navel is known to be the patala (nether world), hence Ulupi is a resident of that region; she is well-hidden there beyond the vision of beings. But who is Ulupi in terms of realities of the body? Beings are tamed and controlled by desire (Kama) so much so that they themselves cannot win over it but be able to do so being graced by Guru. Of course, generally beings never like to win over desire (kama); on the other hand, a human child becomes influenced by desire since its birth and as he grows in body and mind this influence of desire becomes expressive within a broader perspective; with the advent of youth the same desire seeks ova or semen. To reveal the existence of beings, tejas was attracted by Ulupi to saturate the life of beings with desire (Kama) and expressed that she was smitten with love. Ulupi is the energy of inspiration of the faculty of desire (Kama); but her role in the life of beings is thoroughly unknown to them and that is why she remains unidentified to the vision of beings. Passing his night with the new-found inamorata, Arjuna came back to Gangadvara with Ulupi and at the time of bidding farewell to him she blessed him with a boon that he would win oever all marine creatures. It is to be noted that the person who in the previous morning led Arjuna to her palace in the nether world to sate her passion, in the next morning she blessed him with a boon. But why was Arjuna blessed being an itinerant? The marine creatures are the ova of the famine beings, that crave for tejas and surrender to it and also become sated coming in contact with it. The beings, prior to coming into material existence have been instilled the active faculty of desire (Kama). Hence Ulupi is the energy of inspiration of desire (Kama).

Then Arjuna started his journey eastwards. Visiting many places as well as many places of pilgrimage he reached the kingdom of Manipura on the coast of the ocean. There seeing the princess of Manipura he became desirous of her. He approached the king to marry the princess and he was allowed to do so accepting the king's condition. Now, where is Manipura in the body and who is Chitrangada? Manipura is the third nerve-centre in the spinal cord and its place is at the root of the navel and again, it is also the station of tejas too. This centre is responsible for intake of food, its digestion and production of blood and its movement, nourishment of the body by replenishing the waned away realities of the division and disposal of solid and liquid waste of the food taken etc. The energy that performs all these actions remaining in the navel is Chitrangada and the resultant effect of all these actions cannot leave this centre. So the son of the princess cannot leave the kingdom. The bride also cannot go to the father-in-law's house after her marriage for the same reason but the marriage is not impossible as this energy requires to be united with tejas to remain active. The navel is the King of Manipura and the energy is his progeny.

From Manipura Arjuna came to Panchatirtha (five places of Pilgrinage). There he enquired about the desolation of the place and came to know that there was a crocodile in each of the five water bodies there and he was asked to leave the place. But paying no heed to the locals' advice Arjuna got down into the water body at Saubhadra and instantly a crocodile seized his leg. He dragged the creature to the ground and coming out of the water it transformed into a bejeweled apsara. Arjuna became amazed and asked for her identity. She recounted her story in details and requested him to rescue her other four companions and Arjuna did it. Now the question is who are these apsaras? In the first chapter of this book that has been discussed. They are the celestial creatures and live in the heaven. But their movement on earth also is unhindered. They were transformed into crocodiles being cursed although they knew as to how they would regain their former forms. These apsaras of this story are the desires of mankind known to be the Varga or Purusartha. Generally they are four in number; but there is other one which is a very rare indeed, known to be the love. Beings are required to observe their faith (dharma) kindred to them, to know of the surroundings and in that perspective to know of the significance of their existence (artha), to search for the objects of desire to enjoy (Kama) and to lead the life aiming salvation (moksha) according to the law of creation. But the salvation is not the last word; nor does it cause that final liberation in the light of the realization of the Supreme Reality ensuring freedom from the cycle of rebirth. The beings need to possess love as the fifth desire for eternal peace and tranquility as well; but it is not so easy to acquire love which requires a strong resolution and unswerving aim the inspiration for which comes from tejas. The inspiration born of tejas leads the beings to the way of love. This is the deliverance of the apsaras. But why were they transformed to crocodiles? It is said that an austere Brahmin cursed the apsaras to become so being disturbed by them. Who was this austere Brahmin. He is the symbol of the selfish pursuits of austerity of beings while they are ignorant and fail to understand the real significance of the desires (varga). During austerity when their true nature becomes evident to the vision of the mind's eye they think of them to be repugnant to their selfishness and hence they keep them at bay which is suggestive of the transformation of the apsaras to crocodiles. Thus driven away by the ignorant beings, the desires then mislead their austerity by deluding them and ensure their ruin. Hence being inspired by tejas and knowing the true nature of desires the beings need to proceed in their austere pursuits, otherwise, adversity is inevitable.

After rescuing the apsaras the itinerant Arjuna went to Manipura again and procreating a son in Chitrangada's womb, he proceeded to Prabhasa. But why did Arjuna feel the necessity to go to Manipura? As nourishment of the body and the equilibrium of the realities of it are not all; there is something more than that, — that is the meaningful step in the realm of spirituality and the symbol of the conscious energy for this is the son born of Chitrangada. The beings really step into the spiritual world from the Manipura never-centre. However Arjuna left Manipura for Prabhasa — the seat of Guru and there he met with Krishna. On His advice Arjuna prolonged his sojourn there. There once seeing Subhdra he became curiously eager of her. Reading the mind of Arjuna, Krishna said she was His younger sister and encouraged him in this affair. He also advised Arjuna to abduct her. But why did Krishna advise him to abduct her? Who is Subhadra?

It is absolutely necessary to gather the elements of the existence of beings (jivatva) as well as its dharma (nature) to give a comprehensive shape to it. And the aim of itinerant Arjuna is to give a shape to the existence of beings in its entirety. Assimilating some of the constituent ingredients for the existence of beings in his earlier part of the journey Arjuna came to Prabhasa. Prabhasa is to the west of Khandavaprastha and the country as well. The west is the direction of ignorance and on the field of ignorance the beings meet with Guru. So the meeting with Krishna and consequent sojourn at Prabhasa at His insistence denote the beings' acceptance of Guru and the refuge provided by Him. Subhadra is the sister of Him, whom Arjuna is so much eager to have as his wife. When the Supreme Consciousness incarnates himself, He accepts the assistance of Mahamaya (Primordial Nature) and on the same analogy his sister is also born of the same as illusion is also the progeny of Mahamaya. Hence maya is the sister of Krishna, because of her elegance she is suave by nature.

The life of beings or their birth and death are not guided by themselves and they are full of ignorance. Their life and action are always conducted by their ignorance and to do away with it they are expected to submit to their Guru, for which they are not conscious although the saintly persons are always egar to direct them to the right direction as to how they should lead their life and actions while the scriptures are there to guide them to this aim. But things go other way; depending upon the ignorance beings become their own lords in every sphere of life. The role of ignorance in the life and action of beings is no less important and hence tejas had to be united with ignorance to give the existence of beings a comprehensive form. But the will of Guru plays a vital role in the act of this union. Arjuna could not have subhadra as his wife inspite of his love for her had Krishna not been agreeable to it and assisted him divining the means to succeed. Now it is clear that beings become the victims of ignorance being willed by Guru and they themselves desire it. This is the reason for Guru's eagerness to undo the knot of ignorance of beings even if they craved for it.

Subhadra was abducted in an ambience of celebrations; but that did not influence her action at all on the other hand, the bride and the groom spent a year in Prabhasa with the help of the Yadavas. Here the term 'varsa' has been used to mean a field and not the measure of time. Regulated enjoyment of sense-objects is a divine rule; but the insistence of ignorance in respect of unbridled enjoyment of the same may not be defied by the beings governed by ignorance nor does it enhance the respect to Guru by any means. So Arjuna decided to leave Prabhasa for Pushkara where they both spent eleven years. If the term 'varsa' denotes the measure of time, then twelve years elapsed at Prabhasa and Puskara, then how the rest of the period be measured? The text reads. "Thus on completion of twelve years he returned to Khadavaprastha." The reader is to decide in which perspective the term has been used with what significance.

At Puskara Arjuna and Subhadra were engagd in enjoyment of sense-objects for eleven years (varsa) which denotes that the eleven senses and sense-organs and the mind also were activated under the guidance of ignorance for the beings. On completion of twelve years Arjuna returned to

Khandavaprastha, with Subhadra as his period of abstinence was over. His last sojourn was at Puskara. But why Puskara?

Puskara is the stomach of the body. It has been said earlier that the body gets its nourishment from the savours extracted from food and drink within the stomach. The realities of the body wane away owing to activities of the body. This loss is replenished with the similar realities taken from the nature in form of food and drink in equal quantity. But more often than not the beings fail to quantify the requisite requirement of realities to maintain the equilibrium and hence taking less or more than required quantity of realities they either weaken their senses or make them excited as a result of which they become sick. Though not expected at all, yet it is the truth and by this process the beings enhance their ruin activating the eleven Rudras of the body.

The ignorance is the chiefest functionary that helps outline the form of beings and with this the curtain is drawn on Arjuna's abstinence and his exile. He returned to Khandavaprastha. All these events put an end to the chapter on the sequence of creation prior to its formal shaping of beings.

The Conflagration Of The Khandava Forest

Arjuna with Subhadra came back to Khandavaprastha accompanied by Krishna and a good number of Yadavas. The other Yadavas returned to Dvaravati after a short stay. But Krishna remained here. He used to pass his time here by hunting games (with Arjuna) in the Khandava forest on the bank of the Yamuna. After some time Subhadra gave birth to a son alike Krishna who performed post natal rites of the new born and was named Abhimanyu. On the other hand, Draupadi gave birth to five sons one each in a year procreated by her five husbands. The post natal rites of them were performed by Dhaumya, the priest. Later on, they were given under the charge of Arjuna to train them up in arms and scriptures. The Pandavas were passing their days happily and Krishna was with them.

Once on a hot summer day Arjuna approached Krishna saying, "…..The summer heat has grown too much; so let us have some aquatic sports in the Yamuna with our family members; in the afternoon we would return. What do you think of it?" Krishna in reply agreed to his proposal and both of them appeared before Yudhisthira to have his permission. Yudhisthira too approved of the proposal. Then they all reached the royal resort there and except Krishna and Arjuna other members went inside the building. While Krishna and Arjuna were engaged in conversation being seated outside the building there appeared a very tall Brahmin in tattered clothes and having matted locks of hair. Both of them welcomed the Brahmin who prayed to them to offer food to him. He also said, "I am habituated to over eating." On being asked, which kind of food he liked, he said, "I am Agni (the fire god), so arrange the appropriate food for me." he also said, as Takshaka, the friend of Indra, used to reside within the Khandavaprastha forest whenever he tried to burn it every time the fire was doused by Indra with rainfall. So he requested Krishna and Arjuna to assist him in this regard. Listening to him Arjuna said, he had enough arms to fight against Indra but he was wanting in such a bow that could endure the pressure of his hands in the battle-field. So he needed a bow of this kind. "Moreover my chariot is unable to carry the weight of my arms. So I need a chariot as swift as air being yoked to divine grey horses. Krishna's strength is incomparable; he can easily slay the Nagas and necrophagous evil spirits." Lastly Arjuna said to Agni that had the things prayed for been given to him he could help him squarely.

At once Agni remembered Varuna, the god of water and on his arrival Agni said to him, "Please give me the bow, the two quivers and the monkey ensigned chariot that Somaraja gave to you. Partha with the Gandiva and with the wheel perform a divine deed." Varuna gave them all and Arjuna was satisfied with the gift. Agni gave the Sudarshana wheel and a mace called Kaumodaki to Krishna. Krishna and Arjuna boarding the chariot said to Agni (the Fire god) "Now you please ignite the forest all around and burn the forest with a gusto. We both are helping you."

Being assured Agni (the fire) began to burn the Khandava forest heartily being enkindled in seven flames. In a bid to save themselves from the raging fire the avians of the forest tried to fly away from the forest but Arjuna fell them into the fire, shooting them in the sky. The other beasts trying to flee away were shot and thrown in the fire. The blazing flames created so much heat that even the gods became afraid and approached Indra to take some steps to undo all this. Indra at once arranged for dousing the fire with rain-water. But the heat of the fire was so much so that the rainwater became vapour in the sky. Meanwhile, Arjuna made an awning of the mesh of arrows over the forest so that not a single drop of rain fell upon the fire even after angry Indra ordered a rainfall of greater intensity.

On the other hand, Takshaka, Indra's friend was a resident of the forest. Takshaka, a member of the lizard family having a rough skin and is larger than common chameleon. When the forest was in flames he was away at Brahma's but his wife and son were there. Arjuna cut her into two while fleeing. To save their son Indra made Arjuna senseless for a little while with sound of a thunder and the son got a chance to flee away. But both Krishna and Arjuna noticing him cursed not to have any shelter ever. Meanwhile, a wagtail, Jarita by name, fell in a great distress with her four young chicks who were not yet fledged and forshaken by their father. The possibility of their being burnt to ashes was far more great. But they were the sons of a Rishi and well-conversant in the Vedas. Following their advice their mother Jarita saved herself going beyond the range of fire. Observing the fire was advancing towards them, they began to sing hymns in praise of fire and begged of their safe life. In the past Mandapala, their father obtained the word of honour from the fire regarding their safety. The history is this: Rishi Mandapala after his death in his earlier birth when he wanted to know the reasons as to why he was deprived of enjoying the piety of his austerity in his past life, he was informed that he failed to repay the debt to the manes by procreating offspring and hence he was deprived. Then with a view to have more than one offspring at a time Mandapala was reborn as a bird and made love with a wagtail named Jarita and left her when she was carrying; of course, after the forest-fire was totally extinguished he returned to the place, met with his sons and left it with another wagtail named Lopita for another destination.

After the conflagration devastated the Khandava forest Indra came to Krishna and Arjuna and told them, "What a great deed you have performed, even the gods could not do this! Then he desired to accord them with a boon each. Arjuna prayed for the arms of Indra in reply to which Indra said, he would get them all as and when he could please Mahadeva by austerity. Then Krishna said, "See, the bond of love with Arjuna is never snapped." Indra granted it. Then continent Agni came and thanking them took his leave. Krishna and Arjuna went to the bank of the Yamuna.

After a long travelling Arjuna came back to Khandavaprastha with Krishna, Subhadra and the Yadavas. After some time Subhadra gave birth to a son. Being fathered by tejas in the womb of ignorance was born the self-conceit. The charge to educate him was given to Arjuna. The son of a great hero is expected to be heroic like his father and in fact, he became a great warrior. After the birth of Abhimanyu, Draupadi gave birth to five sons in next five years. These five sons of the Self are but the process of Panchikarana (the admixture of the five pure elements producing twenty-five realities necessary for physical creation).

In the early dawn of creation a good number of realities were produced from the Principle of Primordial Nature (Mahattattva) and the five elements were there in pure form; so they were used to be called pure elements. They were unfit for physical creation and hence their admixture (Panchikarana) was necessary. In short, the method of this admixture is as follows; Every element primarily would be divided into two; then one half would remain intact and the rest half would again be divided into four. Each of these four parts would be mixed with the similarly divided parts of other four elements and thus they all produce twenty realities and the remaining half of the each five elements that was undivided would produce five realities necessary for physical creation be existent. On the other hand, it may be noted that as the elements are progressively evolved simultaneously the process of austerity by mankind is also being evolved symbolically.

According to the tale, on a hot summer day Arjuna proposed to take part in some aquatic sports in the Yamuna and Krishna too agreed. Having taken the permission from Yudhisthira they started for the purpose with the ladies and reached there. On their arrival the fire god (Agni) appeared before Krishna and Arjuna and finally burning of the Khandava forest took place. By scanning the sequence of events, one may ask why Arjuna alone was afflicted with the heat and his other brothers or Krishna even did not feel so much heat as did Arjuna! The reason is, when Guru infuses his energy in the heart of the disciple that energy creates a special kind of volatile heat in the body and mind of the disciple, known to be Brahmic heat (Brahma tapa) which appears to be almost unbearable at the primary state to the spiritual aspirant. With the meeting of Krishna at Dvaravati the act of infusion of that energy took place and the outcome of that was felt by Arjuna only. The instance of that heat makes the senses and sense organs restless and under its influence they endeavour vigorously to demonstrate themselves and in the early stage of austerity and some aspirants' spiritual realization fails to achieve the goal. We should mind it that this heat is not meant for energizing the senses and sense-organs but to amend them mostly and restrain the scope and limit of their actions. And Vyasa has created a beautiful perspective to symbolize the cause and effect of the summation of the sequences in this regard introducing Agni, the fire god, making an emotional appeal for his appropriate food as he was debilitating owing to consumption of two much clarified butter offered to sacrificial fire and hence he was suffering from loss of appetite! He is not agreeable to consume clarified butter now although the same nourishes fire too much. Then, here is a contradiction, why this contradiction?

The birds and beasts live a life of three dimensions — food, sleep and coition; they seem to be the slaves of these three. But howsoever their subjugation to the sense-objects, some restrictions are there maintained by Nature herself. They have their intelligence having no conscience and that is why Nature restrains them as and when necessary. So, being the slaves to their sense-objects, birds and beasts cannot enjoy unbridled sense-objects. On the other hand, the humans have conscience in addition to intelligence; they have the capability of deciding the right or wrong, honesty and dishonesty yet that sense of judgement remains dormant in the face of enjoyment of sense-objects under the compulsion of attachment. In absence of such natural restraints the humans are much prone to unbridled enjoyment of sense-objects and the chiefest of them is to enjoy the savour of coition. This kind of enjoyment tells upon the body and in culmination sickness grips it. We have said it earlier that both semen and ova are symbolically regarded as butter oil. In the sacrifice of enjoyment both semen and ova are offered as oblation in the sacrificial fire of passion to have the square satiation. The fire god, Agni spoke of his loss of appetite and weakness pointing to such unregulated enjoyment of sex.

Listening to Agni Arjuna expressed that he had no such bow that could sustain the strength of his arm and such a chariot having the speed of wind that could carry the weight of his quivers in the battle-field. If he got them he could have helped Agni as he desired. In this respect, the persons having material knowledge may think, Arjuna taking the advantage of Agni's helplessness cleverly managed to have the things that he needed; and it was an example of commercial exchange by a Vaishya on the part of a Kshatriya, Arjuna. But what Arjuna wanted to have, prayed for them and did not demand of Agni. He confessed his limitations and what he lacked in. Earlier he had fought and won many a battle and then he did not need have a chariot having the speed of the wind nor a bow like the Gandiva and when they became necessary he prayed for them to a beggar Brahmin. But the fact is otherwise. The begger Brahmin, Agni is the symbol of Divine Grace of Guru and he can give you anything and everything when you need. Earlier Arjuna had fought many battle indeed but the character of those battle was not similar to that of the battle to be fought against Indra, the lord of heaven. Indra is the liege lord of the senses and sense-organs as well as the conductor of the body. Indra is the mind of man. It appears to be a neurosis to fight against the mind with the help of mind that conducts the body. Therefore, Arjuna's task was a serious one and hence Arjuna prayed for the requisite bow and chariot.

Arjuna knew it well that without the grace of Guru, the Lord of the mind, it was impossible for him to win the battle against the mind and he sought to have the grace of Guru in form of Gandiva. The Gandiva is the spinal cord of the human body which can not only sustain the pressure of hands but also any other pressure even. The arteries — Ida, Pingala and Susumna constitute the bow-string. In the field of austerity as much as ignorance is undone so much knowledge is dawned upon the austerer and he becomes blessed also as much. And with the dawning of knowledge on him the austerer becomes wise in course of exerting energy of a particular nerve-centre of the spinal cord and thus he progresses in course of his endeavour. At the same time the mental faculties also undergo change and his ignorance gradually become non-existent. All this happens in course of the journey through the six never-centres of the spinal cord. Hence it is the symbol of Gandiva. The other name of burning of the Khandava Forest is to besieze the faculties of the Chitta.

Apart from all this, Arjuna needed a chariot having the quality to move as speedily as wind, yoked to the divine grey horses; of the number of horses no mention had been made here though, they were four in number. This chariot is the human body. The Primordial Energy covers the human heart from end to end as Faith (Vishvas). The beings are not generally aware of it, yet it exists there in the heart. What the beings take for faith is not the actual faith but a kind of trust lulled by self-assertion and selfish gain which is so fragile that it may be non-existent at the drop of a hat. On the other hand, the Faith in the heart holds the whole of the creation. On the basis of this faith there arises Shraddha (respectful adoration to the Supreme); unbounded gratitude, immense astonishment are the ingredients of this Shraddha. With dawning of Shraddha upon the field of faith, knowledge and Bhakti gradually dawns on the heart. These four elements viz. Vishvasa, Shraddha, Jnana and Bhakti are the four horses that draw the chariot. Then the person realizes that what he thinks to be his own are actually given to him, he is supposed to maintain them cautiously and use them in a disciplined way as and when necessary. This understanding makes him bank on the Supreme. When these four horses draw the chariot of the body the existence of the being embarks upon it and Guru becomes the charioteer. Then the person wins any battle whatsoever. But the chariot Agni gave to Arjuna had the ensign of a monkey. The monkey of the Ramayana is the embodiment of devotion. He is the greatest devotee to his Lord. This ensign denotes, the weight of Bhakti makes the chariot steady and he is the son of Air, the chariot would move as speedily as air. Apart from these, Agni gave him two quivers that stand for (1) singularity of vision and (2) firm attention. He gave Krishna a pleasant discuss and a mace named Kaumadaki. Krishna is Guru indeed, but here in the tale he is a relative of Arjuna and his friend. Therefore, he is to be treated as such moreover he has come here as a member of the sporting party and not to fight any battle and hence he has no arms with him, Observing this Agni gave him the arms. The rotating universe is his discus. He is the embodiment of the energy of attraction, cultivation and detraction which is responsible for the creation springing forth from its source, cultivating it means evolution and its final culmination towards its establishment in Supreme Reality relying on the same process of evolution passing through the phases of subconscious, sentient and fully conscious and it is evident in different states of creation. This discus sees only the good. If anyone does transgress or defy this, the mace would not spare that one as it is meant for maintaining a delightful connexion with the creation. Now, Agni (Fire god) collected the things from the custody of the lord of the water (Varuna) but they were the property of Somaraja. On the material plane the relation between fire and water is not a positive one — coming in contact with water fire becomes doused whereas water becomes vapour coming in contact with fire. They cannot appropriate each other. Hence they are friends and not enemies. Now, let us come to Somaraja, the owner of the chariot, quivers etc. But who is Somaraja? Somaraja and Somarasa both are the same; the origin is the Soma. It is generally held that 'soma' is a kind of divine drink taken by the gods. 'Soma' is the semen which moves upward changing its downward course under the heat of austerity, becomes purified crossing the never-centre between the brows, becomes fragrant with a sweet smell and in course of its still higher movement its drops fall upon the epiglottis and the austere person drinks the same and it is the nectar. This is the savour of soma or somarasa, the divine drink of the gods. Thereafter it turns into prowess, the transformed form of semen vis-à-vis soma.

We have already discussed of the quivers that Agni gave to Arjuna; one of them stands for singularity of vision and the other for the firm attention which are necessary for the accurate use of the arms given by Guru. Guru's advices and directives are the most effective arms in the spiritual realm.

Having got the Gandiva and the chariot, the propitiated Krishna and Arjuna asked Agni, "O Agni! Now you may freely burn the Khandava forest being ablaze all around it and we will be at your service." Agni assumed the 'taijasa' (subtle) form and began to burn the forest being ablaze in seven flames. But why did Agni assume the subtle form and was in seven flames? There are seven strata of knowledge that the beings are required to surpass to establish them in the eighth which enable them to be free of the cycle of birth and death being liberated.

With a view to point to passing over that seven stages of knowledge Agni manifested itself into seven flames. But prior to it the fire god assumed the subtle form (taijasa) as till then the creation was far away. The physical fire cannot burn anything subtle but the physical only. On the other hand, the beings are not supposed to observe the physical fire upon their own body as in that case the physical body will perish. So far the question of burning of the Khandava forest is concerned, the form of fire is subtle and the event is also of the subtle state.

While the forest was burning Takshaka was not at home in the forest although his wife and son were there. Thus Takshaka was saved being absent; but his wife died. His son, Ashvasena while fleeing from the fire, Arjuna became unconscious for a little while as Indra played a cunning trick and the creature saved himself. Apart from him four young chicks of a wagtail still unfledged, were saved. Now let us have their identity in the human body. The mind attached to the sense-objects is Indra and the happiness that follows the enjoyment of sense-objects is the rainfall. The beings running after the enjoyment of sense-objects, do not like to have the Brahmic heat.

The author had the necessity to save Takshaka and his son along with four chicks of a wagtail who were unfledged yet — hence he needed a pretext. Takshaka, his son and the four chicks are but the symbols of universal as well as natural facts. Who is Takshaka in our body? It is a member of the lizard family almost of the size of a chameleon, calls with a sharp tonal sound as tak-khak, tak-khak spreading a piercing sensation. While the human heart pumps blood contracting and expanding itself, emits a sound which may be audible through the medium of an apparatus as loff-doff, loff-doff and the sound is of tender nature. But the rhythm of both the sounds is similar and that is why takshaka is the symbol of human heart. In the tale takshaka, a creature of timid nature having rough deep grey skin on its flattened back is not pleasing to look at, has been introduced as a poisonous snake elsewhere in the tale, but it is not a snake; the use is only metaphorical we would discuss about that in its perspective later on. Generally the creature is a nocturnal one and shy of rain and sunlight.

Both takshaka and his son needed to be saved. So he was not at home. His son fled away from the fire and in course of his fleeing he was noticed by Krishna and Arjuna who cursed him to be destitute of shelter. Ashvasena, the son is the flow of blood through the veins and arteries of the body and he has no shelter to stop and rest. If he halts to rest ever, the thriving life will rest for good. The blood flows through the veins and arteries being pressed by the muscles in them and in a wave-like rhythm similar to the trot of a horse. Hence his name is Ashvasena (cavalry soldier). As the flow of blood in the body is continuous, he flees from the fire. Sometimes, of course, owing to this Brahmic heat the pressure of the flowing blood increases but that is not harmful nor does it cause any disease.

Now, the four young chicks of the wagtail who are very young and cannot fly as they are not yet fledged nor can they move from where they are. They are well conversant in the Vedas means they can perform their ordained duties well. The heat of the fire did not harm them at all nor create any impediment in performing their duty. They four are the lungs, the liver, the gall bladder and the kidney — the four organs of the human body. They remain static in their positions as the bird's chicks do in the nest. The fire does not harm them as they are faithful in performing their duties. Their father rishi Mandapala, with a view to have many offsprings at a time, assuming a bird's form married a wagtail named Jarita and procreated them in her womb and when Jarita was carrying he left her for another destination. It is an allegory. In the realm of spirituality the bird is a symbol of the existence of beings and in terms of the body Jarita is the symbol of applied form of motherhood. It is to note that Mandapala returned to the spot after the fire was extinct and left it with another wagtail named Lopita leaving behind Jarita and her sons. There remained no connexion with them any more and it was their destiny.

There remain things in the body that are not useful for it; and it is the duty of Mandapala to see so that those unnecessary things cannot do any harm to the body. The term 'Mandapala' means he who sustains the evil and of course, in a different way. So, he is to oversee the excretion of the elements harmful to the body remaining behind the screen. It is his duty to keep the body safe and sound. His second wife Lopita is the symbol of unending flow of activity of natural law.

Now, after the death of the wife of Takshaka and fleeing away of his son, the demon Moy was in deep distress. There was none to discuss with regarding his own safety. So long he was a dependent of Takshaka and used to stay with his family. Now anyhow he was to save himself from the rapidly advancing blaze and there was no other alternative but to flee away from it. But in his effort to do so, he fell in the sight of Krishna and Arjuna and Agni too. Agni appealed to Krishna to kill him and instantly the clever demon prayed to Arjuna to save him and Arjuna assured him of life. So Moy was saved somehow. Moy is a demon but who is he in the human body? The mind that infringes the established order or moral code of conduct with a view to enjoy sense-objects, is a demon in us. So, the demon Moy should have been directly related to Indra, the mind; but instead, he was directly related to Takshaka, the heart, being his dependent. The senses carry the message regarding sense-objects to the mind and the mind resolves to enjoy them, if so desires. Again, the fruits of actions remain stored in the chitta as seeds and at times they being transformed into faculties express themselves to excite the ripus and bondages. This excitement inspires the senses to convey similar sense-objects to the mind. All these actions are performed by the nervous system of the body. The nerves remain active by the flow of blood through the veins and the flow of flood is caused by air. On the other hand, the consciousness of the physical body is caused by Atman encased in the body. Again, when the possibility of enjoyment of any long-cherished sense-object or any long awaited gain that remained almost an impossibility becomes a certainty, the blood in the heart seems to spill out of it, being jerked suddenly. This is an action of the mind expressed through this organ. Then the mind is completely under the influence of Moy the demon. Moy is that state of mind when it eagerly craves for any particular sense object being daubed with it that remained a deep secret within it. The beings get it as a sequence of succession that flows with the blood always. The demon Moy inspires the beings mostly in enjoyment of subtle sense objects rather than physical enjoyment and for this subtle enjoyment Moy excites the beings to enjoy them. There remains a strong possibility of enjoying subtle sense objects among the poets, musicians, dancers, dansuses, actors and other artists of fine arts in creating their respective forms of art and in that respect their thought and imagination are the gift of the demon Moy who as such remains hidden in the depth of consciousness; he cannot easily be identified with the physical vision. Because of this secrecy he became a dependent of Takshaka and during the burning of Khandava forest he had to leave the shelter under compulsion. Then he saved himself praying to Arjuna (Tejas) for the same. In comparison to that of Takshaka the refuge of Arjuna was more desireable as he could have given him a greater secrecy and his activities might go on smoothly.

When the forest was ablaze Indra left no stone unturned to extinguish it being assisted by the gods in his efforts, but to no avail as the miserable defeat was his destiny. Indra knew it well that if the beings are blessed with the Brahmic heat by Guru, the unrestricted enjoyment of sense objects on the part of the mind would be impossible. So Indra was deperate to douse the fire but his failure was preordained. Therefore, after the burning was complete, Indra wearing an air of superiority appeared before Krishna and Arjuna to bless them with boons eloquently praising their heroic efforts, having the intention of face-saving. Arjuna prayed to give him all his arms to which Indra said. "When you will propitiate Lord Mahadeva (Shiva) by your austerity. I'll give my arms to you." Krishna prayed for the boon so that there should never be separation between Arjuna and Him. Indra agreed to it. Arjuna's boon was not granted instantly as Indra was aware of the use of his arms by Arjuna; of course, he promised to give them to Arjuna after he would please Lord Shiva. In the world of beings Shiva is Guru and if he be pleased the arms would serve the purpose effectively; otherwise not. The mind is the perversion of the Supreme Consciousness and in the pure part of the mind Consciousness prevails upon it. On the other hand, without the active participation of the mind, success in the spiritual realm is a far cry and the elements for this success are the arms of the mind. When the Supreme Purusha incarnates himself in human form, the mind cannot identify him and it has no such vision. Hence Indra blesses him with a boon taking him for the brother-in-law of Arjuna.

After burning the Khandava forest Agni came to Krishna and Arjuna and expressing his satisfaction told them. "Now I permit you to go wherever you like." Listening to Agni both of them went to the bank of the Yamuna and sat there.

The Khandava forest was reduced to ashes by Agni in fifteen days that make a fortnight. The significance of this conflagration has been discussed. The action of burning the faculties of the Chitta occurs only when Guru blissfully desires that but the austere person cannot know of it then; he may know of it after realization dawns on him. The purport of the period of fifteen days is to denote the end of a fortnight and the beginning of the next one. There are two fortnights in the life of beings—one is the dark fortnight of ignorance for enjoyment of sense-objects and the other is the bright one illumined with knowledge full of bliss. The beings in their dark fortnight begin their journey to achieve the bright fortnight burning the faculties of the Chitta by the energy of Guru for his ascension to the blissful bright fortnight. After Agni departed, Krishna and Arjuna sat down on the bank of the Yamuna. The flowing stream of the Yamuna is the flow of life that being attracted by the bliss moves towards the Ocean of Bliss. The birth and death point to the mere change of body, they both keep the stream to flow. The observation of this flow of life from the bank impartially makes one unveil the mystery of life and death as well as makes him immortal by conquering death. Krishna and Arjuna — the Creator and the creation become one in Bliss — and their presence on the river bank points to that truth.

The Royal Court Of Yudisthira And The Rajasuya Sacrifice

Being saved from the raging fire at Khandavaprastha Moy addressed his saviour, Arjuna, "O the son of Kunti! You saved me from enraged Krishna and the blazing fire; please order me to do a good turn in return." Arjuna said, he had done everything in return and nothing new was necessary and he would remain ever pleased to him. Now he might go anywhere he liked. But Moy was not to be desisted. He said, "...I am the Vishvakarma (the architect of the heaven) among the demons. Only being charmed with your good qualities I am to do something good to you in return." He insisted on to do something for Arjuna. Then Arjuna asked him, "Do something for Krishna in return and then I would be pleased."

Now Moy sought orders from Krishna. He thinking for a short while asked him, ".....Do construct a royal court building for Maharaja Yudhisthira so that being seated there and observing keenly, nobody could imitate it; there the divine, human and demonic motifs be exposed."

Moy was happy.

Immediately after Krishna returned to Dvaraka, Moy informed Arjuna that he would set out for the place where the demons wanted to perform their sacrifice near the Mt. Mainaka to the north of the Mt. Kailasha. There the materials stored in the court of the demon king Vrishaparva, if not destroyed meanwhile, would be brought by him for the purpose of construction. There, in the depth of Vindu Sarovara (water body), was a special mace kept by Vrishaparva, would be a fitting arms for Bhima and he would give that to him. Again, there was a great conch-shell of melodious sound once owned by Varuna; collecting that he would give to Arjuna, — saying all this, he departed to reach the northern part of the Mt. Kailasha. There beside a mountain near the Vindu Sarovara he found out the materials, the great mace and the Devadatta conch-shell and collecting them all, he returned to Indraprastha.

On his return from the Mt. Kailasha giving the mace to Bhima and the conch shell to Arjuna, he engaged himself in the construction of the promised hall of court. The hall, decorated with the motifs of golden trees, was a square one having the length of each arm of it being two thousand and five hundred yards. Like that of the fire god, the Sun God and the Moon god, the court of the Pandavas was delightful indeed.

After completion of the construction in fourteen months Moy conveyed the message of completion to Yudhisthira.

On an appointed day welcoming the Brahmins, munis, rishis and the royal guests, the five brothers entered the court constructed by Moy and began the celebrations. Amidst the celebrations the divine rishi Narada appeared there. While the rishi was advising him on the principles of politics, Yudhisthira asked him whether he had seen such a pleasant court earlier. In reply Narada said he had never seen such alike before. But he described those of Yama, Varuna, Indra and Kuvera and finishing his description he told Yudhisthira,

"Your father on seeing me coming to the world of mortals, said to me after salutation, "O the great Lord, on your arrival at the world of men please tell Yudhisthira that his brothers are in control of him and he is able to conquer the world; the best of the kings now should arrange for the Rajasuya Sacrifice. If he does so, I may pass a long time in happiness in heaven with Lord Indra." After discussing on many a subject he departed.

Now Yudhisthira's only thought was the Rajasuya sacrifice.

His ministers and brothers also were engrossed in that single thought and when Yudisthira opened his mind to them they all gladly said to the king, "We all are your will wishers and we are of the opinion that the time is ripe to perform the Rajasuya Sacrifice and the strength of the Kshatriyas is the key to its performance." Even though such opinions made his resolution stronger, he was not up to perform the act only on the advice of the ministers and courtiers. He decided to have the opinion of Krishna and sent a messenger to Him.

Krishna came to Indraprastha having the call from Yudhisthira and heard of his resolution. He then began to speak gently of the impediments that were in the way of Yudhisthira's performing of the sacrifice. He said of two hurdles — one, Jarasandha, the king of the Bhojas and the other was Shishupala, the king of Chedi, who would by no means accept the supremacy of Yudhisthira. "If you resolve to perform the sacrifice then you are firstly to set free the kings imprisoned by Jarasandha and then try to kill the felon, otherwise you would not be able to perform this sacrifice safely. O the scion of the Kurus! This is my opinion.".

Then Krishna narrated to Yudhisthira the irreligious and unethical behaviour of Jarasandha with evidence and said later he deserved to be killed by approaching him secretly and thereafter the imprisoned kings be set free. Yudhisthira wanted to know about him in details and in reply Krishna spoke about his birth, naming, ascendance to the throne and his rule over the kingdom.

Now to kill Jarasandha was of prime importance to Krishna and speaking on the subject he opined, "Time is come to slay him. Even the gods and demons unitedly cannot defeat him; so he is to be killed by vying....if you believe me then give Bhima and Arjuna to me." Yudhisthira said, "Do not speak in this way. You are our Lord and guide. Now please take steps to accomplish all this quickly."

Krishna started for Magadha along with Bhima and Arjuna with a view to fulfil his mission. They three in disguise being mixed with ordinary people entered the palace. But Jarasandha became doubtful of their identity. They revealed their design in reply to his queries. Instantly wrestling between Bhima and Jarasandha took place and finally Jarasandha fell dead. The imprisoned kings were set free and Jarasandha's son Sahadeva was installed to the throne. Krishna returned to Indraprastha with Bhima and Arjuna.

"Now it is my duty to augment the treasury collecting taxes from other kings," — thinking so, Arjuna set out to the north to conquer the world obtaining permission from Yudhisthira, while Bhima went to the east on the same purpose being permitted by Yudhisthira. Sahadeva and Nakula also went to the south and the east respectively with the same intent. The four brothers collected enough riches conquering many kingdoms. Having a thorough idea of the treasury deposits

Yudhisthira decided to perform the sacrifice and at that time Krishna reached Indraprastha. Seeing Him the pleased Yudhisthira asked for His permission and on getting it he commenced the sacrifice.

Meanwhile, the invited Kauravas arrived Indraprastha. Yudhisthira assigned each of them a particular charge. Bhishma and Drona were given the charge of deciding the duties or otherwise. Duryodhana was given the responsibility of accepting and safe custody of the gifts and presents made by the invited dignitaries. Krishna Himself took the charge of washing the feet of Brahmins.

Once Yudhisthira sought the advice of Bhishma as to who was to be paid the homage of offering in reply to which Bhishma said, Krishna was the right person. He was to be paid the homage. Accordingly, Sahadeva paid the homage to him. Shishupala at once rose to protest being impatient and began to remonstrate Bhishma, Yudhisthira and Krishna. At a time Bhima got angry with Shishupala because of his upbraiding Krishna and readily Bhishma consoled him to allay his anger. But Sishupala was relentless in animadverting on Krishna, Bhishma and the Pandavas as well. Then Sishupala addressed Krishna, "O Krishna, if you like to forgive me respectfully, do it; if not don't do. On the whole, if you get angry, I am to lose nothing; and if you are pleased, I am to gain nothing." Listening to the slight-speech of Sishupala Krishna addressing the present kings said, "O Kings! Listen to Me, the mother of this depraved Shishupala, once in the past prayed to Me to forgive his one hundred offences and I granted it then. Now he has crossed the barrier of one hundred offences. Today I'll kill him before your eyes." Saying this Krishna beheaded him with His discus. Then Yudhisthira installed his son as the king of Chedi and his sacrifice also was performed unhindered.

Moy came to Indraprastha with his saviour Arjuna and of course Krishna was with them. The daubing with sense-objects in the company of Guru and associated with tejas became dauntless and free of any anxiety. Resultantly his sense of gratitude made him doing something in return to Arjuna who was not at all willing to have anything in return as till then Arjuna was unaware of the importance of him. So he asked Moy to do something for Krishna in return and that would please Arjuna too. Then he sought for the orders from Krishna. Then Krishna asked him to construct the court room for Yudhisthira in which the divine, human and demonic motifs be prominently expressive and also even observing them attentively nobody could be able to imitate them. The task was challenging and was accepted by Moy gladly.

As a king Yudhisthira was a new one, he had to establish a capital anew and the construction of a royal court was not illogical. But he is the reality of ether. Sheltering the immeasurable creation into his heart he remains the void as usual. The endless effort to fill it fails, it remains the void as it was. The boundless universe, unending intents (bhavas), the endless thoughts and the faculties are there sheltered in the immeasurable void, yet it is not replete. With a view to express this truth, Krishna asked Moy so that his work of art be inimitable but the divine, human and demonic motifs should be clearly discernible visually; meaning thereby the results of actions of three gunas viz. Sattva, Rajas and tamas should be accurate as the prevalence of a particular guna determines the character of the intents or thoughts. The relation between the gunas and the intents or thoughts is a creation of Moy which is not generally revealed to the beings. Prior to the conflagration of the Khandava forest Moy was secretly active being hidden in the active vital energy without being exposed. But he became bewildered owing to the absence of Takshaka and his wife's death of fire. In absence of a dependable shelter Moy becomes inactive even his existence may be in distress. Hence the demon utilized the chance of praying to save him. Saved by Arjuna and indulged by Krishna he became stronger and more fearless, no doubt.

Moy was entrusted to construct the royal court for which materials were necessary. But he did not ask for the supply of them, rather he shouldered the task of collecting them himself and they were the abandoned property of the demons and left in the kingdom of demons beyond the Himalayas. He decided to bring them to Indraprastha going beyond the Mt. Kailasha and near the Mt. Mainaka where the court of King Vrishaparva exists. Now, the question, is, where is the Mt. Kailasha in the human body? The Mt. Kailasha the abode of Lord Shiva (the third of the Hindu Trinity), is the sixth nerve-centre of the spinal cord which exists between the brows. This nerve-centre is the seat of Guru and Lord Shiva epitomizes Guru. Moy had to go to the north of Mt. Kailasha to reach the kingdom of Vrishaparva, where in his court the materials were stored and also to the Vindu Sarovara in the middle of the kingdom. Now, the question arises how the demon Moy crossed the Mt. Kailasha i.e. the sixth nerve-centre of the spinal cord the Ajna (pronounced as Agga) chakra — a feat not even the mind can perform rather it dissolves there? How then could the demon go there? Not only Moy alone, there is also the kingdom of Vrishaparva, the king of demons and his royal court. How could all this happen?

The demon Moy crossed the sixth nerve-centre which the mind cannot do, as Moy is not a reality which the mind is. The demon Moy is an energy manifested by the Divine Energy. Despite being a demon he cannot perform anything independently and all his actions are behind the screen. Earlier he was dependent on Takshaka and being sheltered by him Moy used to perform perfectly. A demon can be identified by his activities the scope of which is generally very limited in nature. On the other hand, although Moy is a demon, his demonic activities are of a different nature as always his identity remains in the background and his performance is constructive. Now Moy is sheltered by Arjuna and indulged by Krishna. So his scope of action and movement is far and wide. Added to this, he received the order from Krishna, the Supreme Being. Therefore, it was not impossible for him to cross the sixth never-centre of the spinal cord.

Yudhisthira is the reality of void; he is always distressed to be full but is never replete. The creation — both subtle and physical are held in the void and also innumerable esses. Both Chitta (inner mind) and Hridaya (heart) contain and manifest the faculties (vrittee) and esses (bhava) respectively. The Heart and the Chitta both are void but esses spring out of the Heart. The Heart full of esses is the court of Yudhisthira, which Krishna asked Moy to build meaning thereby to expose the splendours of the Heart being daubed with its esses. But to whom should Moy demonstrate the opulence of it? He would do it to the elements (Bhutas), the ripus (cardinal passions), the pashas (mental bondages), the senses and other realities so that they could clearly understand the greatness and importance of the reality of the void. The action to clearly reveal the esses and intents, is the construction of the court by Moy. The search for and identity of each of the esses of the heart as to be revealed in the motifs denote the collection of materials by him. Apart from all this, he promised to do two other deeds. He would procure the mace kept by Vrishaparva in the Vindu Sarovara as well as the sweet sounding conch-shell once owned by Varuna. He would give the mace to Bhima and the conch-shell to Arjuna.

But where is the Vindu Sarovara in the human body? From the sixth nerve-centre the space upto five inches upwards under the skull is the Vindu Sarovara. It is said to be a waterbody as the place is filled with mercury-like almost liquid substance which is called vindu (semen), the quintessence of the body. This region is the field of Guru controlled and guided by him in all respects. Below this Vindu Sarovara the spinal cord is there and the hollow within it between the two ends is full of this liquid. Between the Muladhara and Ajna nerve-centre there are four other such nerve-centres. Among them at the root of the navel the nerve-centre is known to be the Manipura while between the breasts there is the Anahata (unhurt) nerve-centre. This Anahata nerve-centre is the home for the reality of Air (unhurt) and is responsible for vital energy of the body being its basis and home of Bhima (Air). The other name of Bhima is Vrikodara meaning to have fire in the stomach as 'Vrika' means fire and 'udara' means stomach. The terms 'Vrika' and 'udara' being compounded become vrikodara. The fire is born of air and also dissolves in it. The mace is an arms and if used by suitable hands it may be a deadly one. The suffering from the fruits of actions antagonistic to discipline or the directives of Guru, is the striking with the mace and this thrashing is of the mace accomplished by the vital energy.

Just below the anahata nerve-centre is the Manipura nerve-centre, the home for fire which is known as Vaisvanara fire. The Vaishvanara fire is responsible for digestion as well as division of the elixir of food and the waste as well. Apart from this, fire controls the energy of the body and that of the senses too. The mouths of Vaishvana are the mouths of the gods who take the taste of food and drink through his mouths. In specially deep meditation one may discern that a sweet sound produced by the other five nerve-centres coming through the mouth of Vaishvanara becomes audible and as the sound thus audible appears to be that of a blowing conch-shell, it is called a conch-shell. Again, as it comes from the mouths of gods, it is called the Devadatta (gift of gods). Moy said of this conch-shall. Now it is clear that the fire plays specially a very important role in both Anahata and Manipura nerve-centres; in the one it is called Vrika and in the other it is Vaishvanara. The Vrika fire is the mace of Bhima and Vaishvanara fire is the Devadatta conch shell of Arjuna.

Now, the Sankrit term 'Vrisha' means (1) irrigation, (2) conception, (3) opulence. But here it means 'semen'; and the term 'parva' means (1) a knot (2) a knuckle, (3) a joint etc. But it has yet another meaning — celebration. The Vindu Sarovara is a pool of semen and the king of that pool is Vrishaparva, the inspiratory energy of celebrations. The demon is the king of this pool.

It took fourteen months to complete the construction of the court of Yudhisthira. But why fourteen months? A wealthy man is aware of his own wealth but people around him may not know of that; and to make it known to others, the senses, the mind, the chitta and the ego are to act. Therefore, it is necessary to train the ten senses and four other realities so that they may be proficient in this respect to convey the message of the opulence of the heart adroitly to others and Moy took a month for each of the fourteen realities to train them. Hence fourteen months Moy took to complete the construction work. Now it is over. The celebrations started with the stepping into the court by Yudhisthira with his four brothers and ministers. During the celebrations came the divine rishi Narada who is the epitome of human conscience. He profusely praised the royal court of Yudhisthira and then advised him on politics. Then he told on his way to the world of mortals Pandu requested him to convey the message that if Yudhisthira perform Rajasuya Sacrifice, he would be happy. His four brothers and the ministers were firstly aware of the opulence of his heart. All were happy. Meanwhile amidst the celebrations Yudhisthira expressed the desire to perform Rajasuya Sacrifice. Of course, Narada had an important role in this respect. There was neither self conceit nor pride to desire so but it was the natural expression of his Dharma.

But what was the character of the Rajasuya Sacrifice for Yudhisthira? Earlier we have said that he is the reality of ether and holding the boundless universe within the void he is not replete and to be so, his yearning is always intense. This intense yearning to be replete is the inspiration for his Rajasuya Sacrifice. Of the five brothers he alone is entitled to perform this sacrifice. Many a person had encouraged him truly but till then the opinion of Krishna was unknown to him and therefore he sought for it. Being called for, Krishna came and said that there were two great impediments, — one was Shishupala, the king of Chedi and the second Jarasandha, the king of Bhoja. Now, the Rayasuya Sacrifice means the performer should enjoy unqualified and universal recognition of greatness as well as loyalty of all the ruling kings of the country so that the performer be regarded as the lord of them all. But Jarasandha and Shishupala were not to accept Yudhisthira as the king of kings. Krishna then advised him to get rid of these two kings. He suggested firstly to kill Jarasandha and free the kings imprisoned by him. But who is Jarasandha? Though born with a vertically split body he became live and active when two halves of his body had been joined. Jarasandha is the faculty of envy associated with oppression and cruelty. He attacked Mathura seventeen times, but in vain.

It is said that Vrindavana is land of love and Mathura is that of Yoga. After the king of Mathura was killed, Jarasandha attacked Mathura seventeen times and every time he was defeated. The subtle body is constituted of seventeen realities — they are five senses, five sense-organs, five vital breaths, the mind and the intelligence. The yogi is expected to restrain them and make them active as and when necessary following the advices of Guru and Guru assists him in his efforts. On the other hand, the desire (Kama), on his part, tries to engulf the whole of the subtle body influencing the realities of it so that the efforts of the yogi turn to be futile. In such a state Guru diminishes the influence of desire (kama) by killing him (kamsa). Kamsa epitomizes the desire — the volatile desire.

Jarasandha had to suffer from the ignominy of deafeat seventeen times for attacking Mathura as many times yet he could not be restrained. He imprisoned one hundred kings to execute them by beheading. What could be more glaring an example of cruelty and oppression? Advices or aphorisms can not do away with envy and cruelty; it needs the actions of vital energy to undo them.

The living Jarasandha would be a considerable and powerful obstruction to Yudhisthira's Rajasuya Sacrifice; so he had to be removed first. On Yudhisthira's acceptance of his logic Krishna disclosed his plan to Yudhisthira who endorsed it and then on his approbation he set out for the palace of Jarasandha with Bhima and Arjuna. Avoiding the main gate there, they entered the palace through another gate and in disguise. They three come straight to Jarasandha who welcomed them as usual; but the new comers did not accept that. Being doubtful Jarasandha asked who they were and in reply to that Krishna disclosed their identity as also their mission. Krishna also said, "Now we are inviting you to fight; either release the imprisoned kings or go to hell by fighting." Jarasandha opted to fight with Bhima that began at onec.

As a result of this fight Jarasandha fell dead and with him ended the frenzy of envy. When envy ends, love, friendship and modesty prevail which happened on the death of Jarasandha. The imprisoned kings were set free and his son Sahadeva was installed to his father's throne by Krishna. Sahadeva was an epitome of modesty and forbearance. The kings who were made captive by Jarasandha, were all defeated by him and he made them prisoners with the intention of beheading them. The self-assertion of Jarasandha was inflated thus and incited his faculties of oppression.

Krishna returned to Indraprastha along with Bhima and Arjuna after killing Jarasandha. On their arrival Arjuna and other three brothers decided to augment the royal treasury as the Rajasuya Sacrifice was advancing and resolved to set out to conquer the world with the permission of Yudhisthira, to the four directions. This campaign of the four brothers was but a preamble to Yudhisthira's performance of the Rajasuya sacrifice. On the material plane this attempt denotes the collection of taxes and presents from the other kings that would be beneficial to defray the cost of the sacrifice. But spiritually it denotes the establishment of greatness of the supremacy of the element of ether and also to ensure the acceptability of other four elements to the traits and faculties of the mind. As the treasury had been augmented by the four Pandavas Yudhisthira fixed the date of the Rajasuya Sacrifice.

He who performs Rajasuya Sacrifice, is recognized as the greatest of the ruling kings enjoying unrivalled power and authority. Krishna desired it so that Yudhisthira gets this recognition. To this end in view he not only advised them but led them as a leader and stayed with them as a shadow; he knew that the Pandavas belong to the divine side. Being guided by the eldest they were to establish themselves in dharma and righteousness. As Guru he desired that Yudhisthira should hold all the creations in him facilitating their manifestation and evolution. Similarly, the whole of the creation should embrace his dharma to enrich their hearts by recognizing his esses. This was the reason for which he encouraged the performance of the Rajasuya Sacrifice and that was why he played so active a role in this regard.

Now there remained no hindrance to perform the Rayasuya Sacrifice. Krishna came to Indraprastha and obtaining permission from him Yudhisthira was initiated to the sacrifice. Prior to it, the invited Kauravas Viz. Bhisma, Drona. Duryodhana and others arrived and they were given the charge of duty according to their dignity. Krishna engaged himself in the duty of washing the feet of the Brahmins. He who is the lord, should have to be devoid of self-conceit and His actions deserve to be exemplary; He becomes honoured honouring others. Hence he took the task of washing the feet of guest Brahmins. No less is Yudhisthira. He could rightly surmise that the grandsire Bhishma was no longer the undisputed lord of the royal house of Hastinapura; his authority and importance had to a great extent diminished. As Bhishma knew it well, Yudhisthira was aware of it. Hence the reflection of Supreme Consciousness was given the charge of deciding what was to be done and what should not. The military teacher who was the epitome of customary intelligence had an important role to play in deciding what was due to be done — was made an associate of Bhishma. Duryodhana was desire and his vision was directed always towards sense-objects hence he was given the charge of accepting and preserving the presents given by the invited guests. Yudhisthira proved his far-sightedness in distributing the duties and responsibilities among the Kaurava royals according to their nature.

At a time Yudhisthira asked Bhishma as to whom the homage of honour be offered. Bhishma opined that Krishna was the right person to be offered the homage, so let it be given to him. Therefore, as ordered by Bhishma Sahadeva offered the homage to Krishna, which Shishupala could not tolerate. He vehemently reacted to this and began to upbraid Bhishma, Yudhisthira and Krishna openly in the assembly of honoured gests.

Shishupala is the symbol of arrogance. Those who are arrogant emulate in challenge. He should not have forgotten of the deformity of his body since his birth and the oracle on it. He should ever remain grateful to him who removed his deformity but instead he became a challenger to him. Shishupala was not generous enough to accept the truth that Krishna was greater than him. Moreover, he failed to honour the promise of Krishna to condone his one hundred offences, to his mother and his greatness in this respect. There was Shishupala's inferiority complex at the root of all this. His upbraiding, challenge and inferiority complex were the impediments to his improvement in life. Hence his vanity was done away with by Krishna beheading him. This action of Krishna means to detach vanity from its source to impart a lesson to mankind to honour the honourable realizing one's worth for the welfare of human race.

Yudhisthira arranged for Shishupala's funeral installing his son to the throne of Chedi. The son of vanity killed with Sudarshana wheel, is the humble submission.

After the Rajasuya Sacrifice was over, the invited kings and other guests left Indraprastha. Krishna returned to Dvaraka. Still then two guests were there in Indraprastha — one was Duryodhana and the other was Shakuni. Even enjoying the fruits of the Rajasuya Sacrifice, the eldest Pandava could not be free from the clutches of Desire (Kama) and Delusion (Moha). A violent storm was brewing in the horizon for the Pandavas the indication of which remained beyond their ken for the time being.

The Game Of Dice In The Kaurava Court

After the Rajasuya Sacrifice was over and most of the guests left Indraprastha. Vyasa came to Yudhisthira to ask for leave to depart; then he asked Vyasa whether the three calamities viz. divine, supernatural and material as disclosed by Narada, had been done away with the death of Shishupala, Vyasa said in reply, they had not been ended at all, rather, they would persist for thirteen years to come. Hearing this Yudhisthira became melancholic and distressed and he promised to himself to do only endearing deeds for the next thirteen years.

On the other hand, even after the departure of other guests as the Sacrifice was over, two of them remained in Indraprastha; they were Duryodhana and Sakuni. Duryodhana became envious of the incomparable riches of the Pandavas and his sole thought was how to appropriate them and finding no means at hand he became morose. Observing the mind of Duryodhana Shakuni asked for the reason to be so. Duryodhana opened his mind to him; and wealth of the Pandavas had made him restless and eager. Shakuni then opined that they were enjoying their own riches and that should not be unforebearing. But Duryodhana was not to accept any logic; his envy was growing owing to the power and opulence of the Pandavas. When Shakuni said that he had also the power and wealth as the Pandavas had, paying no heed to him, Duryodhana proposed to secure the possession of the Pandavas' wealth defeating them in fight. In reply Shakuni said, "Even the gods are unable to defeat them in fight, but Yudhisthira is fond of the game of dice although he is a novice in the art of the game....hence invite him to the game of dice, I will take with dexterity the wealth of the Pandavas. But you are to make it known to your father and having his permission we shall defeat them, no doubt." Being excited by his maternal uncle's counsel, Duryodhana asked Shakumi to have the permission of Dhritarastra.

Then they both appeared before the king. There Shakuni apprised Dhritarastra of the perversion in body and mind of Duryodhana but Dhritarastra could not make out the reasons for them. Then Duryodhana elaborated as to how he was keen on observing the abundance of wealth of the Pandavas which could only be compared to that of Indra (lord of heaven), Yama (king of death), Varuna (lord of water) and Kuvera (lord of Yakshas). "And seeing such enormous wealth I have lost my peace of mind." He said again, "O king! The expert dice-player, the King of Gandhara is encouraged to carry off all this wealth; please permit." Dhritarastra said, "The wise Vidura is our minister and I am to follow his counsel. Let me consult with him and then I'all conclude." Pat came the reaction of Duryodhana. "If Vidura comes, he will desist you and if you do so, surely I'll die." Listening to him the blind king permitted and ordered to arrange for the game. Later on, Vidura came and Dhritarastra asked him to bring Yudhisthira inviting him for the game of dice despite Vidura's disapproval. On the other hand, Duryodhana continued his untiring efforts to excite the king to bring him to bear Duryodhana's desires; he began to narrate as to which kings had presented which gifts, such as precious gems and other gifts, horses, mules, deer-skin and costly clothes in details and lastly expressed his design to appropriate them all to which, inspite of, expressing his feeble opposition to this Dhritarastra agreed to consent to the game of dice.

Meanwhile, Vidura went to Indraprastha to bring Yudhisthira to Hastinapura. There Vidura proclaimed the order of Dhritarastra to take part in the game of dice with Duryodhana. Yudhisthira was not so willing yet he had to respond to the call of Vidura; moreover, he could not deny any call for the game of dice. So, he agreed and the Pandavas along with Draupadi came to Hastina. Then began the game, of course, prior to it Duryodhana announced that Shakuni would participate on his behalf and the stake would be all the riches. One by one all riches, all the maids and servants, the four brothers even Yudhisthira himself were staked and lost them all being defeated to Shakuni. After all this, Draupadi was staked then and this time also Yudhisthira was defeated. Knowing that Draupadi had been won Duryodhana being jubilant ordered Vidura, "Go and bring Draupadi here. Krishna having no pity at all should now scour and scrub our palace with other maids." Listening to this Vidura began to remonstrate Duryodhana who then sent a messenger to bring her. Then Draupadi told him, "Go and ask the courtiers to let me know truly what my duty is. What those wise and revered persons would ask me to do, I'll do that." But the courtiers remained silent without making a reply to Draupadi because of excessive eagerness of Duryodhana. Then Yudhistira asked the messenger to tell her that crying Panchali should appear before her uncles-in-law in her loin cloth as she was in the state of menstrual period. The messenger was hesitating to go; — seeing this

Duryodhana ordered Duhshasana to go to her to bring her to the open court.

Duhasasana went to Draupadi and said, "O Panchali! You are defeated in the game of dice and look at Duryodhana shaking off year bashfulness" etc. Hearing all this being frightened she begged of help from the ladies of Dhritarastra; forthwith enraged Duhshasana dragged her to the court pulling her hair and her distressed entreaties and protests could not influence him at all. When she said, "O Duhshasana, I am undergoing the menstrual period wearing a single cloth; it is not proper to drag me to the court." Duhshasana replied in indignation, "O Yajnaseni! It is no matter whether you are in menstrual period or wearing a single cloth or nude. Now you have been won in the game and have become a maid to live with other maids. Listening to such harsh and acrimonious language Draupadi began to weep calling the names of Krishna and Arjuna. Overcome with insult and oppression bewildered Draupadi began to rebuke Duhshasana. "O the depraved soul. I am under menstrual period and you are dragging me before the great nobles of the Kurus and nobody is remonstrating you for this vile deed; it seems, they also approve of it. Fie to the dharma of the Bharatas. The disposition of their Kshatriya wisdom has totally been destroyed as the Kurus in the court are observing the flagrant infringement of their dharma unabashedly. Now I understand Drona, Bhishma and high-souled Vidura have no remnant of virtuosity in them as they are ignoring the acts of adharma by Duryodhana without any strain."

On the other hand, Duhshashana began to laugh holding her hair and addressing her as a maid-servant. Karna and Shakuni praised him much. Meanwhile Bhishma expressed his inability to make an answer to Draupadi's question. The persecution and disgrace of Draupadi were going on unabatedly. Observing all this, Bhima lost his patience and attacked Yudhisthira saying, "Today I will burn your hands to ashes." Immediately Arjuna tried to pacify his anger consoling him.

Meanwhile Vikarna entered the court and addressed the present kings "....Consider justly what Yajnaseni has alleged and judiciously tell us your valued opinion otherwise we all have to go to hell. Let the grandsire, Dhritarastra and high souled Vidura speak something on that. I cannot share the view that Draupadi has been won." In reply to what Vikarna had said, Karna putting up many a reason said, "....As Draupadi....has been obedient to many husbands, there is no doubt that she is a prostitute; hence to bring a public woman to the court or to make her denuded of clothing is not an act of astonishment. Shakuni has truly won what Draupadi and Pandavas have; so. O! Duhshasana, Vikarna is a mere boy, You please take all that the Pandavas and Draupadi have." Hearing Karna the Pandavas gave up their scarves. And Duhshasana being highly encouraged tried to denude her. Then she prayed to Krishna who remaining invisible provided her with different kinds of clothes unendingly and tired Duhshasana failed utterly in his bid.

When the kings present in the court were loud in disapproving the acts of Duhshasana, Bhima getting very much furious promised, "O the Kshatriyas of the world, listen to me, if I do not drink blood rending the chest of this sinful evil Bharata, Duhshasana then I should not go to the ways of the manes."

Meanwhile, narrating a tale from the scriptures, Vidura requested the courtiers to make a reply to Draupadi's question. Draupadi also entreated them to reply to her question saying, "thereafter whatever you will ask me to do, I'll do that." Bhishma said that he was unable to reply to her question and suggested to have it from Yudhisthira. Duhshasana asked to have the answer from Bhima, Arjuna, Nakula and Sahadeva. Then Karna said to Draupadi that no longer the five Pandavas were her husbands. So she should better accept someone who would not be defeated in the game of dice. Bhima became more furious to this. At this time, Duryadhana asked Yudhisthira to say as to whether she was won or not and at the same time taking the cloth off his thigh he made an indecent beckoning to Draupadi. This added fuel to fire — already furious Bhima took the oath to break his thigh.

Amidst the controversy as to whether Draupadi was won on not, Dhritarastra called her and said, "Pray for your desired boon from me; your are the best among my daughters-in-law." She then prayed for the freedom of her husbands and at this juncture Karna did not desist himself from persifladging her. At this Bhima grew angry again and wanted to kill the enemies on the spot and Yudhisthira refrained him saying, "Calm down," then he asked Dhritarasta what he should do now. In reply Dhritarasta ordered, "Go with all your wealth and rule the kingdom." Having got this news Duhshasana at once informed Duryodhana that the old king had spoilt the hard-earned riches and now "decide the course of action."

The greatness and importance of the element of ether had been duly acknowledged with honour and respect through the Rajasuya Sacrifice and the two most prime hurdles were over by the Grace of Guru. But the eldest Pandava was not absolutely free from melancholic anxiety. After the departure of the guests Vyasa asked for leave of Yudhisthira to depart, Yudhisthira wanted to know of him as to whether the divine, supernatural and material disturbances as told by Narada were over with the death of Shishupala or not. Now the question arises why even after successful completion of the Rajasuya sacrifice could a person like Yudhisthira who enjoyed perpetual calm of mind ask such a question? Secondly, till the completion of sacrifice Krishna was there in Indraprastha. He could have asked the question to him. He did not do so but asked Vyasa.

Till now the course of evolution was in progress in the domain of the subtle with the aim to create the physical body in absence of which the Divine Leela could not have the culmination. The aim of the Creator is to create the physical body. But it needs the perfect ambience having the necessity to attract the ordinary consciousness towards Supreme Consciousness, through the process of evolution, so that the ordinary consciousness finally becomes one with the Supreme Consciousness. This design of the Lord as amazing as it was extended in time and space. The fully grown human body is necessary to make the consciousness of the inner mind manifests through the progressive evolution of human kind having fixed its aim to the highest perfection. The thoroughly developed human body is the best container of ordinary consciousness (chetana) and the highest realization is possible in it. Even the Creator Himself assumes this body for his leela. But the life of embodied souls are not unimpeded. In the world of matter to lead a life having the physical body one has to endure snags such as pain and pleasure, success and failure etc. Our forefathers have called them to be the three kinds of afflictions — the spiritual, supernatural and material and enduring them in life one becomes purified. Narada warned Yudhisthira of these three afflictions earlier. But Yudhisthira had no comprehensive idea of these afflictions till then nor did he know how to get rid of them. We have said earlier that still the sequence of creation was in the subtle and the necessary preparation was being made for the creation of physical form while these three afflictions remained the constant companions of the beings.

As Yudhisthira was ignorant of the three afflictions to some extent, he enquired of Vyasa as to whether they were over with the death of Shishupala, in reply to which Vyasa informed that they were not concluded, rather they would persist for thirteen years to come hence. Yudhisthira became morose in apprehension of the future distress as Vyasa's word could never be false altogether.

On the other hand, Duryodhana and Shakuni did not show any signs of departure from Indraprastha even after all other guests had left; they had two motives in their mind. Firstly, to have a clear idea of the wealth of the Pandavas and secondly, to find out ways and means to appropriate all of it. It was not very difficult to have a thorough idea of their wealth but not very easy to appropriate it entirely. Secondly, any attempt to seize the Pandavas' wealth would never get the moral support from any quarter and both Duryodhana and Shakuni were well aware of it. Apart from this, such actions were not to be endorsed by the court of the Kauravas. Therefore, they both hanged around if any such faults and failings could be detected so that a hostility could be created through which their wealth could have been appropriated. Kama (desire) and Moha (delusion) are ripus (cardinal passions) and they are born of mind. They need to integrate their desire into that of the mind and then with the help of the mind the action be accomplished. So the mind requires to agree with them otherwise their attempt is sure to fail. When Duryodhana was perplexed as to how he could draw the mind (Dhritarastra) to his favour, reading his mind Shakuni advised him that all the wealth of Yudhisthira could be appropriated by defeating him in a deceitful game of dice having staked all the wealth of him. By hook or crook the blind king should be made agreed to this game of dice. Hence immediately both of them left Indraprastha in their effort to make Dhritarastra a party to the game. Duryodhana could not resist himself to say to the king that the enormous wealth of Yudhisthira was the only cause for his envy and until that riches were appropriated to him, he would not have his peace of mind; he also said that Shakuni, an expert in the game of dice, is encouraged to take it all by deceit. If the king agreed, the game of dice would start. But even the king also might have some delicacy; Dhritarastra said there was the necessity for Vidura's advice. It is to note that there are three characters here : (1) The blind mind in the form of Dhritarastra, (2) Kama (desire) in the form Duryodhana, (3) Delusion in the form of Shakuni. Each of them is expressing its intent commensurate with its nature. The mind demonstrates the will-power. It decides which of the sense-objects be taken and when, but it is blind. Owing to its blindness it cannot visualize sense-objects. Hence it depends upon the senses, cardinal passions and bondages to know of the sense-objects. But the resolution to enjoy sense-objects, is its own notwithstanding the importance of the roles of senses, cardinal passions and bondages. Firstly, Kama (Duryodhana) with a view to bring the mind (Dhritarastra) to his own side placed his proposal before the mind in a straight way so that it could be influenced. But the mind is by nature doubtful and restless, hence Dhritarastra could not agree with Duryodhana. The mind knows the desire well and vice versa; hence the alibi of Vidura's counsel. Vidura is the divine part of the energy of mind i.e. the conscience and Dhritarastra knows it well that by no means Vidura is to consent to any misdeed and both Dhritarastra and Duryodhana know it well. Duryodhana then puts forth his ultimatum, — if the blind king does not permit, he is to commit suicide. Now, the mind becomes doubtless and approves of his proposal; he agrees. Then Vidura, the conscience went to Indraprastha to invite Yudhisthira to participate in the game of dice. Yudhisthira though very easily could not accept the call yet to honour the royal invitation, he set out for Hastina with the brothers and Draupadi. Desire (Kama) and Delusion (Moha) influenced the mind, the divine part of the energy of mind, five elements as well as the self (Jivatma) although they all were not influenced to the same degree. The blindness of the mind makes him subjugated to Kama (desire) through and through. His weakness for the game of dice makes Yudhisthira influenced by desire (Kama). As the eldest is influenced, his following brothers and Draupadi came under the periphery of that influence naturally also Vidura was not an exception as he was the minister of Dhritarastra.

On the arrival of the Pandavas arrangements were made for the game of dice which denotes one of the players being bound by the other should try to overcome the bondage; if he succeeds, he is the winner and retains his stake. If he does not, he loses the stake being the loser which is decided by the cast of dice. It is a gambling. Before the game started Duryodhana declared that Shakuni would play the game as his representative. The delusion is there at the root of every intense desire or in the eagerness of beings to have the sense-objects to enjoy them in an unbridled way. Had not the delusion obscured the vision of the beings, it would not have been possible for the beings to crave for and enjoy sense-objects in an irregulated manner. Therefore, in any kind of gambling the role of delusion is foremost. Secondly, delusion is a cardinal passion (ripu) having an intimate relationship with the pashas (bondages). The beings are to depend upon the grace of Guru to be free from them. Hence there was every possibility of Yudhisthira's losing in the game. In fact, all his stakes were lost and there remained nothing to stake except the wife, Draupadi. Lastly, Yudhisthira began to play the game of dice and the stake was Draupadi and lost the stake. Duryodhana was exulted and ordered Vidura to bring Draupadi to the court as she was won. Now she deserves the dignity no better than that of a house-maid. Vidura cared two figs for his order and began to remonstrate Duryodhana. So an envoy was sent and later on Duhshasana. The sole intention of all this was to disgrace the Pandavas' wife as much as possible and thereby to be self-complacent.

Time and again it had been said that Draupadi was undergoing the menstrual period and such a state a lady should not be humiliated before her senior male relatives in an open court. Her physical state has been mentioned again and again. It means that the fact is a natural phenomenon universally which points to her ability to create a physical body.

Draupadi is the Self (Jivatma), but the beings are not yet created. All these events are of the subtle body. Until the physical body is created, a comprehensive idea of the activities of the Self cannot be manifested. The circumstance is conducive and the existence of beings is necessary for the activities of the Self. On the other hand, the relation between the self and five elements is very close and hence they are her husbands. Any attempt to separate the Self and the elements would surely disturb the course of creation. Hence the oath to drink the blood Duhshasana and that to break the femur of Duryodhana. In the open court Karna, the epitome of avarice and a friend of Duryodhana told Duhshasana that Draupadi was a harlot and she could be denuded in the court. Duhshasana being highly encouraged in a bid to denude her began to pull her cloth. Draupdi then prayed to her Lord and Friend to save her from this barbaric humiliation and the Lord did it by providing her with various types of cloths. There are two sides of this incident which we are to discuss now.

We have said, Draupadi is the Self and five elements are her five husbands. But no sensible person can acknowledge five husbands of a woman, yet this is the fact in this case. In the material world she exists in every human body irrespective of gender and she maintains a close relationship with five elements and hence she is the wife of five husbands. Within the body her abode is the first nerve-centre of the spinal cord known as Muladhara chakra. There she is known as Kulakundalini. The Yogis, saints and Guru say that the knowledge of the Kula meaning the immeasurable universe, remains in the Muladhara nerve-centre. Now, Kula is the combination of knowledge of nine constituents viz. Direction (Dika). Time (Kala), Jiva (the existence of beings), the science of Nature (Prakriti Vijnana) and five elements (Pancha Bhuta). It is said that this knowledge being coiled in three and a half coils remains in the Muladhara; it is also known as the serpent-power. In fine, Kulakundalini is the divine energy to be identified by its activities only. When this energy is stupefied, it cannot be identified as such. To know of this energy it is necessary to be wise of these nine constituents by austerity and then the light of that wisdom will enlighten the austerer through his realization. The cardinal passions (ripus) are incapable of doing all this and hence they cannot denude her. In the body she is enveloped with darkness of ignorance from the first to the last of the nerve-centre and to undo them one is to take up austerity and finally one would be eligible for denuding her i.e. the austerer would be realized and it is to denude her. The cardinal passions (ripus) can never do this with their insolence.

The attempt to denude Draupadi by Duhshasana (wrath) imparted some lessons to Duhshasana along with the courtiers of the court as well as Draupadi. She was the loving wife of the Pandavas and a devotee of Krishna. In the court and in full view of the elders when her brother-in-law was trying to denude her pulling her cloth, she did not get the desired result calling Krishna by different names. She herself attempted to protect her modesty even with her palms which rendered to be futile. Realizing her own inability to preserve her modesty and dignity she raised her both hands in submission to pray to the Lord of her heart to save her from ignominious disgrace and He provided her with various kinds of cloth to save her, remaining Himself invisible. The different kinds of cloth of various hues denote different stages of knowledge and innumerable esses of them and as well of the Kula (the universe). Until and unless one sacrifices one's own authority of action i.e. the ego and surrenders oneself to Him, one cannot be saved by Him in dire distress.

The kings and courtiers present in the court became sharp-tongued when unsuccessful Duhshasana stopped his efforts being exhausted and disappointed. Owing to the disgrace and insult of Draupadi, Bhima became very much enraged and promised to drink his blood rending his chest. One has to endure the punishment for infringing the course of creation by natural law and also by Divine Will. Sometimes such punishments come in form of a curse or a merciless promise of someone.

Meanwhile, none in the court could make any answer to Draupadi's question and when the discussion was going on Duryodhana pulling upward his cloth called Draupadi to show his bare thigh to her. Already wrathful Bhima became much more angry and promised to break his thigh. Even after all such happenings the wise courtiers could not conclude regarding their duty in such a situation. But Dhritarastra asked Draupadi to come to him and told her to pray for any boon she liked which he would grant to her. Draupadi then arranged for the freedom of her husbands. Being permitted by Dhritarastra the Pandavas then returned to Indraprastha with their lost riches. Disappointed Duryodhana again with a greater zeal began to excite the king for another bout of the game of dice, in order to smoothe the way to the universal law of creation.

The Exile Of The Pandavas

Just after the departure of Pandavas for Indraprastha Duhshasana conveyed to Duryodhana that all the wealth so far appropriated, has been lost owing to the blind king. Duryodhana became disappointed but not discouraged at all; rather he tried to excite the king in his favour with a greater enthusiasm. His associates Karna and Shakuni playing falsely endeavoured to make the king understand that the Pandavas fully armoured were advancing towards Hastinapura with the determination to destroy the Kauravas. So another bout of the game of dice was imperative. "You please permit it," said Duryodhana. Next he said, "Now if they observe a vow of exile for thirteen years, we can easily defeat them as you desire."

The mind is helpless under the tutelage of the desire (Kama) associated with delusion and avarice. So, Dhritarastra said, "Let the Pandavas come and play the game of dice". But Gandhari could not approve of this proposal. She endeavoured in many ways to make Dhitarastra disown Duryodhana, the disgrace of the family. Dhritarastra was firm in his decision; his argument was, "Let the sons do what they like to do, the game of dice with the Pandavas should begin".

So Duryodhana said to Yudhisthira ".... Now the father has ordered, come, let us begin the game of dice casting our own dies."

Now it is the turn of Shakuni who told Yudisthira that a new stake has been fixed for this game this time." If we are defeated to you, wearing deer-skin we would go to the deep forest and remain unknown for one year and pass another twelve years also in the forest inhabited by human-folk. And if we become victorious, then you are to go in exile and pass thirteen years in the similar way.

Yudhisthira agreed notwithstanding the protests coming from the courtiers. Began the game of dice and inevitably the Pandavas were defeated; now they would go in exile. Prior to their departure for the forest Dushasana was very much encouraged to pierce the hearts of the defeated Pandavas dispossessed of their kingdom, with the shafts of sarcastic and acrimonious comments. Even to humiliate Draupadi he found no bound of his enthusiasm. At a time he said, "… Yajnasena (Drupada) could not earn an iota of piety by giving his daughter by marriage to the Pandavas as they are impotent. O Draupadi, what pleasure would you have seeing the Pandavas roaming in the forest? Rather, now accept anyone as your husband. At this Bhima lost his composure and said, "… Now as you are driving your sharpened words into our hearts, similarly in the battle-field I shall cleave your cutis." etc.

The Pandavas left the royal court to go to the forest with the oath to destroy the Kauravas. Blessing the Pandavas Vidura said that their mother Kunti would remain in his household during their exile. On the other hand, Kunti bade farewell with blessings to Draupadi having her dishevelled hair.

After the pandavas left for the forest Duryodhana, Karna and Shakuni after a conference confided to give the Pandavas' kingdom to Drona. On accepting the trust Drona warned

Duryodhana and his associates saying, " You will be in distress after thirteen years have elapsed." Hearing Drona's warning Dhritarastra ordered to bring back the Pandavas. But nobody heeded to that.

On being asked by Sanjaya the reasons for his depression glum Dhitarastra said to him how could they be happy as the Pandavas were their enemies? During the discussion with Sanjaya regarding persecution of Draupadi, Sanjaya advised him, "O the king, please do make an alliance with the Pandavas; unite both sides with a free mind and that would be good for you." Dejected Dhitarastra replied, " Sanjaya, Vidura advised me to do so for the well-being of all, but considering the disposition to do good to my sons I rejected it."

In an earlier chapter in course of discussing the divine, super natural and material calamities, we said the sequence of creation was in the subtle state and the physical body was yet to be created. The necessary preparation for creation of the physical body was complete; any time it might take place. If the physical body is not created, the sequence of creation would be highly disturbed as order in Nature is meticulously maintained; any such disturbance which is very few and far between may happen, the consequence is sure to be disastrous. In this particular case, the first attempt to create the physical body proved not to fructify owing to the absence of close co-operation between Kama (desire) and its associates on the one hand and the mind on the other. The leader of them all is Kama (desire) and now he decides to take such a step that must have to be effective. And he was resolute to be enemical to any extent and that would not tell upon his character, in any way, as he was constantly observing his own dharma. Now, a question may arise as to how does come the proposition of the subtle and physical creations in the perspective of two kingdoms of the same dynasty and their union and separation, avarice and retaliation, the game of dice, winning and losing the stakes between the players? It is a pertinent question indeed. We have said earlier, the tale depicts the origination and manifestation of physical body and is delineated with the help of imagery, symbolism and allegory the proper interpretation of which the life-time of the beings. The Pandavas were required to live in the forest for a yuga. This world of the humans is like a forest. As there are tall trees, bushes and creepers in the forest, similarly there are saints and sages in the world of men rising high above, impart various lessons and teach the men and women of the society how to rise above the mundanity of this world and also guide them to attain the eternal peace. Again, like the bushes and creepers in the forest, there are human-folk who in course of their life tread the trodden path to draw the curtain upon their life unceremoniously without caring for durable peace, lofty ideals or high thinking. As there are ferocious beasts and predators in the forests, there are fierce and cruel beings in the forest of the human world, observing whom even the beast of the forests be ashamed. In fine, the world is a forest, no doubt, and the beings are in exile for a yuga in this forest.

But how? The beings are always guided by the mind, cardinal passions and bondages. In the life of beings cardinal passions and bondages are the main players guided by their lord, Kama (desire) and avarice and delusion are its close associates. In fact, life of beings from birth to death is led by Kama (desire). Prior to the creation of physical body life was in the subtle state and had that life been concluded in that stage, the Divine Scheme of Creation would not have been thoroughly accomplished and His Leela too would have been impeded. So at a certain stage life in the subtle required to be evolved into the physical one following the Nature's law of evolution. Indraprastha, their kingdom is their Kingdom of Self and they have been driven out of that Kingdom of Self owing to the conspiracy by cardinal passions and mental traits as a result of which the Pandavas are roaming in the forest as destitutes. During this exile they are to experience the three calamities viz. the divine, supernatural and material and at the same time they are to learn how to overcome them.

Here in Hastinapura Kunti remained under Vidura's guidance. Nobody sought for her exile as that was not necessary. Kunti is detachment (nivrittee). If she accompanies her sons and daughter-in-law in their exile all the while, they will fail to experience the said three calamities squarely and would not learn the ways and means to be free of them. Hence Kunti remained with the divine part of the energy of mind. Apart from this, her stay at Vidura's had a practical side too. Vidura would know of their whereabouts in the forest and at any instance communication with them would be there. So she could be regularly posted with the information of them. So Kunti remained in Hastinapura bidding farewell to the sons and daughter-in-law in tears.

As Kunti had not to go in exile, similarly the other wives of the Pandavas were not required to go in exile. Only Draupadi needed to go. She was the stake in the game of dice that Yudhisthira lost and she had to undergo the indignity as well. For the creation of the physical body she is bound to be associated with her five husbands as she is the Self (Jivatma) and the Self ensures the existence of beings that also ensures the fruits of austerity. And again, the Self causing finally union with the Supreme draws the curtain upon the existence of beings. Hence the Self is the pivotal energy of beings in both spiritual and material planes. So she is a must in physical body.

The exile of the Pandavas was of twelve years added to another year during which they should remain unrevealed. No one should get any information of them during that one year and if it happens, then they are to undergo another thirteen years' exile in the same way. Now, the exile for one year remaining unknown denotes the beings' stay in the mother's womb. Generally it is held that the unborn child remains in the womb for ten months and ten days and even after the child is born, impressions of his state of confinement remain there upon the child's mind for two or three months. If this time after birth, is added to the period of its sojourn in the womb, the result would be one year.

Once Dhritarastra wanted to know of Vidura as to how the Pandavas were going to the forest. In reply Vidura said, they all were going to the forest hiding their visages and assuming various appearances. Dhritarastra wanted to know the reasons for such behaviour. What Vidura said meant that the Pandavas were driven out of their Kingdom of Self being the target of intrigue hatched by the shrewd sons of Dhritarastra and being rendered paupers they would not show their faces. Of course, they went to the forest taking the oath to destroy the Kauravas. It is a fact that the form of pure elements in the subtle does not remain the same in the phenomenal worlds— it undergoes change that can be visualized by the wise with the divine eye.

After the Pandavas went in exile, their kingdom was given to Drona, the military teacher, who was the epitome of notional and instinctive intelligence. It is true that he is incapable of ruling the kingdom of the subtle body, yet his rule of the kingdom is necessary as the beings having physical body become subject to three gunas in the realm of maya and would lead the life entangled in the mesh of sense-objects. Then their subtle bodies will guide them according to their past notions and instincts. So, the role of Drona is important in ruling the kingdom of the Pandavas that is given to him to rule. Drona, even if is the notional and instinctive intelligence, could visualize the future of Duryodhana and that of his own also and echoed the merciless prophecy of Narada at the time of transfer of authority.

Later on, once Dhritarastra in conversation with Sanjaya confessed to him how much unable he was to undo the wrongs by his sons and also by himself towards the Pandavas. The mind, even if is blind, is the perversion of Consciousness and when the perversion is gone, what remains is Consciousness; but in this perspective, the perversion of the mind is not gone at all; only for a little while, in the company of the divine eye the mind sees its own image reflected in the mirror of knowledge but its duration is as momentary as the bubbles upon the surface of water.

With Draupadi the Pandavas set out for the forest amidst the mourning and weeping citizens some of whom expressed their desire to accompany the Pandavas but Yudhisthira forbade them. Only the Brahmins were allowed to go with them although the Pandavas were incapable of their maintenance. When Yudhisthira was expressing his sorrows in this regard, rishi Shaunaka offered some advice to him; Yudhisthira said, he did not crave means for his own enjoyment but to maintain the Brahmins with them. In reply Shaunaka said, persons accomplished in austerity might do anything by dint of their austerity. Listening to Shaunaka Yudhisthira asked their priest Dhaumya about his own duty now.

Dhaumya said in reply, "at first beings born of the elements became afflicted with hunger. Then the sun being the source of their birth was kind enough and attracted heat and savour by means of its rays moving in Summer Solstice, set down in the earth coming in the Winter Solstice. Then the moon collecting heat from the sky and with the help of water produced vegetation. Then the thunder ejected. At last the sun turned itself into food for beings of various tastes and savours being exuded by the moon. This food produced by the sun is the means for sustenance of the beings."

Following the speech of Dhaumya, Yudhisthira began to pray to the sun god. The sun god being pleased, appeared before Yudhisthira and said, "O king, please accept this plate of mine made of copper; the food items upon this plate would not be exhausted before Panchali has taken her meal and ripe fruits, tuber, vegetable and meat — these four kinds of food items would remain inexhaustible in your kitchen. On completion of thirteen years you will regain your kingdom." Examining the merits and demerits of the plate Yudhisthira went to the Kamyaka forest.

After the Pandavas left for the forest once Dhritarastra said, "Vidura! let by gone be by gone, now what is our duty? How be the citizens subjugated to us? O Kshatta! please give us some of your honest advice ascertaining the means so that they do not uproot us altogether."

Now, Vidura said what he had said earlier ending with these words, "... Let Duryodhana, Shakuni and the carpenter's son

Karna seek the refuge of the Pandavas lovingly and let Duhshasana beg forgiveness of Bhima and Draupadi in the court. O king, do install Yudhisthira in his kingdom consoling him. O king, you sought for my advice, I have said what is righteous; now act accordingly and you would be successful, no doubt."

The words of Vidura did not shower honey into the ears of Dhritarastra. Obviously, being annoyed he spoke. ".... You are speaking all this for the welfare of the Pandavas. It is correct they too are my sons but Duryodhana is born of my body....you are offering harming and deceitful advices to me; whether you stay here or go anywhere, that does not matter to me." Vidura realized, "this cannot be done" and muttering these words he left for the Pandavas.

Seeing Vidura coming from a distance they thought that he was coming with an invitation to play the game of dice again. But on his arrival when the Pandavas asked to disclose the reasons for his coming to the forest, he narrated the audacious behaviour to him by impertinent Dhritarastra and said finally — "Dhritarastra has given me up. Now I have come to you to offer some moral advice to you; ....listen to them carefully and do observe them earnestly." Saying this he began to advice Yudhisthrira who also promised to follow them.

Meanwhile, after Vidura left the court, considering his influence upon the Pandavas, Dhritarastra impatiently asked Sanjaya to bring back Vidura saying, "O Sanjaya, highly religious Vidura is my brother and a loving friend of mine....you please bring him back post-haste." Ordered by Dhritarastra he went to the Kamyaka forest and saw the Pandavas surrounded by the Brahmins and after the exchange of good wishes Sanjaya said to Vidura. "O the scion of the Kurus, bidding farewell to the great Pandavas present yourself immediately to the king as per his orders to save his life."

On his return Dhritarastra apologized to Vidura. Then he spoke to Dhritarastra. "Both the Pandavas and your sons are equal to me but seeing the sons of Pandu extremely indigent my mind has been attracted to them. So to be compassionate to them is a sacred duty of mine.

Hearing the news of Vidura's return and his cordial reception by Dritarastra, Duryodhana being extremely anxious began to confer with Shakuni, Karna and Duhshasana. Duryodhana said, Vidura, the minister "is a dependable friend and an earnest well-wisher of the sons of Pandu.... If I see them returned again. I'll be extremely afflicted and swooned no doubt. What more to say, rather I would die by hanging, or of poison or by arms or of burning, but I won't like to see them fortunate ever by any means. Listening to Duryodhana Shakuni said, "Pandavas are truthful, they are not to return at all, if they come, it would not be difficult to find fault with them." Then Karna said, "If they come back then it would not be impossible to defeat them in the deceitful game of dice." Next, understanding that Duryodhana could not subscribe to his views, Karna proposed, "Now let us go unitedly to the forest to kill the Pandavas." Duryodhana liked the proposal of Karna and started for the forest to kill the Pandavas.

Meanwhile Vyasa could know of this with his divine vision and forbade them. Appearing before Dhritarastra he warned him saying, "Find out a way for the well-being of you all."

The physical out of the subtle does not mean that the whole of the subtle be transformed into the physical one and then only the physical would exist and the subtle be non-existent, that is not the fact. Rather, the subtle would remain as such and in addition, the physical then thrive in full form in the sequence of creation. These circumstances were quite new and unknown then and most of the players, of course except the wise ones, failed to get the measure of this phenomenon and could not comprehend as to how the physical be existent while the subtle was there. As till then there was no physical creation prior to the exile of the Pandavas, the players of the subtle body could not squarely discern the significance of it; but Yudisthira understood that well and when the weeping citizens of Hastinapura were desirous to follow the Pandavas, he desisted them from doing so. Those ordinary citizens were the traits of mind (vritti) and they could not assume the physical form until otherwise ordained by the Divine Will. Added to this, the subtle body is the conductor of the physical body and the traits of the mind have a vital role to play in the active physical body. Hence Yudhisthira forbade them to follow him. On the other hand, he took the Brahmins with them. As the Brahmins are wise in the knowledge of Brahman and they can make others wise imparting that knowledge as they are repositories of the esses of the heart (Vava), they are needed always for the uplift of the ordinary consciousness of the beings in the journey of life of the humans intended to be blessed with the knowledge of the Supreme.

But in the phenomenal world Yudhisthira was wanting in the means to maintain the Brahmins with them and while he was expressing sorrows regarding his inability, rishi Shaunaka offered some advices to him in reply to which he said, he wanted nothing for his own enjoyment but for the accompanying Brahmins only. Rishi Shaunaka is an esse of the heart and esses become well-nourished by kindred esses and knowledge also. But in that early dawn of physical creation knowledge did not develop in a flourishing bloom and hence Yudhisthira was anxious for their maintenance. So he had to approach Dhaumya, the customary earnestness who advised him to pray to the Sun. The Sun is the source of creation and also the source of nourishment of the created. The sun god being pleased with the singing of hymnody by Yudhisthira in praise of him, gave him a plate and said that everyday the food in whichever quantity be cooked would remain in that plate inexhaustible being replenished from time to time till Draupadi had taken her meal. The plate was made of copper. In reality, the sun provides food for beings upon the surface of the earth, symbolically said to be the copper plate. This plate never exhausts in vegetation and if ever a kind of vegetation exhausts, then it is replenished by the other kind. So the plate is full of food always.

But this plate is not made of copper but earth. This is the tale of Dvapara Yuga. There is a legend that the beings of Satya Yuga used the plates of gold, those of Dvapara used the plates of copper and those of Kali Yuga are to use the plates of iron. Therefore, the sun's copper plate in those days appears to be justified.

Now, the second one; — the Sun of innumerable suns is Guru. He is the source of our existence also. The sun which we see everyday is but the representative of that Greater Sun and a symbol too.

The plate given by the sun god to Yudhisthira, was nothing but the Sun of Knowledge radiant in the firmament of the heart. The knowledge that dawns on the heart, nourishes the esses (bhavas) in the heart. The nature and manifestation of this sun of knowledge is obviously perceived by the element of ether (Yudhisthira) and also the energy of Kulakundalini (Draupadi). But the nature and manifestation of the esses dawned on the heart are not the same at all times and in every perspective. Once on acceptance of a particular esse another kind of esse would occur naturally. Now the intervening span of time between the acceptance of a particular kind of esse and the consequent appearance of another kind of that denotes the emptiness of the plate after Draupadi had taken her meal.

The Pandavas set out for the forest northwards. Having been blessed with the boon of the sun god Yudhisthira reached the Kamyaka forest along with the brothers and Draupadi and the Brahmins. We have said earlier that the exile of the Pandavas was actually the sequence of evolution of life from the subtle to the physical having a body of five elements. And the forest is the phenomenal world where this life is supposed to thrive, where beings having the body of five elements, will lead their life primarily being guided by Kama (desire). The evolution of creation from subtle to physical became possible for the inspiration of Kama at the root. This exile is an outcome of losing the stake in the game of dice played with delusion (moha) as proposed by Kama (desire) and to honour the agreed conditions. So, the role of desire (Kama) is a vital one. The desire is the sole inspiration to live a bodied life here on earth. One of the peculiarities of this exile is to reveal and manifest the existence of beings and one is required to embrace the desired sense-objects for the purpose. So the Kamyaka forest was adopted by the Pandavas at first.

Dhritarastra knew the Pandavas well as he knew Duryodhana, Duhshasana, Karna and Shakuni. Again, he knew well of Bhishma and Drona too. The Pandavas distressed in insult and persecution gradually became fearful to him. The valiant warriors like Bhima and Arjuna who are sheltered by Vrishni Vasudeva and to whom Srinjaya Drupada is related by matrimony, are never expected to accept gracefully the insult and reproach to Draupadi and to roam in the forest like beasts without taking revenge for the insult and outrage to Draupadi — such a possibility was not there even in any wild imagination of Dhritarastra. So he is very eager to know how they are planning the measure to retrieve their lost kingdom and also to avenge the insult meted out to them. With this end in view once he called for Vidura and wanted to know of Vidura's advice as to how the interest of the Kurus be safeguarded.

What Vidura said earlier, said this time also. His suggestion was to forget enmity, envy and cruelty and on the basis of love and forgiveness, the Pandavas be installed in the kingdom calling them back from the forest. But the blind king was in no mood to listen to lessons of morality. He wanted to know as to how the subjects of the Pandava kingdom be subjugated to the Kauravas and in which way the Kauravas could ever remain unharmed. He who asked the question was the blind mind attached to the sense-objects and he who was asked the question was bhakti — the truthful part of the mind. They were poles apart. Hence Vidura could not satisfy the blind king with his reply as was desired by the king.

Resultantly, Dhritarastra grew irritated and remonstrated him. He said Vidura might go anywhere else he liked leaving the court. Mortified Vidura left for the Kamyaka forest. On the one hand as the esses of the heart build a bridge between the subtle and phenomenal existence in the life of beings, likewise the part of the truthful energy of the mind does the same at times. With the expression of anger and disgust on the part of Dhritarastra, Vidura comprehended that the blind mind was antagonistic to any step being taken for the sake of truth other than those which it is interested in and serve its own purpose. Therefore, the truthful part of the mind associated with the truthful Pandavas and narrated before them how Dhritarastra rejected his suggestion towards the welfare of both the parties. Had it been possible, the truthful part of the mind could have stayed with the Pandavas in the Kamyaka forest. But that was not ordained as the constant presence of the truthful part of the mind with them could have diminished the influence of the blind mind upon the beings and resultantly the required development of the existence of beings according to necessity would have been impeded. Only for this reason, Dhritarastra deputed Sanjaya to Vidura in the forest to bring him back to Hastinapura. The mind though blind, knows well that enemies should not be allowed to be adiposed. Had the truthful energy of mind remained associated with the existence of beings, it would have been propitiating to the existence of beings which was not at all desired. So it necessitated to separate the truthful energy of mind from the beings, at least for the time being. Therefore all pervasive true knowledge was called for embassy, because the truthful energy of mind would not trust any other messenger.

At the behest of Dhritarastra Vidura came back. On his arrival Dhritarastra apologized to him for his behaviour. Whether this apology was an acting or not, his sole intention was to ascertain Vidura's stay at Hastinapura; had this not been done, the development and manifestation of existence of beings would have been hampered and at the same time the role of the house of Hastinapura would have been restricted. Hence the effort is to maintain an equilibrium between two sides and pointing to this Vidura said, the Pandavas and the Karavas were equal to him but the Pandavas did attract much of his attention because of their penury now.

Having the news of Vidura's return to Hastinapura, Duryodhana became distressed and began to confer with Shakuni, Karna and Duhshasana apprehending the Pandavas' return through Vidura and had that happened the consequences would have been disastrous to Duryodhana who had but to commit suicide. At this juncture, as per the counsel of Karna, it was decided to kill the Pandavas in the forest. So Duryodhana started to proceed to the forest to kill the Pandavas. Imprudent Kama (desire) failed to understand how the Pandavas were engaged in fulfilling the Divine mission in exile and had they been killed in the forest then what harm would inflict upon His Leela. On the other hand, Kama (desire) was ignorant of the importance of his own role in this Leela.

Vyasa did comprehend how much childish was this resolution to kill the Pandavas in the forest. He desisted Duryodhana and later on expressing his annoyance he spoke to Dhritarastra to find out a beneficial course by all means.

But does the cardinal passion Kama (desire) or the mind subjugated to it, know the real weal and the duty to be performed to that end? Even that is unknown to them, but ever conscious Guru warns at the proper time.

The Life Of The Pandavas In Exile

After Vyasa had doused the flames of ill conceived design of Duryodhana, Dhritarastra requested Vyasa to chastise him.

"Holy Maitreya will be coming here to see us after having met with the Pandavas and he will reprimand your son Duryodhana for the welfare of your clan," — said Vyasa to Dhritarastra.

Came the muni Maitreya. In course of conversation with Dhritarastra, he concluded his speech saying, "O king! I say, do conclude an alliance with the Pandavas and don't indulge your wrath."

Duryodhana being present there and hearing the advice of the muni ignored it abominably. Observing Duryodhana the enraged muni cursed him saying. "....Bhimasena, the valiant warrior will break your thighs in a devastating war to be waged against you in not very distant future." Then he said, "O king! If your son enters into an alliance, then the curse would be futile, otherwise not."

On the other hand, having the news that the Pandavas had been to the forest, the friends and relatives belonging to the Bhoja, Andhaka and Vrishni families came to see the Pandavas in the forest to sympathise with them. Among the visitors there were Dhristaketu, the king of Chedi, the great Kaikeya and also Krishna. After they had been seated,

Krishna addressed Yudhisthira, "O Dharmaraja, it is sure that the earth will drink the blood of these four depraved souls — Duryodhana, Duhshasana, Karna and Shakuni and slaying them in the battlefield....we will install you in your kingdom." In course of discussion on this subject Krishna appeared to be very angry and in order to allay his passion Arjuna began to sing hymnody praising him. After some time when his wrath subsided to a great extent, he said, "O Partha, you are mine and I am yours....in fine, there is no difference between you and Me."

Draupadi, after Arjuna began to sing hymns in praise of Him and endeavour her singing saying, "Now let me express my sorrows lovingly to you" and began to speak, "O Krishna, am I the subject to insult and persecution by Duhshasana in the court being the wife of the Pandavas, a sister of Dhristadyumna and a loving companion of yours even? I was in loin cloth then observing femine formalities. Fie to the strong arms of Bhima and the Gandiva of Arjuna as they easily ignored my ordeal by an insignificant fellow.... O the kind-hearted! Now I think, I have no husband, no son, no friend, no brother, no father and even you are also non-existent for me." The next moment she said, "O Krishna! Only you are protecting me relying on relationship, glory, companionship and your Lordship." Hearing her lamentations Krishna consoled her saying, "Truly I say that you would be the queen, no doubt. Even if the sky falls upon the earth, the Himalayas become shrivelled, oceans dry up and the earth becomes fragmented, My words must fructity."

After consoling Draupadi Krishna addressed Yudhisthira, "Had I been to Dvaraka then you would not had to suffer in such a way." Saying these words he again said, had he been there he could have stopped the game of dice by any means. "Women, the game of dice, hunting and drinking of alcohol — to these four luxuries born of desire (Kama) men lose their fortune. The wise count them to be the harbingers of suffering and noxious too. After discussing for a while he concluded his speech saying, "Aha! What a hardship you are undergoing." If the bridge is broken the impact of the water-flow cannot be resisted easily." Then he started for Dvaraka. Dhristadyumma, Dhristaketu, the king of Kekaya returned to their kingdoms after the departure of Krishna, Gradually the subjects of the Kurus left the forest.

After they all had departed, Yudhisthira called his brothers and told, "We are to stay in the forest for twelve years. So find out such a place that is full of games and birds and resided by honest persons so that we may pass off happily." In reply Arjuna said, "Nearby there is a forest resided by honest persons, having waterbodies, full of fruits and flowers and also attended upon by the Brahmins, named Dvaitavana which is but a sanctimonious place; if you permit, we may live there for twelve years easily." Listening to Arjuna Yudhisthira said, "I agree to what you said; now let us go to the Dvaitavana."

The delusion and avarice are cardinal passions; so also is the desire (Kama). In association with delusion and avarice how much arrogant and powerful could desire be is approved of its disregard to morality, scornful contempt to justness and its speed to implement its own designs. Whatever it likes to do, does that whiffing off the admonishments of two grandsires — Vyasa and Bhishma, uncle Vidura, military teacher Dronacharya and well-wishers; to its disregard, they all seem to be the fallen leaves since dried up. How is it so powerful, so arrogant? Why is it so indomitable? — Such questions may arise into the minds of the readers of the Mahabharata. On the other hand, the author has arranged the argument in such a manner that the king of passions viz. Kama (desire) has himself tarnished his own image.

But is it so?

The tale of the Mahabharata holds a mirror up to a split picture of Lord Krishna's Leela. Yet inspite of its division, the picture of the human world as well as human life has been painted in such a way that clearly depicts the stages of creation on the one hand and on the other, it contains the lessons for its culmination blooming forth like a lotus step by step. The courses of Leela and reality are different indeed; but at times and under the influence of circumstances they both meet at a single point. Duryodhana of the Leela and Kama of reality have been correlated in such a way that it appears to be that owing to the importance of its own role, Kama (desire) in form of Duryodhana, is the important inspirational factor for apportionment of creation from a certain state of it and this cognizance is not false altogether.

The world is perishable, so also the life of beings. But the beings (Jivas) are not at all conscious of this impermanence. Hence throughout the life they crave for sense-objects meaning thereby life is squarely dominated by Kama (desire) and to put the life of beings to this domination in all respects the role of Duryodhana is a vital one. So Duryodhana is so all-devouring, so insolent. But it is astonishing that even the wise rishis could clearly understood this truth — such an evidence is absent in the tale. Of course, both of them were active participants of this Leela and knowing the truth they did not disclose it in view of the further progress of the Leela.

In the royal court of the Kauravas when Dhritarastra requested Vyasa to admonish recalcitrant Duryodhana, Vyasa did not agree rather he deftly devolved that task upon rishi Maitreya to do so, because he knew well that his own blood was running through the veins of Duryodhana. Had he been insulted or ignored it was not possible for him to take any effective step against Duryodhana. But it was not difficult for Maitreya who did it well afterwards. Vyasa is a symbol of the energy of Guru who never punishes or curses anybody. Maitreya came and advised the king which Duryodhana ignored and Maitreya cursed him. He let him know his inevitable fate.

Having the information the Pandavas had been exiled, friends and relatives came to see them in the Kamyaka forest. With Balarama Krishna also came. He told Yudhisthira that He was not in the know of the facts when the game of dice took place. Had it been known to Him, He could have stopped the game and Pandavas also were not to suffer such difficulties in the forest. Of course, earlier He said the earth would drink the blood of Duryodhana, Duhshasana, Karna and Shakuni; and "We will install you in your kingdom."

Krishna did know nothing about the game of dice and the sequence of events thereafter and now on the basis of hearsay he had come to see them. What could be more amazing than this? How is it that Krishna knew nothing? He Himself is the incarnation of Supreme Consciousness. He is the source as well as the conductor of every creation yet He was not in the know of the happenings. But why?

Krishna is an incarnation of Supreme Consciousness and regarded to be the greatest of them all. Everything is in His knowledge and nothing is unknown to Him but He cannot disclose it all. Assuming the human form when He performs His Leela on earth, His divine entity remains as such but He never allows his divinity to be exposed to ordinary men and women; rather he presents himself like a common man as if He is one among them. But at times, He lets a few devotees know of his Divine identity with a view to advance his Leela to a certain degree. But such instances are very few and far between. Generally he behaves like a common man. In this instance a particular stage of creation is being evolved to the next one in search of its culmination and being guided by His Will. But Krishna said He was unware of all this; but why? The answer is, if the truth was revealed His Leela would surely have been impeded to a great extent and such kind of hiding the truth is also a part of His Leela. On the other hand, His listeners, even Draupadi herself failed to raise the question that had the event of the game of dice and its consequences been unknown to Him, how could He provide Draupadi with clothes in the Kaurava court? But His listeners were so transfixed to His speech that they forgot to question. Such type of acting is necessary on the part of avataras and yet another instance of such acting now follows. In course of discussion. He feigned to be very much angry with those whose unjustness caused so much hardship to the Pandavas. Observing His anger Arjuna began to sing hymns in praise of him to allay his passion. Having been assured that His feigning had not been detected by Arjuna but appeared to be real. He consoled Arjuna saying that there was no difference between them two and also said, "You are Mine and I am yours" and he calmed down to be serene. After Arjuna, Draupadi singing hyms in praise of Him began to lament as to how she was insulted and tormented notwithstanding having five husbands and Krishna, her friend and in the next moment shaking off her despair and with full of confidence she said that only Krishna lovingly saved them from all harms always. Krishna then consoled her saying that surely she would be the queen. But He did not utter a single word regarding her ordeal and tribulation. His behaviour with Draupadi was but formal denoting a distance between them. And that was true. There exists an intervening distance between the two as there is a difference between God and the beings in this world.

After consoling Draupadi Krishna began to converse with Yudhisthira taking the cue of the game of dice and expressed his sorrows for the Pandavas resultant to the ill effects of the game of dice and also expressing His inability to do any weal to them immediately saying, "If the bridge is broken, to resist the impact of water is almost impossible." By His last words he meant to Yudhisthira that there was no immediate relief from the ongoing misfortune that befell to them and at the same time they would be subject to the ordeal of divine, supernatural and material disturbances. That was His Will.

After departure of Krishna and other guests Yudhisthira called on his brothers and asked them to find out such a forest that would be full of deer and birds as well as abundant in flowers and fruits so that they could spend twelve years there. Hearing Yudhisthira Arjuna said there was such a forest nearby known as the Dvaitavana where they could go. Yudhisthira agreed to go there.

When the existence of beings was manifested the forest became its shelter. Sometimes it is Kamyaka forest, sometimes the name is Dvaitavana — the forest of dual existence. This world of man on earth consists of two sides — on the one there is the Creator and on the other there is the creation and both are correlative. Generally two opposite intents, actions and reactions are there to form the human world such as honesty and dishonesty, truth and falsehood, day and night, justice and injustice, birth and death etc. and with these elements Maya, the expert weaver, is weaving a multicolour fabric of human life to become the target to the three disturbances said earlier and having this life men and women raising their hands in the sky pray to God in distrees and fear, which is very dear to the Lord to whom human life is the pawn of his play known to be his universal Leela. In this Leela there is none other than 'You' and 'me'. This world of duality is the Daitavana of the Pandavas in exile where they are to live for twelve years. Nobody can grant freedom to them out of turn.

Interaction Of Yudhisthira With Draupadi & Bhimsena

The visitors had departed. There remained the Pandava brothers and Draupadi enduring the angst for exile that befell to them through insult and persecution and which had to be accepted for the sake of love for truth. Yudhisthira was not agreeable to take any retaliatory step against the Kauravas until the time was up. Such a firm stolidity on the part of Yudhisthira appeared to be astonishing to Draupadi. So she entreated to excite him to requite the misdeeds of the sons of Dhritarastra. She spoke out to him, "Seeing you were not at all pained for the distress of the brothers and mine, I understood that you are sans wrath indeed.....it is not at all fair to forgive the enemies, rather they should be uprooted showing your prowess."

Perceiving the air of distraction in Draupadi Yudhisthira in course of consoling her explained the nature of wrath saying, "He who restrains anger, he finds weal around him; but he who cannot do this, anger becomes the cause of his own peril, anger that exterminates men from the root." Saying many other things he again began to say, "He who can restrain intense wrath with the help of his intelligence and who has not even a little of anger in his heart, — the wise call him a man of prowess. To him it is not wrath but proper to forgive in all circumstances." Later on he spoke, "In forgiveness is established truth, Brahman, Sacrifice and the worlds." Lastly he said, "O Draupadi, the extremely terrible time has come for the destruction of the clan of the Bharata dynasty and I perceived it earlier. Suyodhana (Duryodhana) is miserably incapable of ruling the kingdom and he will not have the recourse to forgiveness, but I am the ablest of them all and hence forgiveness has taken refuge in me.....No doubt, now truly I will have the recourse to forgiveness."

Draupadi could not rely upon what said the eldest Pandava. She said, "Action is the means that ensures attainment of the best, better realms and also ensures fruits of action." Then she said, "You know nothing dearer than dharma, rather dharma is dearer to you than your life." Again she said, "The king who protects dharma, dharma protects him but I see dharma is not protecting you.....your judgement affected so adversely in the terrible defeat in the game of dice that your opposition took away your kingdom, treasures, arms, the brothers and me too easily...Now observing such of your unredeemable distress I being bound by delusion cannot control my outburst of grief."

Praising Draupadi's ability to argue Yudhisthira said to her, "What you said is tender and well said, but it is expressive of atheism. Now what I say now is ascertained in the Vedas that you should never have any doubt about dharma.....O Queen, you should not disregard dharma and the Creator guided by your mistaken notion. The boys think that the wise are insane but they never search for evidence being doubtful of observance of dharma." He concluded saying, "Please give up your atheistic view; do never scorn the Creator of elements. Better try to know His Excellence, salute Him; do not express such views ever. Never do insult Him."

Being unable to contradict Yudhisthira she spoke in reply. "O Partha! I did never scorn or upbraid dharma, nor can I insult the Lord of the elements; but I lament only being stricken with sorrow and I'll do that further, listen to it." As she could not bear with Yudhisthira's forgiveness and forbearance by any means she clarified her position saying, "Beings get the fruits of actions performing actions on the basis of the past fruits of actions, so engage yourself in performing actions without weariness and do them always to achieve success." Speaking elaborately on the performance of action and also on divinity and manliness she lastly said "apprehension is the root of every evil; performance of action with unsuspicious mind must yield the desired result. But such persons are the rare of the rarest." Speaking much more of the performance of action she concluded, "Prowess is the mainstay of success by performing action everywhere; so to do your action, do it with sobriety."

Vyasa tells us, short-tempered Bhimsena grew more furious in wrath and exhaling a long breath began to say to Yudhisthira, "Without dispelling your dharma be an honest person to retrieve your kingdom. Just see, what is our necessity to live in the forest devoid of dharma, artha (riches) and Kama (desire)? Depraved Duryodhana did not have our kingdom by dint of his prowess; he had stolen it by deceitful game of dice." "....why you for the protection only of a little bit of dharma, are plunged in the ocean of sorrows leaving aside the source of dharma and Kama (desire) and also of artha (riches) in form of your kingdom.... O king, you love dharma, only to please you we all are in distress. Following your steps and words we with self-restraint are enhancing woe to our friends and mirth to our foes. Nobody will welcome your present state; neither Krishna, nor Arjuna, nor Abhimanyu, nor the Srinjayas, nor me, nor the sons of Madree. Only for the sake of dharma always observing vow will you pass your time taking the path of renunciation like a man lacking in vigour? Just see, we despite being able to defeat the enemies, have taken the way of forgiveness, it is sorrowful than to die in fighting." "Dharma is the fountainhead of wealth which also is the cause of dharma as the cloud and sea nourishes each other, similarly dharma and artha (riches) nourishes each other....Kama rises up in the human Chitta (inner mind) and it has no body of its own....The desirous gets the desire propitiated, but there is no possibility of attaining any other fruit of it. Desire produces love which is its fruit.

With a view to get Yudhisthira excited against the Kauravas, Bhimsena addressed him, "O king, resorting to their own sense-objects which satisfaction the five senses, the mind and the heart enjoy, is called the Kama and that is an excellent product of dharma." ..... "It is proclaimed in the scriptures that one should observe dharma in the morning, act for earning money in the noon and in the evening cultivate Kama. .....You are well aware of the essence of dharma and practise it always and knowing this your friends are inspiring you to Karma (action). As the king of heaven along with the gods, killing the demons retrieved the kingdom of heaven, similarly please do retrieve your kingdom from Duryodhana exterminating the foes altogether."

Listening to Bhima pained Yudhisthira replied, "With an intention to steal away the kingdom of Duryodhana I took part in the game of dice and sensing my intention sly Shakuni partook in the game to play with me being the representative of Duryodhana. When I observed that the dice were being united and separated according to his will, then I should have desisted myself from the game but a sudden rage engulfed me and I lost my fortitude. Hence I could not desist from the game. The loss of fortitude in a man cannot be controlled even by prowess, assertion or heroism. Methinks it was the destiny; so I cannot take exception to your words." Yudhisthira opened his mind to Bhima saying, "To a civilized person it appears to gain a kingdom transgressing dharma more painful than death." Lastly he said, "Kingdoms, wealth, sons and fame cannot be equal to even a particle of dharma."

But Bhima is his own self. To him Yudhisthira's reasonings bear no worth at all. To him, as the beings are not in the know of their span of life and if that ends within these thirteen years then the kingdom can never be reclaimed. So the Pandavas should endeavour to regain their kingdom right now depending upon their prowess. Yudhisthira in reply says, "Actions performed with dauntlessness appear to be full of deadly sins;" the warriors on the side of Duryodhana such as Bhishma. Drona, Karna, Kripa, Ashvathama, Bhurishrava, Shalya et al are not to be slighted. Therefore in a state of penury and without military strength it is not possible to retrieve the kingdom.

In the earlier chapter we have said that the forest of the human world is the domain of duality and the excellence of it can only be traced here. Here it consists of 'you' and 'me'. But we do not know properly this 'you' and also 'me'. What we know of 'you', know by inference and as much we know of 'me', that much we know by vanity. The inference and vanity are the two manifestations of the energy of life. The more vanity is inflated, the more influence is stretched out; but when vanity is contracted, inference becomes controlled and it becomes controlled coming in contact with argument in search of truth; not by any passionate action of vanity. This truth is revealed in the conversation of Yudhisthira and

Draupadi. The Self in the form of Draupadi is but a woman in this world of matters. Her intent is to incite Yudhisthira to inflict retribution upon her tormentors for insult to her womanhood and her persecution in an open court. But that cannot be avenged as the tormentors are powerful enough and her husbands are roaming in the forest in penury. Moreso, Yudhisthira is bound by his oath to pass twelve years in exile and another year too remaining unrevealed. If this condition is infringed to wage a war against the enemies for revenge, that step may yield two possible results — one, even being honoured as dharmaraja Yudhisthira would fall from his dharma and two, there is the possibility of defeat than victory and in that case all hopes to retrieve the kingdom would be dashed. In which step the possibility of retrieval of the kingdom is slender, Yudhisthira cannot adopt such a measure as it is but an impetuous one. It is not a fact that he does not realize the necessity to reclaim the kingdom but he is to wait for convenient time and opportunity.

The insult and persecution that Draupadi had to undergo in the court of the Kauravas was far more great than that of the Pandavas. She had to hear that she was a prostitute and how much derogatory this calumny was! Added to this, attempts were made to denude her in the court before her revered seniors. No logic can measure the indignity caused by the meanness and inhumanity of the attempt. To drag older sister-in-law to the crowded court holding her hairs, is never endorsed by any civilian code of conduct. But such a torment was meted out to her with the intention to incite the energy of the Self so that it can be inflamed to the maximum extent in the time to come in order to initiate her husbands to the act of retrival of the kingdom of the Self avenging for all the misdeeds. Her say was well designed that the enemies should not be forgiven but to be uprooted altogether.

It is not a fact, what Draupadi understands, Yudhisthira cannot comprehend. He is not agreeable to avenge right now as Draupadi desires. So in order to soothe her distracted mind he said to her, performance of any impulsive action being guided by wrath may entail harm rather than weal. On the question of taking revenge for the insult and to retrieve the kingdom the role of Yudhisthira is most important. He is the king and his decision is final but that requires to be rational and approved by scriptures. He is not to take any indiscriminate action at once.

On the other hand, Draupadi being afflicted with insult and persecution wants to revenge herself right now. She is up to inflict punishment upon her tormentors, namely Duryodhana, Duhshasana, Karna and Shakuni immediately. Knowing the facts well she is not to understand that there is no immediate possibility of it now. Yet she desires to be so because of her self-respect. She is the proud daughter of Drupada and she cannot think that even insulting her the Kauravas evade punishment. Her inability is caused by her vanity and absence of her impartiality. Beings can never be impartial. Both Bhima and Draupadi analyse the chain of events in the light of their self-respect and vanity. Yudhisthira cannot subscribe to their views. His vision is impartial and hence he is to wait for the opportune moment to wage the war against the enemies and to win it.

In comparison to the impartiality of Yudhisthira that of Bhima and Draupadi was short lived as the colourful sunset in the dusk.

Arjuna Receives Celestial Weapons

Neither Draupadi nor Bhima had the earnestness to and reliance upon Truth and Consciousness that Yudhisthira had and hence his character could not be clearly evident to them. Sometimes their evaluation of Yudhisthira's character was not justified at all. The eldest Pandava had no equal to his forbearance and remained steadfast in pain and pleasure. He was never perturbed during his interaction with Draupadi and Bhima; he simply clarified that their logic bore no veritable substance. They also being unable to refute his argument rather finally subscribed to that at last. While he was discussing with Bhima regarding retrieval of their kingdom Vyasa came there. He told Yudhisthira, "I will arrange for the redressal of your apprehension in respect of Bhishma, Drona, Kripa, Karna, Ashvathama, Duryodhana, Duhshasana by performing acts following the edicts of scriptures." Saying this Vyasa advanced to Yudhisthira and taught him a mysterious art saying, "Later on Arjuna having it from you, if practise with austerity and strives for weapons, will be blessed with the grace of Mahadeva (Shiva) and Mahendra (Indra)." He also said, Arjuna would perform very commendable deeds having weapons from Rudra (Shiva) and Indra and the Lokapalas (the guardian deities of the corners of the earth to prevent corrupt practices). He said again that the Pandavas should now live in another forest leaving this one.

Obeying Vyasa the Pandavas went to the Kamyaka forest near the river Sarasvati. After some time Yudhisthira told Arjuna that Bhishma, Drona, Karna and Ashvathama had squarely mastered themselves in the art of archery and they would show their mettle in favour of Duryodhana when the time would come. So to repel them it needed proper training in application of arms. Then he taught him the art he received from Vyasa and instructed him to go northwards in the guise of a mendicant muni but being fully armoured holding a scimitar in hand. Bound by the oath to uproot the Kauravas, Arjuna started as ordered by Yudhisthira.

In course of his speedy journey towards the north at a certain place in the Himalayas, he suddenly heard a voice saying "halt" and looking around he could find an austerer having long matted hair. He asked Arjuna, "Who the newcomer are you fully armed like a Kshatriya but dressed as a muni in this peaceful atmosphere of the austere Brahmins who are calm and whose wrath has been subdued? There is no necessity of arms here. You may throw away your arms." Then he asked Arjuna to pray for a boon disclosing his own identity — "I am the king of gods, Indra." Then Arjuna prayed for the boon saying — "I have come to you for training in all your arms, please be kind enough to grant it." "There is no necessity of arms here — as already you have reached here" — said Indra. Arjuna said in response that he never ran after avarice, enjoyment, godhood or happiness; he had come for the cause of defeating the enemies and any exception to it would rather be disgraceful for him. Indra said, after meeting with Shamkara he would get all the divine weapons. Now he should pay earnest attention to meet with Shamkara, saying this he disappeared.

Following the advice of Indra Arjuna began his severe austerity to meet Shamkara. The severeness of his austerity made the great rishis anxious who informed of it to Shamkara who told them that they had no cause for anxiety. "I am aware of his prayer and in no time I will fulfil that."

Then Shiva in the guise of a primitive hunter came to the place where Arjuna was and saw that to kill a wild boar Arjuna shot an arrow; instantly Shiva too shot an arrow aiming that boar. The hunter told that he would kill Arjuna for flouting the rules of hunting. Arjuna said, he had struck the boar earlier than the hunter did. But the hunter was adamant and claimed the hunted to be his. As a result a fight between them ensued. With a view to kill the hunter Arjuna shot as many arrows as possible but his unhurt rival asked him gracefully to shoot more arrows. Gradually he took away the Gandiva from Arjuna and lastly both were engaged in wrestling in course of which Arjuna fell senseless. Then Arjuna began to worship Shiva making a clay idol but to his wonder he saw that the garland he offered to the idol was showing around the neck of his rival. Seeing this Arjuna fell prostrate at the feet of the hunter singing hymns in praise of him. Shiva asked him to pray for a boon. Then Arjuna prayed for his "Brahmashiro" weapon. Mahadeva said, "O Partha! I do give you the arms of mine which you will be able to hold, shoot and hold back." Then he ordered him to go to the heaven and disappeared. Immediately after there came Kuvera, Varuna and Yama to see Arjuna and gave him their weapons. Later on Indra came and asked him to go to the heaven to perform certain ordained deeds there and said that

Matali was coming to take him there boarding Indra's chariot. Came Matali and Arjuna went to the heaven. In the realm of gods Arjuna was now a man among them.

Yudhisthira was aware of the rationality, judgement and necessities of the phenomenal world despite his reliance upon Divine Will and this awareness of him sprang of that reliance. So notwithstanding his difference of opinion with that of Draupadi and Bhima regarding revenge, he lauded their logical analysis of the perspective which would be evident in the next instance.

While Yudhisthira was conversing with Bhima, Vyasa appeared to him to offer a mysterious art to be given to Arjuna to mitigate the fear of the Kaurava heroes consequent of his getting weapons of Indra and Shamkara. The author Vyasa had an important role to play as Vyasa the character in the tale. Time and again he appeared before the Pandavas at the time of crisis and guided them to attain the goal. This role of Vyasa is of much importance and symbolizes the energy of Guru. It is to note that at the time of the game of dice he was not present there nor did Krishna. There was a dire necessity of the Pandava's defeat and loss of their kingdom. Had they not lost their kingdom and not been exiled, the physical body could not have been created and at the same time, the preparation for austerity and its culmination through the uplift would have been a far cry. So to guide them properly Vyasa came to the forest to meet Yudhisthira and disclosed the modality to become free from the fear of the great Kaurava heroes, of course, not for Yudhisthira but for Arjuna who having received the divine weapons by dint of that mysterious art, could defeat the

Kaurava heroes and dethroning Duryodhana, would retrieve the kingdom.

Again and again Vyasa endeavoured to make the Pandavas understand that the exile was not the last word while in exile and that was not applicable to the Pandavas only but to the whole of human race also. The Pandavas symbolize the humankind. It would not be possible to be saved from the three disturbances, of course, that might happen if the duration of the exile would have been minimized while there was no chance of it in immediate future. Deliverance from those three disturbances was possible by retrieving the lost kingdom. But there was a question of a war to reclaim the lost kingdom, which ensured the necessity of weapons. The Pandavas were languishing in penury; they had no financial or other support for the preparation of a war. It was not a fact that Vyasa was not aware of it, yet his intention was to inspire them to prepare themselves depending upon the divine and the Pandavas did follow him earnestly.

The mysterious art which Vyasa bestowed upon Yudhisthira aiming Arjuna was given to him after some time. He was instructed to go northwards being fully armed in the guise of a muni. Arjuna did so. He is the reality of tejas and it is possible for him to go to heaven passing through the nerve-centres one after another in the spinal cord. His necessity to go to heaven has already been said. He was to propitiate Indra and Mahadeva (Shiva) and to get their weapons to be used to win the war to retrieve their lost kingdom. He started his journey northwards for the purpose. But why to the north? The heaven is to the north of the body i.e. upwards. So his journey was northward. It is the direction where all questions are solved and that is the upper part of the body.

To the north i.e. upper part of the body, if human energy is directed, newer understanding and realization enrich the human heart and that has been narrated in the tale as the conversation between Indra and him primarily. On the prayer of Arjuna to have all the weapons of Indra, he told Arjuna prior to that he was to endeavour first to visualize Shamkara (Shiva). Arjuna began his austerity as until and unless one is surrendered to Guru one cannot dominate over one's mind as an overlord meaning thereby one would then be capable of commanding one's mind and this is the weapon of Indra (the mind). But Indra did not offer him the gift instantly, only assured of that. These weapons were meant to be used for retrieval of the kingdom of Self. The mind (Indra) knows that Arjuna is his son who is to inherit the weapons of his father.

Obeying the advices of Indra Arjuna engaged himself in sadhana and in course of it he met Shamkara, of course, in the guise of a primitive hunter and to whom he was miserably discomfited. He lost his weapons, his Gandiva and also his self-pride of physical strength to an ordinary huntsman. He even became senseless in wrestling with him and when he came to his senses he could know that the opponent wrestler was none but Shamkara who came to Arjuna in disguise and wrestled with him only to test him and make him understand how far worthy his mettle was. When Guru puts a disciple in any ordeal, His sole intention is to control his pride and to make him conscious of his own self. However, as Arjuna prayed for his weapons he gave them to him and disappeared. Then came one by one Kuvera, Yama and Varuna who gave him their weapons to him. These gods are revelations of the lustre of Guru, they are born of this lustre and manifest the lustre of Guru. Then came Indra (mind) who now requested Arjuna to go to heaven and arranged for his journey too. The mind is Indra, the lord of heaven and it is the mind that is the main recourse to every endeavour of sadhana in either of the material or spiritual realm. The mind is Indra, the king of the celestial world and to go the heaven, to have its support is absolutely necessary to attain the heaven and hence Indra sent his chariot to take Arjuna there.

Arjuna In Heaven And The Love Tryst Of Urvashi

Obeying Shamkara Arjuna came to heaven. There the gods and other residents welcomed him with love and fondness. Indra himself offered his own seat. Having received all the weapons of Indra viz. the thunderbolt, lightning etc. he began to stay there happily as desired by Indra remembering his brothers. Thereafter once knowing that he had learnt the art to use the arms given to him Indra asked him "to get training in all types of dance, music and also the training to play the musical instruments under the guidance of Chitrasena and that would be beneficial to him". So Arjuna began to get lessons in those branches of art.

After pretty some time once Indra surmised that Arjuna was deeply enamoured of Urvashi and calling Chitrasena advised him confidentially to go to Urvashi and tell her "Coming here she should satisfy the desires of Arjuna" and also said, "As being appointed by me you have trained him in the application of my weapons, please train him in the like manner to make an expert of him in femine gesture and deportment." Ordered by Indra Chitrasena rushed to Urvashi and narrated what Indra said. Responding to Indra's message to her she said, "I have accepted him in my mind already.... Surely I'll go to Arjuna today, no doubt." On that day in the evening after darkness fell love-sick Urvarshi reached Arjuna's residence. Seeing her at his door-step surprised

Arjuna said, "O Apsara! I salute to you, here is your servant, tell me how can I serve you?" Urvashi became dumbfounded in amazement having been greeted in this fashion by Arjuna. However, after a little while coming to her senses she said what Chitrasena told her. Once in a musical soiree in heaven Arjuna looked on Urvashi again and again. Observing Arjuna Indra took it for granted that Arjuna was in love with Urvashi. So he asked Chitrasena to convey his order to Urvashi, "Do accept a valiant man of prowess, Arjuna as your husband," and ended with unfolding her mind to him saying, "I eternally cherish my desire to have you as my husband."

Lestening to Urvashi Arjuna became very much shameful and blocking his ears with fingers said, "I am quite unable to do what you say and even not to be heard. You are as venerable to me as the wife of my Guru. Like high souled Kunti and Indrani you are also adorable to me, no doubt... Now listen to me the reason for my looking on you again and again. I looked at you because I took you to be the mother of Paurava dynasty and there was no ill motive in my look, O the good lady, Paurava dynasty came into being of you and therefore you are my venerable Guru."

Urvashi replied, "I am an ordinary feminine being, it is not fair on your part to call me your Guru. Stricken with love I have been attracted to you so much. Now please requite my love satiating my passion, please". But Urvashi's solicitations could not move Arjuna who said, "lowering my head I am offering my salutations to your feet; you are equally adorable to me as my mother is and to be saved by you as your son. So return to your place."

Arjuna's rejection made the most beautiful apsara furious and angry. She cried, "O Partha, ordered by your father and being victim of my passion I came to you who rejected my proposal. I curse you to pass your time as a hermaphrodite among the women like a bull" and she left the place angrily.

After her departure Arjuna hastily went to Chitrasena and told him what had happened between him and Urvashi including being cursed by her. Chitrasena at once took him to Indra. Listening to Arjuna in details he said, "Today I come to know that Pritha should be a proud mother having an honest son like you. You have even made the rishis ashamed with your forbearance and restraint. The curse of Urvashi will also be beneficial and meaningful to you, no doubt. In course of your exile in the thirteenth year when you are supposed to pass your time unrevealed, you are to remain among the ladies as a neuter being and after that one year you shall regain your manliness." Arjuna is happy now.

Arjuna is the reality of Tejas and is determined to win the war. To collect the divine weapons he has come to heaven where he is a welcome guest whom the gods have received cordially, — we have said it earlier. But the reason for his warm reception in heaven is that he who diligently endeavour to be established in his own dharma, manhood, is blessed by his Guru. Those who are so blessed by Guru are welcome by one and all. How ill fated are they who do not search for the means to pass over the three disturbances and those who do it are very dear to Guru and this happens to Arjuna. Of course, not only Arjuna alone is determined to pass over these three disturbances but his other brothers also do the same and he is their reprenstative and symbol too. So in order to smoothen his course of future action Indra asked him to have lessons in songs, music and dance from

Chitrasena and said in addition, these lessons would benefit him. Arjuna did so and Chitrasena became his tutor.

The Gandharvas, expert in all kinds of arts, are but the symbols of energy of action sprung of the fruits of actions of past births.

Once Indra asked Chitrasena to impart lessons on the demeanour of ladies to Arjuna after he had been accomplished in the art of music and dance and for this purpose apasara Urvashi would be the fittest one. Apart from this, he surmised that Arjuna was attracted to her and therefore she could impart lessons to him easily. But Indra did not clear the air either to Chitrasena or Arjuna as to why such a lesson was necessary for Arjuna. The weapons for which he had come to heaven, were necessary for winning through the war to retrieve their lost kingdom of self cutting asunder the raging ignorance; but how the lessons of gesture and deportment of ladies could be related to that purpose he could not make out. On the other hand, having been informed by Chitrasena the apasara appeared at his doorstep to be stupefied receiving the welcome of Arjuna. Yet she earnestly entreated him to satiate her passion but stolid Arjuna did not change his stand, rather she was the first mother of the Paurava dynasty to his eyes. He could not do what she asked for. The love-lorn apsara turned to be furious and cursed him that he was to move as a neuter being among the ladies like a bull and she left Arjuna's dwelling. Indra succeeded in his bid.

It is commonly natural that the unctuous ova do attract the manly semen and vice versa. Here in this instance it is neither unnatural nor surprising that the vigour of Arjuna attracts Urvasi although Arjuna does not feel any attraction for her knowing her another identity. He knew that Urvasi was the first mother of their dynasty and hence she deserved to be revered. The celestial apsara failed to attract a worldly man in whose memory she got a recess curved with reverence. Hence she was venerable. Indra was well aware of the difference of outlook between them two but kept it a secret without divulging it to any one and he used deftly to assure the future security of his own son. Now having the evidence of his extra ordinary forbearance gladdened Indra told anxious Arjuna that the curse of Urvashi would turn to be a boon for him during the course of exile in the thirteenth year and on completion of that course he would regain his manliness.

The war to retrieve the kingdom of Self is actually the war of austerity and to win through it while the role of the mind is very important. In the preparatory stage some indications of it has been exemplified in this chapter. If one takes a plunge in the war of sadhana, Guru then helps him through someone or other to win the war and it is his grace bestowed upon that one. In this particular instance, the mind in form of Indra helped Arjuna through Chitrasena and Urvasi to advance the progress of Arjuna's preparation for the war as an example of God's Leela.

The Thoughts Of Armed Conflict In The Kaurava And Pandava Camps

Once Arjuna was acquainted with Lomasha Muni in the court of Indra in heaven. There Arjuna requested the Muni to come to earth to meet Yudhisthira in the Kamyaka forest and convey to him the message of Arjuna's well being. The Muni agreed.

On the other hand, then wise Dhritarastra listening to the narrative of Arjuna's expedition to heaven from Dvaipayana, addressed Sanjaya, "O Sanjaya! I have heard of the activities of diligent Partha and I think, you too are aware of that....My son, vile Duryodhana is addicted to performing evil deeds and inebriated in rustic culture. So he will soon be thrown out of the kingdom. The great soul who neutrally speaks the truth on all subjects and whose warrior is Dhananjaya, surely will be the lord of the three worlds, no doubt. The evil souls in form of my sons will die in the armed conflict with the indomitable Pandavas. They all are full of prowess and expert in the art of using arms and good warriors too. It is impossible to defeat them and they expect to gain supremacy being victorious. Until Arjuna or all of them is dead, there will be no peace." These sayings of Dhriturastra to Sanjaya are nothing but the expression of his own repentance and Sanjaya too admits of it. Dhritarastra having a companion at times of weal and woe can unfold his mind to convey his anxiety and sorrows to him. Again he told Sanjaya, "It is very strange that Dhananjaya wrestled with Mahadeva and people saw what Damodara (Krishna) and Falguni (Arjuna) jointly did to have the patronage of Vanhi (Fire) in the Khandava forest. So if Bhima, Arjuna or Vasudeva become wrathful in the theatre of war my sons even being united with the courtiers and Shakuni are not supposed to win." After a little while he said, "They are aggrieved of the persecution of Draupadi and never will they pardon us.....Earlier I did not pay any heed to the good counsels of friends being subjugated to Duryodhana but now I am to remember them all."

As the say of Dhritarastra got the approval of Sanjaya, for a little while the charioteer becomes the adjudicator of the king. He says, "O king, despite being able you did not prevent your son, rather ignored his misdeeds; it was very much condemnable." The king did not take any exception to the remark of the Charioteer, rather he continued the conversation as if to support him. He said, "At the time of the game of dice Vidura told me", "O king, if you defeat the Pandavas in this game of dice, then the Kuru dynasty will face its fearful end in the stream of blood." Now I see the words of Vidura are being fruitful. On expiry of the promised period of time a great war will take place, no doubt."

When anxious Dhritarastra afraid of the Pandavas, is busy with conversation with his charioteer regarding his fear and anxiety, then in the Kamyaka forest Yudhisthira with his brothers and Draupadi is distressed because of the absence of Arjuna. Meanwhile, Bhima praising Arjuna said. "Knowing his prowess I did not kill the sons of Dhritarastra along with Shakuni in the court then. We are here restraining our anger being strong enough only awaiting the directive from Vasudeva." Next moment he said, "We being the great in war have been thrown in this pitiable condition owing to your love for the game of dice." After a while he said, "You should observe Kshatriya dharma, to pass your time in exile is not the dharma of a Kshatriya. Defying twelve years' exile and that of one year to remain unrevealed, we should get Janardana (Krishna) come here and kill the sons of Dhritarastra before thirteen years are over." "....They say there is no apprehension of sin to kill a deceptive person with deceit and the wise say so by the name of religion."

Next, regarding the exile remaining unrevealed, his opinion was that there was no such place where the spies of Duryodhana could not intrude to collect information of them and they were to suffer again thirteen years' exile if the same did not remain unrevealed in the thirteenth year of exile and if it remained unreavealed then playing the game of dice with Yudhishira and defeating him they would snatch away the kingdom again. It was better then Yudhisthira should accord consent to Bhima to kill the sons of Dhritarastra declaring war against them. Yudhisthira quietly replied on expiry of the stipulated time along with Arjuna Bhima would kill them. To Bhima time was ripe but to Yudhisthira it was not; he was not to take the refuge of falsehood; Bhima could inflict death to Duryadhana.

Howsoever great may be the extent of happiness in heaven, Arjuna was wide awake of the thought singular to him i.e. the war and to win it. He never desired to be in heaven leaving his brothers and Draupadi in the forest yet he had to do so under compulsion. But never was there any separation between the forest living brothers with Draupadi and Arjuna.

Both of the sides were united with their anxiety and thoughts. The anxiety expressed by Arjuna for the brothers and Drupadi as well as their anxiety for the well being of Arjuna in heaven are but the outcome of one single aim — victory in the war after exile.

Really, since the commencement of the Pandavas' exile, the war was the only subject of discussion and also the object of thought in both Kaurava and Pandava camps. But the difference of outlook between the camps be noted. Again, in the Kaurava camp the thinking of Dhritarastra regarding the inevitable war and that of Duryodhana or his associates are of different characters. Though blind the mind is, consciousness remains afloat in it. So the mind can sense the air of what is yet to come and at the same time it can perceive the fruits of actions done by it and its associates. In this perspective Dhritarastra and Sanjaya were exchanging their views while they were engaged in conversation.

While Dhritarastra and Sanjaya belonged to the subtle state, with Draupadi the Pandavas were on the material plane. So due to this difference, the character of thought of both the camps was not the same. The Kauravas had nothing to lose even if they were defeated; at the best they were to return the kingdom appropriated deceitfully. Of course, the Kaurava heroes might have to lay down their lives on the ground of battle but the possibility of death in a battle should not make a Kshatriya fearful and anxious. Yet Dhritarastra is fearful and anxious, why?

The mind is not only zealous to enjoy sense-objects but very much eager to preserve and protect them for future enjoyment also. In this instance it is not otherwise. The mind knows it well that kingdom of the Pandavas had been appropriated wrongfully, but it never wants to undo this injustice, rather it never thinks of returning the kingdom to the Pandavas, nor had it the power to do so because though he was the king the authority to rule had been given away to Kama (Duryodhana) to whom he had subjugated himself and Kama rules the kingdom with authority. Then, was Dhitarastra feigning of fear and anxiety? No, he was not feigning. The mind, even if subjugated to Kama, has the flow of consciousness within it and resultantly, can deliberate on right and wrong, honesty and dishonesty and at the same time it becomes aware of the fruits of action evil or good. Dhritarastra understood clearly that the appropriation of the Pandavas' kingdom by Duryodhana was not just but he was undone to remedy it. His inability pricks his conscience and his angst found an expression in scolding Duryodhana in his conversation with Sanjaya.

Dhritarastra well understood that the persecution of Draupadi in the open court and the deceitful appropriation of the kingdom of the Pandavas, —these two were the seeds of destruction of the Kauravas. It was not unknown to him that after thirteen years' exile the Pandavas would not get back their kingdom on demand nor was it unknown to him that the war was inevitable. The hero of that war is now enjoying the hospitality of the king of heaven, successfully collecting the desired weapons there. Arjuna's expedition makes Dhritarastra anxious and fearful. He knows the future of Duryodhana and he repents that the advices of well-wishers were not honoured at the right time.

When Dhritarastra in the palace of Hastinapura was engaged in conversing with Sanjaya about the war, then stricken with grief of the absence of Arjuna Draupadi and other Pandavas were discussing on the same subject in the Kamyaka forest, of course, from a different angle of view. Bhima was of the opinion that before the expiry of thirteen years' exile they should declare war immediately getting Krishna come to them. Bhima is the reality of air which is always restless; it can not be stationary; stolidity goes against its nature. But Yudhisthira is reality of void, it can never be restless. So Yudhisthira is firm and streadfast. He cannot endorse the emotional form of war cry of Bhima. Again, Bhima is not diffident in advising Yudhisthira saying that to dwell in a forest is not the dharma of a Kshatriya. His opinion is to annihilate the Kauravas declaring war right now. He thinks that to remain unrevealed during the thirteenth year of exile shunning the sight of evil Duryodhana's spies is impossible and if that becomes true then they are to undergo yet another thirteen years' exile and the hope for retrieval of the kingdom will be crushed. So one should be deceitful to behave with a deceitful man declaring war at once to retrieve the kingdom.

It is of prime importance to retrieve the kingdom of Self by waging a war and the role of Guru in conducting that war is inevitable. Bhima was not oblivious of this truth and hence he sought the presence of Janardhana (Krishna) for his guidance. But there remained the question as to whether the time was ripe. On the other hand, King Dhritarastra at Hastina was afraid of the possible death of his sons, which is expressed in his conversation with his charioteer. He sought the welfare of his sons even after preserving the right to the deceitfully appropriated kingdom which the Pandavas are eager to retrieve. The conversation between Yudhisthira and Bhima and that of Dhritarastra and Sanjaya were the expressions of thoughts of mind but different in character depending upon the objective conditions around of the same mind.

Dhritarastra is the mind and Sanjaya is exhaustive knowledge. Yudhisthira and Bhima are elements and these elements have been presented to us as human characters. Hence all human qualities have been attributed to them including the mind. Therefore, these are the exercise of the mind.

What a peculiar reality this mind is!

The Tale Of Bhima, Nahusa And Yudhisthira

After being blessed with the divine weapons, having lessons of dance and music, being cursed by Urvasi and residing in the heaven for five years when Arjuna was returning to the Kamyaka forest almost midway near the Gandhamadana mountain he met with his brothers who were then out for a pilgrimage. Arjuna too was included in the group.

After the union with Arjuna, once Bhima alone went out for hunting but he did not return after a long time and Yudhisthira became anxious for his safety. Leaving Arjuna, Nakula and Sahadeva at the hermitage with Dhaumya he went out in search of Bhima and saw he was constricted in the coils of a large python. Fenced Bhima appeared to be utterly helpless. Seeing Bhima in this state Yudhisthira sought to know as to how all this happened and who the snake was. Bhima in reply said, "I have been taken by this snake as his food. He is the great souled rishi King Nahusa resting here as a python".

Yudhisthira then requested the python, "Please leave my brother, I am to provide you with other kind of food." The snake replied that he had caught the prince to be his food. If Yudhisthira did not leave the place immediately, he too would turn to be his food tomorrow. He was not to leave Bhima nor had he any appetite for other kind of food.

Then Yudhisthira somewhat forcefully said, "O snake, be a god, a demon or a snake, whatever you may be, Yudhisthira is asking you, speak truthfully why have you grabbed Bhimsena? Tell me, what you like to know to be pleased? Tell me, which kind of food should I give to you and by which means would you leave Bhima?

The snake replied, "O king, I am your ancestor being the son of Ayu and the great grandchild of Chandra, my name is Nahusa. By performing sacrifices, austerity, the study of the Vedas, restraining the senses and with prowess I acquired all the opulence of three worlds without any labour and became arrogant of my wealth so much so that I used to engage thousands of Brahmins to carry my palanquin by insulting them and because of that crime of mine by the curse of rishi Agastya I have been in this state. But my earlier wisdom is not destroyed yet... By no means I am to give up my prey and I have no such desire to do so either. Now if you be able to reply my questions, I may leave your brother."

Yudhisthira said that the snake might ask him questions at random. If it seemed to him that his answers could propitiate him who asked the questions, then he would make answers. But he was to know first as to whether the snake was in the know of Purusha irrespective of knowable of Brahmins and after being confirmed of it he would make his replies. The snake replied, "Listening to your words, you seem to be intelligent. Now please tell me who is a Brahmin and who is the knowable? Make a reply to them."

Discussing the characteristics of Brahmins Yudhisthira said, "He attaining whom men do not become the subject to pain and pleasure, that solitary Existence known to be Brahman is the only knowable. You may say if there be anything more."

The python said in reply, "Vedic behaviour may be discerned not only in Brahmins alone but in that of Shudra too and what you said to be the knowable is not existent anywhere."

Discussing the characteristics of Brahmins and Shudras Yudhisthira said, "To me the Eternal, Imperishable and beyond all pain and pleasure the Almighty is the only knowable." After a long discussion on the scriptural dicta between them, the python said to Yudhisthira, "...I think you are well-experienced of the knowable. So I will not gulp your brother." Then after a discussion on spiritual subjects for a while between the two the python said, "O king, addressing me politely you have made me free of the curse which was hard to dispel, performing an uncommon action."

Arjuna had to pass five years in heaven. The heaven in the body is between the brows and to stay there one has to cross the other five nerve-centres below. The fields of those five nerve-centres have been treated as years. In Sanskrit the term 'Varsha' means a year and also a field. Now the necessity of weapons is over and his security also is confirmed. The battle that entails necessary weaponry and also security that caused anxiety in the Pandava camp, will take place upon the earth and the hero of that battle, Arjuna is a symbol and representative of the beings of this earth. So he is to come back here.

Arjuna met Yudhisthira and others on his way back home while they were on a pilgrimage. The purpose of his expedition to heaven was fulfilled and everyone was happy now. Meanwhile, one day Bhima alone was out for hunting and did not return timely causing alarm among them. After a long absence of Bhima, Yudhisthira going out with Dhaumya in search of him saw that Bhima was helplessly enclosed under coils of a great python. Observing Bhima's helplessness Yudhisthira wanted to know how all this happened and who the snake was. Bhima replied that the python was their ancestor, king Nahusa who being cursed by rishi Agastya had metamorphosed as a great python living in the jungle. But how could the python have made a prisoner of a strong man like Bhima — asked Yudhisthira in reply to which the snake said that whenever it coiled anybody instantly his vital energy got lost. This was the effect of the curse of the Brahmin.

The python is the symbol of ignorance of beings. Whenever ignorance engulfs the beings they lose their vital strength; ignorance confirms the existence of beings. Notwithstanding having been empowered in all respects, the beings actively assist the ignorance to grow keeping aside all their energies. Ignorance at the first step makes the beings powerless and then compels them to follow its own course. Bhima is the reality of air and manifests the active energy and that active energy under the influence of ignorance fails to guide the performance of ordained actions, rather it attracts the beings to rush for their destruction.

What is the nature of ignorance and why does it attract the beings in such a way? We have said it earlier that two antagonistic forces and esses are always active in the world of beings. As the high and ebb tides are there naturally, likewise knowledge and ignorance are there to remain in the human society; but in comparison to knowledge, ignorance is greater in proportion. This world is comprehensible by sense-perception and the mind. The mind resolves and dissolves too but the area of resolution is far wide than that of dissolution. Resultantly taking the refuge of mental resolution ignorance thrives in the human world and in such a state the vitality and vital energy are bound to follow the course of ignorance.

In course of disclosing his identity the snake said obtaining plentiful of wealth without labour he became proud and because of his pride he appointed the Brahmins insulting them to be the bearers of his palanquin and he was cursed by rishi Agastya. When he was cursed, his performance of sacrifices, of austerity and restraint of senses and also the study of the Vedas could not ward off the effect of the curse. But why did they fail? In the material world sacrifices, austerity, restraining the senses are but the traditional religious activities of stock notions that ensure the prospect of enjoyment of sense-objects in the realm of desire. Such activities do not make a man wise of the Almighty nor do they offer him peace and Ananda. The knowledge that desists a man from unscrupulous enjoyment of sense-objects, until that knowledge dawns upon him he cannot come out of the cycle of death and rebirth. But such religious activities of stock notions are incapable to do so, yet the attraction for such kind of activities of the beings knows no bound. King Nahusa was a successful man in this kind of activities, who did not hesitate to insult the knowers of Brahman which meant that he insulted Brahman and the Brahmins should never condone this audacity. They cursed the king who became repentant of his own misdeed and knowledge finally dawned on him and he was released from the curse.

One should think of the means to overcome the ignorance that conceals even the active energy of beings. Firstly, one is required to identify ignorance as such and then to repent for it. Struck with repentance one understands the nature of ignorance and with this sense one seeks freedom from ignorance. In such an instance beings are required to search for the refuge of Guru who is beyond both ignorance and knowledge. But beings are unable to find out Guru, yet he appears before them at the time of need. Here in this instance Yudhisthira came to Bhima when he was constricted by a large python who was indeed ignorance symbolically.

Now, Yudhisthira's immediate duty was to save Bhima from the gulp of the python. But Yudhisthira observed that ignorance sought answers to his questions from Guru. Guru decides first after observation as to whether the questioner is getting delight with the answers given to him, if not, he may decline to make any reply. This delight is the binding string that establishes the relation between Guru and the disciple. Ananda is the nature of Guru. Yudhisthira tells the python, if his questioner becomes delighted with his answers then he will do that. He also said, "Without knowing as to whether you have known the solitary Purusha, knowable of the Brahmins, I am not to make any answer to your questions." At the end of the question-answer session with him being fully satisfied the python freed Bhima.

We have said that Nahusa in the form of a python was ignorance and to Bhima he said that he was Bhima's ancestor. Let us see whether there is any propriety between the two. With the passage of time owing to our extraneous vision we become more and more attracted to enjoyable sense-objects and create a distance between Consciousness (Chaitanya) and ourselves. This tradition is continuing since the days of our ancestors. The result is ignorance and the ancestors have become synonymous with it. Crossing the barrier of ignorance we should move forward to knowledge and that should be the aim of ours — the future generations.

Duryodhana's Expedition To Dvaitavana

Once a wandering Brahmin came to Hastinapura with the information of the Pandavas after visiting them in the Dvaitavana. He narrated the sufferings of them to Dhritarastra who then became very sorry for them, even expressed his repentance too. Dhritarastra was rueing alone but at a time he began to think aloud. "Dice-loving Shakuni being lured of the game of dice, had done a very evil deed; and the Pandavas had done a very disagreeable thing then by not exterminating Duryodhana and others. I too had done many an act of crime being obedient to my evil-souled son, now it seems that the time is ripe for total destruction of the Kurus indeed." After a while he again said, "Dhananjaya going to the realm of Indra from the forest and collecting four kinds of celestial weapons, has come to the earth; so his prowess is quite extra-ordinary, who can endure his prowess? ...Is there any man going to heaven with physical body does ever wish to come back to the earth? So it seems that the Kurus cursed by their fate be uprooted by Arjuna alone, no doubt." When Dhritarastra was thus repenting aloud, Shakuni heard his lamentations.

Along with Karna, Shakuni at once closeted with Duryodhana and said. "Maharaja, you have made the valiant Pandavas roaming like mendicants, now enjoy this empire like the king of gods. .... You alone with your intelligence appropriated the wealth and kingdom of Yudhisthira and for some time your rivals are passing their days in penury; so you have enough leave to enjoy the happiness....O the greatest of the Kurus, they are now deposed from their kingdom and poor; but you are the king, prosperous; so this is the time to meet with them and that is obligatory on your part and they will look at you to see the rare nobility and an all round benefactor in you as King Yayati, the son of Nahusa." Lately he said again, "As one gets delighted having a son, wealth and kingdom, likewise it is rare a pleasure to see the utter poverty of the enemies. Being successful you will be pleased to see Dhananjaya wearing tree-bark or deer-skin and when your beloved ladies well-dressed with costly materials, will meet sorrowful Draupadi wearing deer-skin or hide then she will surely censure her poor life and herself too.

Listening to the words of Karna and Shakuni pleased Duryodhana said, he also had the same thoughts in mind but Dhritarastra was not permitting him to go to the Pandavas as he knew "...we have no other motive to go to Dvaitavana except to extirpate the Pandavas." He again said, "O Karna, what would be more delightful than to see Drupadi in ochry clothes in the forest. I would be very much happy and my joy will know no bound if Yudhisthira and Bhimsena look on me as a man of extra-ordinary power and wealth. But now what should I do? By which means should I go to Dvaitavana? How to get the permission of the king? Please find out a means to go there conferring with Shakuni and Duhshasana.

Next day Karna informed Duryodhana, "O Maharaja, an expedient has been arrieved at, listen to me! It is your immediate duty to look after the milkmen's colonies there in Dvaitavana and let us go there on the plea of inspection. King Dhritarastra will surely permit us to go there considering the obligation to that effect. Conferring with Karna on his proposal it was planned as to how to get the permission of Dhritarastra. According to the plan Karna and Shakuni approached the king saying that the milkmen's colonies were in a very pleasurable place and it was the right time to ascertain the age, colour etc. and to accord serial number to each of the calves there and Duryodhana was also very much desirous of hunting, so he should please be permitted to go there. Initially Dhritarastra declined, saying, "The human tigers in form of the Pandavas are there." Then Shakuni approached him adducing various reasons and finally saying, "we have no desire to meet the Pandavas there. We would not go to their dwelling nor oppress them by any means."

After having their word of honour Dhritarastra permitted them to go to Dvaitavana. Duryodhana started for Dvaitavana with his retinue and solders and reached there. A large water-body around which Yudhisthira was residing making huts there. Duryodhana ordered his men to build a pleasure-house on one side of that water body. But the ground was on the path of the king of the Gandhavas that led to the water for his sports. Duryodhana ordered to build the house on that very spot and the Gandharva guards forbade them. On being reported to Duryodhana regarding this interdiction, he ordered his men to teach the Gandharvas a lesson and sent his soldiers with them.

Meanwhile, Chitrasena, the king of the Gandharvas was informed of Duryodhana in details. Angry Chitrasena ordered his soldiers, "Go post-haste and teach those non-aryans a good lesson." Therefore a fierce encounter ensued between the forces and the Kaurava soldiers being afraid of the prowess of the Gardharvas left the battle-field. Karna alone fought valianty and killed many Gandharva soldiers. At a time when the Gandharva force become somewhat weak, King Chitrasena joined his forces and made Kauravas so much fearful applying illusory tricks, that they left the battle-field being weak and frightful. Karna was still fighting; but after a while he too fled and Duryodhana was left alone. He was made a captive while his wives were abducted. Being driven by the Gandharva forces the Kaurava soldiers took the refuge of the Pandavas and told. "O Pandavas, the Gandharvas have captured king Duryodhana, Durvishaha, Durmukha, Durjana and the royal ladies, now please rescue them."

On getting the news of Duryodhana's defeat and captivity Bhima became happy and he said, "What we relentlessly could have done by collecting horses and elephants with much hardship, has been done today by the Gandharvas." Putting a stop to Bhima's elation Yudhisthira told him, "O Vrikodara, the Kauravas being fearful and distressed have taken our refuge; how can you say all this? ...The Gandharvas are smearing our family by capturing Duryodhana and abducting the ladies forcefully. So now save the sheltered person and the honour of the family, get up and be armed. O

Bhima, uniting with Arjuna, Nakula and Sahadeva please release Duryodhana from the clutches of the Gandharvas."

Ordered by Yudhisthira the four brothers started for the battle field. At first in a light warfare the Gandharvas did not react so much. At a time Arjuna asked them, "O the movers of the sky, please release my brother Duryodhana." The Gandharvas replied, "O Sir, we act obeying single mindedly the orders of our king and accept his rule, as he has ordered us, we act accordingly. We have no other ruler than he." As a rejoinder Arjuna said, "It is highly unbecoming of the Gandharva king to abduct others' wives and to be intimate with the humans. If you do not free them easily I will do that by showing my prowess, no doubt."

But Arjuna's warning could not yield the desired result. Therefore, a fierce fighting ensued between the sides and after a while wounded Gandharva king revealed his identity to Arjuna saying. "O Arjuna, I am your loving friend Chitrasena." Surprised Arjuna asked Chitrasena how he could be a party to the coercion with the Kauravas. Chitrasena said in reply that Duryodhana intended to see with his own eyes the wretched condition of the Pandavas in the forest and to ridicule Draupadi showing his retinue and opulence. Indra in heaven could know of his intentions and ordered me, "Go immediately and bring captive Duryodhana to me." now they were to go to Indra with captive Duryodhana. Arjuna said, "If you like to do any good to me, then release Duryodha; he is our brother and Dharmaraja (Yudhisthira) earnestly desires his freedom." Chitrasena replied. "...this evil-soul cheated Dharmaraja and Drupadi. He could not know of his evil intentions. Let us go to him to apprise him of the happenings. Then what he says, would be done."

They all came to Yudhisthira who thanked the Gandharvas for their good treatment to the Kauravas and bidding adieu to them turning to Duryodhana he said, "O Brother! Never be so daring as the persons of rare feat of daring can not be happy ever. However, go back home happily without having any anxiety in mind."

Since the Pandavas have been exiled, the Kauravas used to gather information of the Pandavas and the Pandavas also did the same about the Kauravas encouragingly and in a regular course. The cause was of course war. Both sides were certain that on expiry of the period of exile the war was inevitable. One side was seriously intent on winning the war while the other was egar to do away with the possibility of war but they did not know how to do it.

On the other hand, at Hastinapura having the news of Pandavas' difficulty in exile, Dhritarastra became distressed thinking of the hardship Yudhisthira was undergoing. At the thought of Yudhisthira's daily life was full of hardship, Dhitarastra was pained at heart and repented for the past misdeeds of his sons while admitting of his own role too was intertwined in all that, he became fearful of the certainty of the total destruction of his line. While he was speaking out his thoughts mixed with jealously, by chance, Shakuni heard his soliloquy. The mind is blind indeed but it can visualize the consequences because of the influence of consciousness inherent in it.

This thought of the mind was perchance revealed to Delusion (Shakuni). Delusion observes the thought process of the mind meticulously and whenever it perceives that there is a possibility of enjoyment of sense-objects, it activates its influence to make this possibility brighter. In this instance the same has happened. When the mind is repentant for its past misdeeds, it may free itself of the influence of delusion and desire at any moment by changing its own resolution while delusion never approaches of it. Hence on hearing the soliloquy of Dhritarastra expressing his repentance, Shakuni became active and accompanied by Karna went to Duryodhana to incite him against the Pandavas without telling anything about Dhritarastra. Addressing Duryodhana he said, the Pandavas were now lost of kingdom, wretched and in exile. But Duryodhana now was the king of kings, graceful and opulent. If wealthy Duryodhana now could meet them in the forest, he would be happy; especially to see Draupadi clad in ochre clothes would be a matter of delight.

Duryodhana agreed. He too liked to go to Dvaitavana but the only obstacle was Dhritarastra. He knew why Duryodhana was desirous to go there and so he did not permit him. But desire too was not to be silenced. As Duryodhana knew this truth, Shakuni and Karna also knew it. Therefore, they three conferred and resolved that hiding their actual intention they would approach the king for his permission advancing an ordinary alibi and it was that in the milkmen's colony at Dvaitavana they would go to prepare a statistical document of the cows and to mark the calves with serial numbers, of course, after finishing this job hunting could be taken up. Dhritarastra permitted them to go on the eagerness and assurance given by Shakuni. This is but a game of hide and seek settled amicably. The mind knew it well that neither Shakuni nor Duryodhana would honour the promise given to the king but Dhritarastra was bound to permit them to go to Dvaitavana. The blind king was undone.

At any time Duryodhana can go beyond Dhritarastra to fulfil his desires for enjoyment, but he does not do that. He gets Dhritarastra's permission on each of his occasions and Dhritarastra too permits him under compulsion. Why is an insolent and arrogant son like Duryodhana so much obedient to his father? The reason is howsomuch powerful the cardinal passions be, they cannot attach themselves to sense-objects let alone the question of enjoying those sense-objects. The senses become attached to the sense-objects and of course, being permitted by the mind. Whether the sense-objects carried by the senses, will be accepted for enjoyment or not will be decided first by the mind and then on being permitted by the mind, the way to enjoyment will be decided and then being permitted by the mind, those sense-objects will be enjoyed by the mind with the help of the senses and sense-organs. The cardinal passions (ripus) are only the inspiration for enjoyment of sense-objects. So Duryodhana is to wait for Dhritarastra's nod of consent.

On being permitted Duryodhana started for Dvaitavana. On reaching the destination Duryodhana's only duty was to belittle the Pandavas, to oppress them mentally and show his wealth to them. So he ordered to build a pleasure-house on one side of the water body around which the Pandavas used to live in their makeshift huts. The plot selected for the pleasure-house was on the way which the king of the Gandharvas used to go to the waterbody for sports with the apsaras and being guarded by the Gandharva guards. As the place was near the Pandava's habitation, Duryodhana selected the plot. But the Kaurava men were resisted by the

Gandharva guards from constructing the building at the initial stage.

A water-body may happen to be in a forest and on its bank men may live too by making huts there. But what the significance of this water-body in the tale? The life on earth from birth to death is not a fountain of milk and honey; there are mutually contradicting energies and esses and their actions and reactions as well as the three disturbances to endure. Yet every life revolves round a central belief which being amalgamated with the existence of beings in its deep depth makes him do his ordained actions at the proper time. Any ideal, any morality even a particular life-style having the basis of Dharma may become a centre of belief. However, it is a truth born of Dharma, — its formal exposition may be different.

Water is essential for life. On the bank of the water-body the huts are the symbol of existence of the Pandavas and the water-body symbolizes the centre of their belief surrounding which they live on. If this centre of belief is harmed by someone with misdeeds then that will hurt the Passdavas' belief. In that case the beings' life on earth will be prolonged and Kama (desire) spreading out its influence will cause delay in the possibility of retrieving the kingdom of the Self. Having this view to that end Duryodhana wanted to build the pleasure house on its bank. But the Gandharvas created the impediment; their king used the path for his water-sports and that would have been obstructed had the building be erected there.

Kama (Desire) may be the king of the existence of beings, but not that of Manhood. The pre-condition of attaining manhood as well as the retrieval of kingdom of the Self will be a far cry if the centre of belief is disturbed. On being aware of the evil design of desire (Duryodhana) the Gandharva king ordered the Gandharvas to fight against the Kaurava forces. In that fight Karna saved himself fleeing from the battle-filed and Duryodhana was made a captive along with his wives; he was to be brought to heaven before Indra.

But how is it that the king of the Gandharvas partakes in water-sports with the apsaras in the water-body that symbolizes the centre of belief of men?

The Gandharvas are heavenly beings. We have said earlier that they are inspirational energy of notional actions. The relation between the inspirational energy of notional action and belief is a very close one. Hence the Gandharva king comes to the water-body to partake in water-sports to be invigorated with the savour of belief. But the mischievous actions of unbridled desire undoubtedly would make the transparent ambience of the confluence of three streams of belief, manhood and outcome of notional actions polluted. So Indra ordered Chitrasena to bring him to heaven.

On the other hand, some of the Kaurava soldiers observing that Duryodhana became a captive and others were fleeing from the battle-field, came to Yudhisthira with an appeal to set Duryodhana free. Bhima became elated hearing of Duryodhana's humiliation. Yudhisthira mildly scolding him asked to remove the smear on the family first, then to think of the family feud. He ordered the four brothers to set Duryodhana and the ladies free from the clutches of the Gandharvas.

Knowing of the mischievous intents of Duryodhana Indra ordered to bring him to Indra in heaven. But had the order been executed the effect would have been disastrous as captive Duryodhana and restrained desire (Kama) are but synonymous. If Kama goes to heaven being restrained the possibility of enduring the brunt of three disturbances by the beings in the material world be more and more slender because the source of those disturbances would be dried up and at the same time the Divine Leela would be very much hampered. Yudhisthira realized this truth and ordered so.

In a fight for a short while, Chitrasena revealing himself to Arjuna said to him of the evil design of Duryodhana and the order of Indra to him. Inspite of that Arjuna requested him to bring captive Duryadhana to Yudhisthira and what he would say would be honoured. In his ashrama Yudhisthira thanked the Gandharvas and bade farewell to them; then letting Duryodhana go home with warning not to recur such happenings any more. Duryodhana left Dvaitavana bowing head heavy with the burden of shame.

Karna, Duryodhana And The Vaishnava Sacrifice

Although starting for Hastina Duryodhana could not enter the capital, so ashamed of and hateful to himself he was. On their return journey they had to halt for passing the night on the way. Next morning meeting Duryodhana Karna said to him, "It is our great good fortune that your life is not lost. You have defeated the fierce Gandharvas" etc. and then describing his own flight from the battle field he said, "There is none in this world who can do what you have done to-day so valiantly in the battle field."

In reply Duryodhana said, "O Radheya (Karna), you know nothing of our fighting and so I am not getting angry with you. You have thought we have defeated the Gandharvas with our might, but that is not the fact." Then the narrated his fight with the Gandharvas and how he along with his wives was captivated. Then his soldiers appealed to the Pandavas to free them, who then arranged to set them free. Meanwhile Gandharva Chitrasena disclosed "all my evil designs to Arjuna." Now he had no means to cover up his shameful face. The death in the battle field was far better than this ignominy.

Duryodhana's only thought was what he would say to Dhritarastra and other principal persons of the royalty of Hastina; his death was more preferable. "I do not like to live in the perspective of the thoughts of mine disclosed, ridiculed and insulted by my enemies at the time of crisis."

So Duryodhana resolved to die of fasting and also decided to install Duhshasana in his own place. Knowing of the decision of Duryodhana, Duhshasana began to cry even. Meanwhile Karna came there. Advising him to have patience and to console him Karna said, "Today I come to know that you are a very light minded man...." "The Pandavas are the subjects of the Kaurava kingdom. If they do some desired actions for their lord that should not be the cause of anxiety to you. The Pandavas have done their duty but that need not be considered to be the cause of your thoughtfulness." Then he said, "If you do not pay any heed to my words. I am but to engage myself to nurse your feet. I cannot live without you." But no change of view became perceptible in the behaviour of Duryodhana.

Then came Shakuni and said, "I see you are behaving just the opposite to that pining for the facts which should make you glad and the Pandavas be sorry for. Now calm yourself and do not commit suicide, rather return the kingdom to the Pandavas being satisfied with their service; then you will be placed on your dharma and your fame will be spread everywhere." He again said, "... Return their paternal kingdom and live happily for ever." But Shakuni's requests could not make Duryodhana change his resolution. Purifying himself he sat on a seat of kusha grass and forshaking all his activities and concentrating his mind.

On the other hand, the demons being defeated by the gods and driven to hell performed a sacrifice out of which there appeared a peculiar-looking serving goddess who asked the demons, "O Demous, how should I serve you?" The demons requested her, "Please bring fasting Duryodhana to us." And he was brought to hell. There the demons consoled him saying, "Just see! Persons committing suicide go to hell and become infamous among men you please give up the idea of committing suicide that enhances the happiness of the enemies and destroys dharma, wrath, happiness, fame and powers. You are not a natural human but a divine superman...." "Maharaja! Earlier we get you as a graceful boon of Maheswara (Shiva). The frontal part of your body is made of thunder which cannot be pierced through with any arms. The rear part of the body is made of flowers by the Goddess herself beholding which the feminine mind be charmed; so your body is not a human one."

The valiant kshatriyas like Bhagadatta, expert in handling divine weapons will uproot your enemies; so give up your moroseness. You have nothing to be afraid of and only to help the demons to have come to the earth. The other demons while bewitch them such as Bhishma, Drona and Kripa etc. will fight with your enemies being kindless. Then they will not consider the relationship such as father, son, brother, friend, relative, kinsmen, boy and the old and fight without forgiving them. Owing to severe demonic influence they will fight against all fiercely, no doubt."

"O king! We have found out the way to allay your fear of Arjuna."

"The soul of Narakasura slain in the past has assumed the form of Karna who will fight against Krishna and Arjuna and defeat them in the war remembering the past animosity of his earlier birth.... As the Pandavas are the minions of the gods, likewise you are our only refuge; so be restrained please from this ill-intention of yours and go home never opting for any other mission."

Listening to the words of consolation of the demons Duryodhana gained back his self-confidence regarding defeating the Pandavas. Next morning Duryodhana ordered to start for Hastina being confident to some extent in the words of the demons but keeping them a secret.

Arriving at Hastina he had a chance meeting with Bhishma. He said to him that he had forbidden him to go to Dvaitavana but he did not pay any heed to his advice; going there Duryodhana even being rescued by the Pandavas from his enemies, he had not been ashamed a bit. He also added, "The carpenter's son, Karna fled away from the battle field in full view of your army and this fact approves of the prowess of the Pandavas and that of the evil minded carpenter's son." Bhishma's opinion was to make a treaty at once.

Being angry with the straight comments of Bhishma, Karna said to Duryodhana, "Bhishma always upbraids us and praises the Pandavas. To disparage you means to disparage me. He always demean me in your presence. Surely I am not to digest his praises for the Pandavas in your presence to disparage you. So please permit me to conquer the world. Strong four Pandavas had done it earlier, I'll do that alone."

Duryodhana became pleased with the heroics of Karna and he at once permitted him. Karna too set out at once to conquer the world and returned after conquering many a kingdom collecting huge amount of levies. Pleased Duryodhana warmly welcomed him and said, "O Karna, may you be blessed. What I did not get from Vahlika, Bhishma, Drona and Kripa, today I get it fully from you. Moreso, I am to grow under your shade. Neither the Pandavas nor are the other powerful kings equal to you."

Seeing the eloquent welcome to Karna jealous Shakuni thought that certainly he had defeated the Pandavas.

And Karna said to Duryodhana, "Duryodhana, you have no more enemy in the world. Now you may rule the world like Indra without any fear." In reply Duryodhana said, "Seeing the Rajasuya sacrifice of the son of Pandu I also desire to perform it. Please arrange to fulfil my desire."

But the priest when called for, opined, "Maharaja, so long Yudhisthira is alive none of your family is eligible for Rajasuya sacrifice; more so, your father is alive; so it goes against you. But there is another sacrifice as important as Rajasuya sacrifice which you may perform easily. It is known as Vaishnava sacrifice." It was then decided that it would be performed. So along with arrangements for the sacrifice, the guests were being invited. Duhshasana ordered a messenger, "Go to the Dvaitavana and invite the evil-souled Pandavas and the Brahmins residing there with them." Yudhisthira however declined to accept the invitation on the plea of non-completion of thirteen years of exile.

Performance of the sacrifice was concluded. Karna said to Duryodhana, "O Maharaja, now you have performed the sacrifice without any hindrance. But when you will perform the Rajasuya sacrifice with pomp and grandeur defeating and uprooting the Pandavas, then I'll serve you much better, no doubt. Later he said, "I'll not wash my feet nor take a drop of water to drink before I kill Arjuna. I will take up the asura vow from today. If anybody comes to pray for anything I'll give away that to him. I am to dishearten none at all.

Having the news of Karna's vow Yudhisthira became anxious.

There is an adage that a shameless person neither be made ashamed nor can be insulted. But facts approve of Duryodhana's shamefulness as well as his sense of insult. He cannot deny the series of facts that happened to him but they were very hard to accept. Firstly, his defeat and captivity by the Gandharvas, secondly, he had to buy his freedom being desired by Yudhisthira and at the cost of the prowess of Bhima and Arjuna. Thirdly, forgetting all his misdeed, forgiving Yudhisthira behaved with him humanely. Proud Duryodhana could not concede that the king whose kingdom he had appropriated by playing the deceitful game of dice and who had been compelled to go to exile for thirteen years, that tree-bark-wearing Yudhisthira had become the saviour of the proud Kaurava. The more the truth comes to his mind the more his glory and the serenity make his own existence meaningless. This mental torment induces him to commit suicide. After death there will be no compulsion to bow down the head before the magnanimity of Yudhisthira.

But that was not to be.

Firstly, the arguments and requests of Karna and Shakuni failed to prevent Duryodhana from his resolution of committing suicide. If Duryodhana dies then the lord of the cardinal passions is sure to be inactive and in that case the demons will be orphaned. Realizing this truth the demons of the hell began to perform a sacrifice. After offering the final oblation to the fire of sacrifice a goddess came out of that fire. This sacrifice of the demons is but the preparation for enjoyment of erotic pleasure; and the goddess is but the inspiration for erotic actions. That goddess was asked to bring Duryodhana to hell. The significance of bringing him to hell is to prepare for and enjoy erotic pleasure; if Kama remains absent the inspiration for enjoyment is bound to be futile. Hence he is to come to hell. But why the demons were so eager to save Duryodhana? They would be orphaned only, if so, what does it matter to the Lord of creation? Yes, it does matter.

Gods and demons are but two sides of the same coin; the gods belong to the heaven and demons to the hell. But both gods and demons are the active energies of the creation. Both are important in the realm of creation. Moreover, the creation has not yet reached such a state that extrovert Kama be made introvert by restraining to be put to order. Rather to maintain the extraneous efforts of the demons for continuing the creation desired by God. The demons' efforts became successful.

After his arrival at hell the demons consled him and said he should not commit suicide and he was to give up such an evil resolution. Later they said, "You are not a natural man but a great man..." according to them he was born of the grace of Lord Shiva. The frontal part of the body was made of thunder and no weapons could pierce it and the rear part of it was made of flowers by the goddess and viewing that the women would be charmed. So Lord Shiva and his divine consort were his actual parents. The father had created the front part of his body with thunder and was impenetrable. The rear part of it was made of flowers by the mother and it was soft but charmed the women. So on both sides he was unconquerable.

The demons say Kama is a heavenly great man. How? The change in both form and character is possible. When he is a dweller of hell and the lord of demons, he is the symbol of eroticism — a symbol of extreme extroversion and when the same Kama changes its form and character as well it becomes divine love being introvert and expressing the greatness and glory of the Supreme, so he is a great man indeed. Such a great man should not have either fear or doubt. The brave Kshatriyas under the spell of the demons will destroy all his enemies fighting valiantly. Apart from this, the soul of Narakasura engrossing Karna will enable him to fight against Krishna and Arjuna and kill Arjuna. He will die by the hands of avarice and cruelty. Thus the demons in hell consoled him and Duryodhana gains back his self-confidence.

After the return to Hastina grandsire Bhishma shot the first gun. He forbade him to go to Dvaitavan and as a result of ignoring Bhishma's advice Karna fled from the battle field and Duryodhana was defeated and became a captive, who had to earn his freedom by the Pandavas which could not make him shameful. In his opinion it was just to conclude a treaty with the Pandavas.

Had Duryodhana ever upheld justness?

But Karna reacted to the words of Bhishma. Looking down upon him comparing with the Pandavas, made him angry and to prove his prowess he proposed to set out to conquer the world for which he sought Duryodhana's permission which he readily accorded.

Grandsire Bhishma is the ego — a very important reality. Duryodhana is Kama (desire), Karna is avarice and Shakuni is delusion — these three are cardinal passions and they three rule the kingdom of Hastinapura. Among these three Duryodhana holds the mace to rule though he is not the king, — Dhritarastra is the king but blind. Bhishma does not like this arrangement to rule the kingdom and he had no confidence in any of them nor any affection. So he shoots the shafts of sarcasm aiming to them as and when chances permit him and they also endure them. But this time his caustic comment pierced through the heart of Karna because of his fleeing away from the battle-field, which was not an act of heroism, he knew. So to redeem his glory he decided to go to conquer the world and Duryodhana at once accorded his consent. The avarice is spread all over the body and it has no bar to conquer the world.

Duryodhana praised Karna profusely on his return conquering the world as he collected huge levies. Hearing the praise of Karna Shakuni became jealous, he thought as if Karna had defeated the Pandavas.

Karna told that now Duryodhana had no foes any more and he could rule the kingdom peacefully. Then Duryodhana told Karna that he was desirous of performing Rajasuya sacrifice as did Yudhisthira but the priest opined that it was not possible so long Yudhisthira and Dhritarastra were alive. Hence another sacrifice of the like could of course be performed — the Vaishnava sacrifice.

The significance of performing this sacrifice was to establish indomitable influence of Kama (desire). But it could not become a square one as the Pandavas did not accept the invitation. His influence remained unfulfilled to them. Karna understood this truth much more than Duryodhana. So he said when Duryodhana would perform Rajasuya Sacrifice destroying the Pandavas, he would serve Duryodhana better. Then after taking the oath to kill Arjuna, he said, he would take the demonic vow henceforth and he would give away everything that would be begged for. Taking the oath to kill

Arjuna he at once nullified the oath in the same breath unknowingly.

What an irony of fate! Yudhisthira was anxious for nothing.

Rishi Durvasa And The Forest-Dwelling Pandavas

The Pandavas were passing their days happily in the forest — such a piece of information reached Duryodhana. He along with Duhshasana and Karna thought that it would be just to devise a mischievous prank to disturb the Pandavas there; and a chance came in hand.

Once Rishi Durvasa with his ten thousand disciples became Duryodhana's guest. Duryodhana giving up his indolence served the rishi as he could do. Being pleased with his service the rishi wishing his well-being asked him to pray for a boon saying that nothing would be unavailable as he was pleased.

Duryodhana gladly prayed for the boon saying. "O Brahmin, King Yudhisthira is the eldest and greatest in our family. He is a man of qualities and humility. Now he is living in the forest with his brothers. I would pray you to be his guest with your disciples as you have come to us. But you are to go there when Draupadi feeding her husbands and Brahmins and also taking her meal will be happily resting. Please show me this grace." "I must do this for my love to you," said Durvasa and departed.

Thereafter one day Durvasa with his ten thousand disciples appeared before Yudhisthira knowing well that the Pandavas and Draupadi were resting happily after taking their meal. Yudhisthira received them cordially and requested to be his guests for the day and said, "Please come soon after completing your diurnal ablutions and rituals of worship." Durvasa thought how could he be able to arrange the meals for so many persons? However, he went to the river for his daily washing and prayer.

Now Draupadi was in dire distress. Everybody had taken the meal. There should not remain anything on the plate. When she was bewildered as to how she could serve meals to ten thousand and one guests she remembered the Almighty. She earnestly prayed to Krishna to save her from this distress. Responding to her earnest call Krishna at once came to the Pandava's ashrama. Draupadi informed Him of Durvasa. Without heeding to her words He said He was very much hungry and to arrange for His food immediately. Draupadi pleaded that she had already taken her meal and nothing could be had of the plate. Krishna emphatically told her to bring the plate to show Him right now without cutting any jokes. She brought the plate to Him. There was a small particle of food attached to the edge of the plate and taking that He said to her, "Let the Universal Soul be pleased and propitiated with it" and asked Bhima to call for the Brahmins to take their meals.

The Brahmins engaged in washing in the river water began to belch of full stomach and addressed, "O Rishi...we are so full of stomach that we are unable to take food any more; for nothing the cooking is going on there." In reply Durvasa said, "We have committed a sin for this meaningless cooking. Lest we be turned to ashes in the fire of the ire of the Pandavas; so let us flee away from this place. Once the fire of their anger be inflamed, it will burn us like the fibres of cotton wool. So let us leave this place without anybody's knowledge." They all dispersed to all directions.

Now, coming to the river bank Bhima could see none of the Brahmins and in course of search for them he knew they all had disappeared. He thought that they would be coming at night to their distress and on his return he informed of that. Then Krishna narrated the whole story to the Pandavas and lastly said that "Being afraid of the energy of the prowess of the Pandavas they had departed."

The extraneous Kama desires that the beings be extraneous. The more the extraversion of beings be grown, the more beings be fallen under the influence of Kama (desire) along with avarice and delusion. To bring the actions of beings under the purview of Kama, it gains the assistance of other cardinal passions — disciplined or indisciplined that may be — it gets the liberal support of the mind. So its deceit and mischief become boundless. It becomes indomitable.

Earlier in the chapter of 'Kaunteya Karna' we have said that short-tempered and ill-speaking rishi Durvasa was the symbol of the energy of Guru. The heart within the body is the region of Guru and the esses sprung of that manifest his energy as well as his importance but all such esses do not manifest His glory and importance equally everywhere and always. Some of the symbols of Guru expose the said importance in such a way that they are glorifying themselves rather than Guru. But it is otherwise in fact. Owing to our blurred vision and limited intelligence we think so. Durvasa is such a character. He became a guest at the palace of Hastinapura and Duryodhana himself shouldered the responsibility to treat the guest and his ten thousand disciples to fulfil his ill-design which was not unknown to the rishi —

we may assume; but he kept it so secret that Duryodhana could not guess even an iota of it. Accepting the service of Duryodhana the rishi offered him a chance to bow down his head before a symbol of truth despite his selfish and mischievous intent. At the time of departure he asked Duryodhana to pray for a boon knowing well that he would not ask for any boon beneficial to his own self or any other yet the rishi granted boon prayed for knowing that owing to this boon Duryodhana would have a lesson of being restrained at least for the time-being. Not only the rishi granted the boon but to activate that he came to Kamyakavana. Having the reception and invitation of Yudhisthira he became thoughtful of how could he feed him and his so many disciples?

He knew that at such an inopportune moment Yudhisthira was unable to arrange for the provision to feed so many persons. Next moment he discarded the thought as it was a problem for Yudhisthira and he was to find out the solution.

Draupadi, on the other hand, became bewildered. At last finding no way out she decided to take the refuge of Krishna who came to Kamyakavana and heard what Draupadi told Him and at once He asked for some food as He was very much hungry. In reply Draupadi said that there was no food at all in her store. He insisted to bring the plate that was given by the sun. She brought it to Him. A food particle was left on the plate. Taking that Himself Krishna said, "Let the Universal Soul be pleased and propitiated with it."

The untimely arrival of ten thousand and one guests at the ashrama could not make Yudhisthira moved nor was he anxious at all. To remain stolid in any situation was his characteristic. He thought that somehow some arrangements would be made, but how, he had no idea of that nor Draupadi too had any. So to search for the means to overcome this critical problem she depended upon the Lord of husbands than on her own husbands. He came and solved the problem of His devotee. It is an instance of the revelation of Supreme Consciousness being attracted by the individual soul (Jivatma) and the attraction is the bhakti of a devotee. For the second time he responded to the earnest call of a devotee in person while in the first instance he remained invisible in the royal court of the Kurus to save his devotee at the moment of crisis. Of course, the nature of distress in both occasions was different. Here in the forest He came and said He was hungry but Draupadi was running short of food. He asked to bring the plate given by the Sun to Him and taking a food particle from that He said, "Let the Universal Soul be pleased and propitiated with it."

The Brahmins in course of their bath could not understand when they began to eructate with their full stomachs and they were unable to take any farther food. Lest they be burnt like cotton wool in the fire of the Pandavas prowess, they dispersed to different directions in fear.

In the tale the dimension of Duryodhan, Durvasa and Draupadi — these three characters, is but 'D' which stands for Damodara, the other name of Krishna, the Supreme Consciousness and not only these three but the whole of the creation which is being evolved all the while towards its culmination. No creation has its own independent will. In the immeasurable universe every form is His form which means all the forms are His Form and likewise there is a single body in the universe having a single soul, a single mind, single sense and all these belong to Him. Whenever he expresses his will that will becomes activated in individual minds. So when he says, "Let the universal soul be pleased and propitiated," everyone was propitiated and the truth was only known to Him and realized by Draupadi.

Duryodhana is deceitful, malicious and extremely jealous; Durvasa is wrathful, ill-speaking, visionary and truthful and honours the austerity of others. Draupadi is the subtle body (Jivatma). She is the guiding force of the beings; but this energy of her to guide the beings is but a gift of the Supreme Consciousness. The Leela Krishna performed in a forest hut was unique indeed, the significance of which was realized by Draupadi alone instantly while Durvasa even could not. He could have realized it later through medition had he desired so. But to realize it by any means and at any time by Duryodhana was quite impossible. The author held up three different mirrors to his readers to comprehend His Leela to honour the bhakti of His devotee.

The Abduction Of Draupadi By Jayadratha

Once Jaydratha, the king of Sindhu being desirous of marriage was out with some other kings in search of a suitable bride and roaming here and there came to the Kamyaka forest. Incidentally he could see Draupadi standing in front of their make shift hut. At the first sight he fell in love with her and decided to marry, of course, taking her to his capital. With this view he deputed an accompanying king, Kotikasya to gather information regarding her and to observe the proceedings between the two he himself remained standing at a distance beside a water-body. Kotikasya coming to Draupadi disclosed his identity and then showing Jayadratha he said of his identity. Knowing that Kotikasya was the son of Suratha of the kingdom of Shivi, Draupadi said, "O Shaivya, I am the daughter of King Drupada, my name is Krishna. I have taken Yudhisthira, Bhima, Arjuna, Nakula and Sahadeva as my husbands. At present they have gone out for hunting leaving me here." Then she invited them to be her guests.

Meanwhile, looking Draupadi from a distance and listening to her identity Jayadratha on the plea of seeing her, came and entered the make-shift hut and began to converse with her. In response to her hospitality he said, "O Lady, there is no necessity to remain the wife of the sons of Pandu enduring so much hardship. Better be my wife leaving them and then you may enjoy happily the whole of Sindhu and Sauvira kingdoms.

Sharply protesting to his words she began to pass time saying sweet words. But Jayadratha had no necessity to pass time. So he attracted her holding her cloth despite her forbiddance, then she shoving him off made him fall upon the floor. But rising from the ground he held her and forcibly took her to his chariot and went away with her. The only witness to the incident was Dhaumya. After a while the Pandavas returned and hearing from Dhaumya of the misadventure of Jayadratha, followed him and began an encounter with him. Many of his soldiers were slain. Being afraid of the Pandavas, Jayadratha himself fled away getting down from the chariot leaving Draupadi alone. Bhima asked Yudhisthira to go to the ashrama accompanied with Nakula Sahadeva and Draupadi; he with Arjuna would follow Jayadratha to award him a condign punishment. Getting him from his cover they beat him much and made five cupolas with tufts of hair upon his head brought him to the ashrama. On request of Yudhisthira and Draupadi he was allowed to go.

Being insulted and humiliated Jayadratha became broken-hearted and going to Gangadvara began severe austerity. Lord Shiva being pleased asked him to pray for a boon. He chose the boon to defeat the Pandava brothers. Shiva said that he might defeat the four brothers except Arjuna.

Krishna, the daughter of Drupada is a friend of Krishna. But the earlier history of this friendship is unknown to us. It may be assumed that it commenced with her marriage to the Pandava brothers, of course it is a factual assumption only. Krishna as Supreme Consciousness is the friend of all creatures, indeed, although we cannot realize this truth in our materialistic knowledge. Secondly, the relation between Supreme Consciousness beyond all realities and the realities sprung of Supreme Consciousness is undeniable. But individual soul (Jivatma) is not a reality but the manifestation of the Supreme Being. So the relation between the two is beyond all questions and inevitable.

Despite this friendship between Supreme Consciousness and individual soul the beings are not free from fear; they are always driven by fear. The fear is the second attention of beings. Six fears are driving the beings always — they are fears of pain and pleasure, of hunger and thirst and of birth and death. Among these six the fear of death is the principal one. The beings think that everything perishes in death; there will be no scope for enjoyment of sense-objects and no pleasure too on that score. Within the body Jaydratha is the fear of death. But what was his necessity to abduct Draupadi?

The exile for the Pandavas was tenured for twelve years (one yuga). We have said it earlier, that is actually the life-time of beings ranging from birth to death which has been termed as one yuga (aeon). When this tenure is over death is inevitable and with the touch of death the body is rendered to be the disposable waste only. But the arrival of this inevitable is necessary otherwise how will the beings have their new bodies?

Jayadratha is the son-in-law of Dhritarastra. He wandered here and there in search of a bride and finally came to the Kamyakavana. There seeing Draupadi sitting on the threshold of her hut, he became so charmed that instantly he resolved to marry her. To know of her identity he sent his envoy Kotikasya a tributary king. Why did he not come to Draupadi?

Jayadratha is not death but the fear of death. All on a sudden death normally does not come to the beings. When the body becomes weak and worn out because of disease or old age it comes to the beings as the scope for enjoyment becomes circumscribed more and more.

On the other hand, the subtle body is the conductor of the physical body. If the subtle body becomes ill, the physical body shows the signs of illness. When the physical body becomes weak and worn out the fear of death engross the subtle body and the physical body becomes weak more and more. To the beings death is a disastrous culmination of life. So they are afraid of death. The fear of death comes to the subtle body first, but prior to that it becomes affected with disease. Therefore any disease comes to the subtle body first and then comes the fear of death.

So the symbol of disease, king Kotikasya was first sent to Draupadi to have her identify while the fear of death was awaiting at a distance having the view of what was going on between them. Having the information from Kotikasya regarding her identity Jayadratha came to Draupadi. But now was it possible that the husband of Duhshala, the brother-in-law of Duryodhana did not know Draupadi? Again he says, "Don't remain devoted to the Pandavas who have lost their kingdom and wanting in wealth."

Knowing well that she was the wife of the Pandavas he attempted the abduction by charming her with verbal suggestions and used his force when the first attempt failed. But how could he gather his courage to be so bold?

Physically it may be said that he was influenced by Duryodhana though it is a mere possibility. There is another aspect of the fact. The time for the Pandavas' exile was due to expire soon. We have said that the Pandavas' exile was actually the span of life of beings on earth from birth to death. On expiry of time of exile, death is a certainty and if that does not happen the exile is there to continue. If death comes naturally its beckoning becomes perceptible to the beings and they become fearful of death. The meeting of Jayadratha and Draupadi and later her forceful abduction denote the fear of death and their being fearful of death for the time being.

Now it is evident that had there been any impetus in this regard from Duryodhana or not Jayadratha's coming to Draupadi, his becoming charmed with her beauty and his forceful abduction of her — all these bear testimony to the universal law of Nature and irresistible.

The time was propitious for Jayadratha. In presence of the Pandava brothers all this could not have been happened. When they were away and busy with hunting, it was not a very hard task to abduct their wife from her home. Temporarily detached from the prowess of the Pandava brothers, Draupadi could not resist her abduction. What she could have done that she did in the Kaurava court and at the instance of Durvasa, that did not come to her mind. She could not seek the refuge of Krishna. Did she not seek his refuge willfully? No, she failed to do that. Providence did not allow her to do so. Had she taken his refuge, the series of events that happened could not have happened. So she had no conscious failure.

Meanwhile returning from hunting the Pandava brothers heard of what happened to Draupadi and followed Jayadratha to rescue her. His prowess was no match to that of the Pandava brothers.

To go to hunting by the Pandava brothers leaving Draupadi alone is symbolic of the oblivion of the physical body in respect of the subtle body. Natural law waits for none and comes the fear of death and abducts Draupadi that means the fear of death engulfs the subtle body. In such a state to detach the subtle body from the grip of the fear of death points to the fight between the Pandavas and Jayadratha. When he realized that his strength was very much insignificant before that of the Pandavas, he alighted from his chariot making Draupadi also do so and tried to run away under cover. It means the fear itself for the time being reduced its influence. Now the subtle body is free from fear. Seeing all this Bhima (vital breath) asked Yudhisthna to return to ashrama with Nakula, Sahadeva and Draupadi i.e. the reality of water and that of the earth — the two main realities necessary for nourishment of the body to be placed properly for replenishment of decay of the physical body.

On the other hand, Bhima and Arjuna observed that Jayadratha was running for cover toward the forest. Following him Bhima caught Jayadratha and asked him to identify himself as the slave of the Pandavas making signs of slavery upon his head; Jayadratha agreed. They did not kill him as Yudhisthira did not like that. Vitality and death are hostile to each other and in other words, they are the two poles of the same energy. There is the seed of death in Vital energy and that of vitality in death. But this truth is not equally revealed to the beings. So the beings are up to keep the fear of death at bay and sieze vitality with love. Hence vitality and death are each other's enemy to the understanding of the beings. So vitality cannot let loose the chance to insult and humiliate Jayadratha but did not kill him being forbidden by Yudhishira. The reality of ether is Yudhisthira who shelters everybody. Secondly, as the fear of death is regarded as the second attention, it cannot be done away with and if so happens the order of creation is sure to be disturbed. Hence Yudhisthira's alibi is he is the son-in-law of Gandhari and the husband of Duhshala.

Whatever might be the offence of Jayadratha the eldest Pandava forgave him and made him free saying. "....Never do step in the vicious way again...." But Jayadratha failed to express his gratitude to him because of his revengeful attitude. Shiva granting a boon after his austerity told him that he could win over other four Pandavas but not Arjuna; he should remain undefeated. The lord had armed Arjuna with his own weapon. Arjuna's defeat would be his own defeat. How can he grant such a boon to him? Of course, this is the logic of common understanding. The reality of tejas can ingest everything including the fear of death. So why should he be afraid of death?

Shiva explained elaborately the Leela of the Supreme Lord and concluded after speaking on Vamana Avatara, that "....Lord Vishnu....has incarnated Himself in form of Krishna....and always protects Arjuna; so even the gods cannot defeat him. How can a man defeat him?"

The Unrevealed Exile Of The Pandavas

Being unsuccessful in his attempt to abduct Draupadi, baffled and insulted Jayadratha remained inactive having the boon of defeating four Pandavas. After some time of this event the period of twelve years' exile was due to be over. Meanwhile two events took place; one was the taking away of the armour and earrings of Karna by Indra and the testing of virtuosity of Yudhisthira by Dharma.

However, on passing of twelve years the exile unrevealed was due to begin. Conferring with the brothers Yudhisthira decided to pass a year in disguise and assuming pseudonyms in the kingdom of Matsya and it was also decided that the eldest Pandava would remain there in the court of the king Virata as his courtier as an expert in the game of dice assuming the name of Kanka. Bhima would stay there in the royal kitchen in the guise of a cook. Arjuna said identifying himself as a hermaphrodite he would entertain the ladies in the palace and also impart lessons in music and dance to them. Nakula said, being an expert in horse-training and keeping, he would be the keeper of the stable concealing his identity. Sahadeva said as he was an expert in milching, bovine therapeutics and statistics he would conceal his identity and would become the keeper of the royal byre. Last of all Draupadi said, she would be tressing the queen's hair and wreathe garlands for her in the name of Sairindhri and thus it was decided to hide themselves.

As planned the Pandavas with Draupadi entered the Matsya kingdom. But before entering the capital they had to hide their weapons in such a way that they would not be visible to others and remained in tact. Having the consent of Yudhisthira it was decided to keep them on a branch of a large silk-cotton tree near the crematorium. Ordered by Yudhisthira Nakula climbed up the tree and kept the weapons and five bows binding them with the branch of the tree where rain-drops used to fall aslant. Lest someone being curious comes near the tree, a dead body was also fastened to the branch and a rumour was circulated among the herdsmen that owing to observe certain family rituals a dead body of an eighty year old woman was kept there upon the branch.

After keeping the weapons securely Yudhishira began to pray to goddess Durga singing hymns to her and the goddess being propitiated said to him, "O Pandavas, being sated I tell you that while you stay in the capital of Virata neither anyone of the capital nor would the Kauravas know of your whereabouts." After being graced by the goddess Yudhisthira wrapped the dice in a cloth went to the king in the court of Virata and said. "O king, being robbed of all my belongings, I am before you for a livelihood."

Listening to Yudhisthira king Virata sought to know his name, the origin of his family, livelihood and wherefrom he was come.

Yudhisthira replied, he was a Brahmin, Kanka by name; "Previously I was a close friend of Yudhisthira and I am an expert in the game of dice." Hearing his reply the king accepted him.

After Yudhisthira Bhima came in the guise of a cook carrying equipments for cooking. Coming before the king he said, "O king! I am a cook and my name is Vallava. I can prepare very delectable food dishes. Please take me at your service." Looking at his robust physique the king became doubtful. Observing this Bhima said, "Earlier I was working at King Yudhisthira's Kitchen. Not only am I a good cook but a good wrester also of rare qualities.

The king appointed him as a cook.

After Bhima Draupadi came in the guise of a housemaid. Present men and women became charmed with her beauty and asked, "Who are you, what do you desire?" Draupadi replied that she wanted to be engaged in any job. But nobody could believe her to be a maid. But the queen Sudeshna began to like her; she asked Draupadi, "O lady, who are you and what you like to have?"

Draupadi replied, "I am Sairindhri; he who will engage me in any job I'll leave that well-done..."

But the queen's doubts were not removed in Draupadi's words. After a long conversation she told. "...I'll offer you a residence of your liking. You are not even to touch the left-over of anyone's plate."

After Drupadi was appointed as the maid of Sudeshna, Sahadeva entered in the guise of a milk-man. He said, "O King, I am a Vaishya, Aristanemy by name and was the keeper of the Kaurava's byre and was engaged in preparing the bovine statistics. Presently the whereabouts of the lions in form of the Pandavas are not known to me and am jobless now. You are the greatest of the Kshatriyas and like to be employed by you and none other else." He was appointed in the byre.

Then came Arjuna dressed as a woman. Seeing Arjuna the king said, "O the great, you look like a woman wearing earrings, bracelets made of conch-shell and decorated armlets and setting free your tresses notwithstanding being armoured carry shafts and bow and looking so beautiful... from today you would be equal to my son or to me. I am old now and unable to perform all my royal duties; so you please rule the Matsya Kingdom presently."

Arjuna said that he was an expert in singing, dancing and playing on instruments. He might be appointed as a dance instructor to princess Uttara. His name was Vrihannala.

In response to his prayer the king said, Vrihannala, I do fulfil your desire. You please train my daughter and other ladies in the palace like her in the art of dancing and make them deft artists of it.

At last came Nakula as a desirer. He addressed the king saying, "O king, let you be crowned with victory. I am an expert in equestrian science whom the kings search for. I like to be the keeper of your stables." He too was employed as such by Virata.

Thus began the unrevealed exile of the Pandavas and Draupadi in the palace of Virata and it was peaceful for some time. Then once the king's brother-in-law Kichaka saw Draupadi in the palace and at once became smitten with passion. He desired her company. Draupadi with a view to caution him said, "O man, don't be deluded. Why should you lose your life for nothing? Five violent gandharvas always guard me. they are my husbands. If they become angry surely they will kill you."

But Kichaka was not a man to be restrained by good advices. He requested his sister Sudeshna to make Sairindhri come to his terms. As planned by both of them to take advantage of her he once tried to drag her to an empty chamber holding her hand while Draupadi with a forceful jerk freed herself and the impact caused him fall on the floor. She at once rushed to Yudhisthira; Kichaka also followed her to reach the court and there he kicked her letting fall on the ground holding her hair. A rakshasa sent by the sun-god let him fall on the ground hitting him. The kicking of Draupadi by Kichaka in the court happened before the eyes of both Youdhisthira and Bhima and Bhima being angry with the insult of Draupadi attempted to take revenge instantly but Yudhisthira dissuaded by gestures. On the other hand, Drauapadi prayed for justice to the king who replied, "I know nothing of the quarrel in detail between you two. How could I decide?"

Draupadi while desiring the death of Kichaka in her mind thought that she would have the desired result by going to Bhima. So she went to Bhima to plan to kill Kichaka by inciting him. As was planned Draupadi would invite Kichaka to come to the empty dancing hall at night. Kichaka agreed. Bhima would be lying that night in the hall. Kichaka came in the hall as planned and was received by Bhima who made a lump of flesh of him.

Next morning even if the death of Kichaka appeared to be unbelievable in such a manner, when the arrangements were being made by the Upakichakas (the brethren of Kichaka)

Draupadi was sighted and the Upakichakas decided to burn her alive along with Kichaka in the fire of his funeral pyre and led her to the crematorium. On the way she began to cry loudly saying, "They are taking me to the crematorium." Bhima heard the lamentations and began to follow them. Seeing Bhima they took him to be a grandharva and freed Draupadi.

On her return to the palace the queen said to Sairindhri, "You may go now where you like." Draupadi prayed for thirteen more days to stay.

The life of beings in this world revolves round the sense-objects and extraneous vision. So long the beings are extrovert cannot be endued with Self Knowledge. They are required to change the direction of vision and until the extroversion of vision turns to be introvert, the knowledge of the Self does not dawn on them. Hence the change of the direction of vision is absolutely necessary. It is an axiomatic truth that beings come to the earth only to die. In fact, the beings are ignorant of their origin, the reason for their existence, what actions they are supposed to perform or how long they would stay here as such. So long they are in exile on earth they remain oblivious of their Self. If they remain oblivious, how could they know of their origination, the purpose to have a human life or the worth of it? How could they know of the Source of Origination? So while in exile Guru inspires them to come out of the cocoon of oblivion showing the ways and means. This is known to be the search for truth and this efforts begin in their exile. This search is known to be the war of austerity the preparations of which begin while in exile. It becomes clearly evident in exile. The principal hero viz. Arjuna collected the weapons necessary for this war while in exile. The collection of weapons and to learn the science of their application are two most important features of this exile. One may ask why was the unrevealed exile necessary for the purpose? The answer is to keep it a secret so that the enemies could not have any air of this effort.

The oblivion referred to awhile ago is the main characteristic of the existence of beings. As Guru provides the inspiration to come out of it, that does never mean to be infructuous and following his guidance beings succeed. Now the Pandavas are to go to the exile unrevealed in the kingdom of Virata which is but the realm of the self in the body. In the world of matters Yudhisthira is the element of ether; he may be entrapped in bondages and may become free of them in the world of matters. But how could he be entrapped with bondages and be free of them in the realm of the self? The ether is the first of the elements and its being fastened with and freed from bondage is his game of dice which is continuing always. And in the realm of the Self his play of dice is going on. He is being bound with numerous esses and is being freed from that bondage. This is the game of dice in the kingdom of the self. While he is being free from one bondage of a particular esse he assimilates that esse thoroughly. This is going on and on and it is his delightful game of dice. The reality of ether is also known as Dharma and Dharma does never become fastened.

Next come Bhima to have a refuge taking a pseudonym, Vallava. He was a cook and also a wrestler. He is the reality of air that acts as vital breath being divided into five in the physical world. But in the subtle region when the mind dissolves in vital breath, it widens the passage for the upward journey of existence of being. The dissolution of the mind in vital breath is Bhima's act of cooking and the widening of passage through the Susumna artery for the upward journey of the existence of beings is his wrestling.

Then came Draupadi in disguise taking the name of Sairindhri to conceal her identity and was engaged as queen Sudeshna's maid. The result of actions performed by the introvert vital energy is reflected upon the subtle body and so she followed Bhima which was necessary and at the same time she remained secluded in the inner part of the palace so that not to be seen very much.

Then came Sahadeva in the guise of an expert in equestrian science. He too was appointed in the king's stable as the keeper. Sahadeva is the reality of earth. How could the earth be hidden in the realm of subtlety? In Sanskrit 'saha' means 'with' and 'deva' means 'divinity' and also 'play' both. Howsomuch you trample the earth under your feet, it endures that without protest. Not only that, mixed with water it offers you food grains and medicinal plants also. Endurance and forbearance are the nature of the earth. The physical body is made of earth but it cannot activate itself. It becomes activated by the mind. The horse is the symbol of mind in the body and Sahadeva is the expert of it. There are dharma, vital energy and the subtle body too and the mind is now added to them all.

After Sahadeva came the reality of tejas in the form of Arjuna. In the sphere of spirituality tejas is the most important reality. In absence of tejas, entry into the realm of spirituality is a far cry not to speak of its inspiration. But Arjuna came in form of a hermaphrodite. The beings are expected to be devoid of all desires to become successful in the field of austerity. Even an iota of desire may render your success elusive in the realm of spirituality. Hence Arjuna came to Virata as a neuter being. He was appointed as the instructor of dance and music to the princess and ladies of the palace.

Last of all came Nakula — the reality of savour and identified himself as a cowherd. He became the keeper of king's byre. Savour gets things soft and wet. The result of the functions of realties is the delightful savour that comes at last and there is no exception of it even in hiding.

The Pandavas' days were passing peacefully but one day this peaceful life was disturbed. The Kings' brother-in-law Kichaka, the prince of the Kekaya kingdom was the commander of Virata's army, once saw a new maid in the palace returning from a battle and he at once became smitten with passion. The maid was Draupadi in hiding assuming the name, Sairindhri. The feminine beauty does not become unrevealed in disguise and the result was as usual. He conspired to enjoy her forcefully but he could not have any idea of the consequence at all.

To save herself from the lustful passion of Kichaka she sought the help of Bhima and both of them planned to kill Kichaka. It was decided that Sairindhri would invite Kichaka to meet her in the lonely dancing hall at night and instead of Sairindhri, Bhima would be there to receive Kichaka in the darkness of night. Kichaka was killed by Bhima. Kichaka's brethren who arranged his funeral decided to kill Sairindhri in the fire of the funeral pyre. But seeing Bhima on the scene there they were compelled to free her. On her return to the palace the queen on the advice of Virata, asked her to leave the palace to which Sairindhri prayed for thirteen days' time.

Both king Virata and queen Sudeshna could not make out as to how a physically strong man like Kichaka could meet such a pathetic end. But they clearly understood that Sairndhri was not an ordinary woman and began to believe her claim that five powerful gandharvas were her husbands who always save her, was true. If at any time dissatisfied Sairindhari asks her husbands to be antagonistic to the king or to kill him, they would do that. So the frightened king asked the queen to tell her to find out a new shelter anywhere leaving the palace. The queen obeyed the King and Sairindhri prayed for another thirteen days' time as thirteen days were yet to be passed to complete the year of their hiding.

And during that period of thirteen days there were extensive cumulated events in the kingdom of Virata.

The Theft Of Bovine Herd Of Virata

As the royal personages and the ladies were astounded and extremely stunned because of the death of Kichaka, likewise the principal royal persons were extremely anxious for a different kind of reasons at Hastinapura. The spies of Duryodhana failed to gather any information regarding the Pandavas. If they could not be found out during their exile unrevealed and if that passes unhindered Duryodhana had to return their kingdom which was an anathema to him. The arrangement of deceitful game of dice was not made to return their kingdom after the completion of the exile unrevealed unhindered. Duryodhana is now in a dilemma. Hence it was decided to search for them again sending the spies.

Meanwhile, the king of Trigarta who was defeated again and again by Kichaka, the general of Virata, having the news of Kichaka's death, became very much glad and proposed to declare war against Virata. A good amount of cash and also hamlets, cattle could have been gained apart from the loss of military strength of Virata, would cause augmentation of wealth and prosperity of the Kauravas. Both Duryodhana and Karna accepted the proposal gladly, of course Duryodhana asked Duhshasna to fix up a date in consultation with the elderly persons. Conferring with them it was decided that the day on which Susharma would attack the Virata's Kingdom, the day following the Kaurava army would attack it to steal the bovine herd of Virata.

Susharma attacked the kingdom to steal the cows — such a news reached the capital. The king at once began to prepare himself to fight against the invader and at the same time as the thought that Kanka, Vallava, Aristanemi and Granthika would also assist him in the battle-field, he ordered to make arrangements for their armours and arms. The Pandavas fighting valiantly repulsed Susharma. But suddenly he attacked Virata to fight a duel. Yudhisthira realizing the gravity of it, asked Bhima to free Virata from Susharma's grip extending his helping hand. Susharma being overwhelmed by the prowess of Bhima, took to his heels. But Bhima caught him and drew him to Yudhisthira who ordered to free him. When the king was busy with recovering his stolen cows after sending the message of his victory to the palace, on that very day the Kurus led by Duryodhana stole away sixty thousand cows crossing another frontier. The herdsmen being beaten up sent a message to the palace through their head man there. But then prince Uttaro was the lone male member in the palace. He became happy with a prospect to fight in absence of his father especially while on the other side the hostile party consisted of the renowned Kaurava heroes. The emotion and imagination of an adolescent boy instantly glorified him as the victor of the veteran Kaurava war-heroes, of course, only to his own self. He began to boastfully say had there been a well-trained charioteer he would have the Kauravas defeated to him. In such a moment of crisis, he should have to help the king, their benefactor — thinking so Arjuna sent a beckoning through Draupadi that he was not unwilling to be his charioteer. Draupadi went to Uttaro and told, "Dhananjaya defeated the elements in Khandavaprasatha with the help of Vrihannala. There is no charioteer equal to her."

But Uttaro thought it to be below his dignity to seek help of a neuter person and he sent her sister to do that. On the request of Uttara Vrihannala agreed and Uttaro set out to fight against the enemies being charioted by Vrihannala. Coming out of the capital Uttaro said, "Vrihannala, please draw the chariot to the Kauravas forthwith. I'll return to the capital rescuing the bovine herd defeating the sinful souls." As ordred Arjuna drew the chariot below that silk-cotton tree. There seeing the array of Kaurava army and charioteers Uttaro said, "I don't dare fight the Kauravas' army....seeing them my heart is shuddering, my mind is losing zeal and the body is getting fatigued, let alone fighting with them."

To encourage the fearful boy Vrihannala said, "What sort of deed had they done that you are so frightened of them?"

Uttaro replied, "Let the father scold me even, but I am not to fight them by any means" — saying these he jumped off the chariot and began to run away from the battle-field and his charioteer began to run after him to get hold of him. A prince wanted to leave the battle-field and his hermaphrodite charioteer wanted to make him fight forcefully — such a scene howsoever be humorous and amusing to the soldiers, the Kaurava generals became anxious seeing the charioteer of the prince. They doubted him to be Arjuna and could not make out how he did become a neuter. On the other hand, Duryodhana became elated on the identity of the charioteer to be Arjuna, because if he was revealed prior to full one year's unrevealed exile then another twelve years' exile be confirmed. But none of them could be sure of the identity of the charioteer.

On the other hand, getting hold of Uttaro Vrihannala began to encourage him saying what the great actions the Kauravas performed that in fear of them you want to leave the battle ground? But Uttaro was resolute in his decision; come whatever punishment, he would not fight being induced by Vrihannala. At last Vrihamala said, "....being a Kshatriya why are you being so depressed before the enemies? I'll bring back the cattle fighting with the Kauravas." Thus consoling him Vrihannala asked Uttaro to climb up the silk cotton tree to bring down the weapons kept high above the tree branch.

Obeying Vrihannala Uttara brought down the bundle from the tree and astonished Uttara asked to know of their owner. Vrihannala then identified the weapons one by one including the Gandiva. Then even more curious Uttaro wanted to know where were the Pandavas now with Draupadi? Vrihannala then said. "I am Partha, Arjuna; King Yudhisthira is your father's courtier; Bhimsena is the cook in your kitchen assuming the name of Vallava; Nakula is the keeper of the royal stable and Sahadeva is the keeper of the byre. For whom the evil-souled Kichaka died, she is Draupadi and passing her time as Sairindhri."

Uttaro was amazed. All this seemed to be unbelievable. He said, "Partha has ten names, it is heard. If you can enumerate them all then I'll believe in all that you said. Arjuna then recounted them and explained his ten names. Listening to him Uttaro became overcome with emotion and said "....today I am extremely fortunate and to see you I am gratified. Please forgive me for my unreasonable words spoken out of ignorance." Now he had no objection to accept Vrihannala as his charioteer and said, "I am dull headed and cannot ascertain the things; I think, you are holy Shulapani (Lord Shiva) or the Gandharva king Chitraratha or Indra of heaven."

Arjuna said, "O prince, please don't take me for an actual neuter being. Ordered by the eldest brother I had taken this vow for a year and now the period of the vow is over." Hearing him more curious Uttaro asked him, "O Kaunteya, you are alone and the Kauravas are many who are experts in using all kinds of weapons, how would you defeat them, thinking this I am getting afraid?

In reply Arjuna assured him and said, "Do the duty of a charioteer fearlessly." On the other hand, listening to the sound of blowing the conch-shell and that of the twang of the Gandiva the Kaurava side discerned that they were to be that of Arjuna. They could not make out as to whether the period of one year of the unrevealed exile was over or the Pandavas revealed themselves earlier. Duryodhana was glad regarding the prospect of another exile owing to the contravention of conditions was to hand.

While Karna and generals were debating on Arjuna. Bhishma addressed them saying, "Arjuna has almost come, we should have to fight unitedly." In reply Drona said to him, "O the son of Ganga, think of the safety of Duryodhana, lest Partha can attack him or lest being deluded he becomes under grip of the enemy. Had thirteen years not been elapsed, Arjuna could not have revealed himself. He has come to recover the cows, he will never forgive us." In reply Bhishma calculated the time for the exile unrevealed and said that it had become five months and six days more than the stipulated time; so Duryodhana had no reason to be glad. Now it is the duty to fight. Please, arrange to fight immediately.

Bhishma advised that Duryodhana should return to the capital taking one fourth of the army with him. The stolen cows be herded to Hastinapura by another one-fourth army and Bhishma, Drona and others would fight against Arjuna with the rest half of the army. Bhishma's proposal was accepted by all unanimously.

Coming to the battle-field in front of the Kaurava army Arjuna saluted Drona with two shafts and shooting another two he sent his message. Drona became happy. But Arjuna saw that Duryodhana was nowhere in the battle-field. He thought surely Duryodhana was fleeing with the stolen cows towards the south. So he was to be found out first. Observing Arjuna's movement when the Kauravas saw Arjuna was advancing towards Duryodhana Kripa asked Drona to arrange for Duryodhana's safety. Understanding Arjuna's intention Karna came forward to resist him. But he had to leave the battle-field being wounded.

After Karna fled away from the battle-field, Arjuna's aim was again fixed to Duryodhana and the Kuru generals perceived it rightly. So they unitedly tried to repulse him. Arjuna fighting with Drona, Kripa, Ashvathama and Bhishma, lightly pierced two ears of Karna. Till then Duryodhana was beyond his bound, hence he had to fight with other Kurus. He fought against Kripacharya, then Dronacharya, then Ashvathama one by one and they all left the battle-field being defeated. Then again Karna came to fight and after a terrible encounter between the two Karna being defeated became senseless. Arjuna advanced towards Bhishma. Seeing his advancement the Kuru soldiers rushed to attack Arjuna unitedly but failed to earn victory for them, rather they all were defeated and fell senseless. The charioteer of Bhishma carried away senseless Bhishma from the battle ground. Duryodhana came back to fight again but fled away. Arjuna cleft off his diadem.

Leaving the Kaurava soldiers to flee Arjuna arranged to return to the capital with the stolen herd of cows. At the same time he advised Uttaro to send a message to the palace that uttaro was victorious.

Earlier we have said that the Pandavas' exile unrevealed was actually their confinement in the mothers' womb. But how can some adult men and a woman be in a mother's womb unitedly? We have also said that the unrevealed exile is but to live in the realm of the Self. This world of the Self is the womb of the Universal Mother Nature which is the mother of all creation. To remain in the mother's womb connotes to dwell in the womb of Universal Nature. Mother Nature is the mother of all indeed. But once born of a mother, what is the necessity to be born of the Mother Nature's womb? The precondition of a life in the world of matter is to have the birth of a mother's womb, likewise to have a spiritual life one is required to be born of the womb of the Universal Nature.

The enemies of the divine side namely, the six cardinal passions, eight bondages etc. would never find out the beings while living in the Mother Nature's womb. But they would strive heart and soul to find out them so that the divine side be made an offender for infringement of accepted condition. Hence Duryodhana is so eager to find out the Pandavas in the exile unrevealed sending his spies to all corners.

On the other hand, Susharma, the King of Trigarta resolved to attack the kingdom of Virata to avenge his insult made by Kichaka inflicting defeat upon him time and again. Duryodhana accepted the proposal at once. It was decided that the day Susharma would attack the kingdom of Virata, Duryodhana attacking the kingdom from another side would take away the herd of cows of Virata by stealing them on the following day.

The function of the navel, genital organ and anus is to enjoy sense-objects and to excrete them. These two functions keep the body sound but if they function in a disordered way then the body may become ill. The amalgamation of these two functions is Susharma; in other words, addiction to much eating and carnal pleasure. The term 'trigarta' means three cavities. The consistency of the functions of these three is the king of trigarta kingdom which is a tributary kingdom to Duryodhana. So Susharma, the king is subjugated to Kama (Desire) and he was defeated by Kichaka time and again. Kichaka is the embodiment of the instinct of attachment to sensual pleasures. There is no significant difference between Kama and the instinct of attachment to sensual pleasure, yet then the instinct of attachment to pleasure is up to dominate over the addiction to sensual pleasure and in this regard Kama (Durryodhana) remained unperturbed because of the characteristic similarity between the two. Hence Duryodhana heartily approved of the attack of Virata's kingdom and he himself too decided to do so. His sole intention was to strew thorns in the way to spiritualism upon defeating the king and stealing away divine esses symbolized as cows from his kingdom and also imbuing the subjects with the instincts of attachment to carnal desires. The emperor of Hastinapura is the overlord of the realm of Chitta and he looks forward to the kingdom of Hridaya to fulfil his ambition to dominate over it and he knows it well that the road to Hridaya is not smooth at all. So he advised his brother to fix a date for the invasion conferring with those who were skilled in warfare and wise in the art of it. It was decided that Susharma should attack the kingdom of Virata on the seventh lunar day of the new moon and on the next day the Kaurava forces would attack it from another direction. But what was the significance of attacking the same land by the two forces on two different days? The answer is, the instinct of attachment to sensual pleasure rose to acquire upto the seventh stage of knowledge while the king of cardinal passions, Kama aims to establish its authority upto the eighth stage of knowledge.

Neither the Kauravas nor Susharma had any information that the Pandavas were in their unrevealed exile in the court of Virata nor could they even dreamt of the possibility of stretching their helping hand to Virata at the moment of crisis. Hence Susharma had to sustain a lamentable defeat in a day's war. His life was saved by the grace of Yudhisthira, of course, he had to accept the suzerainty of Virata. The fundamental reason for saving the life of Susharma by Yudhisthira was that the attachment to carnal pleasure remains there in the life of beings upto a certain state and hence he was not killed but his activities be circumscribed by his overlord to a great extent.

On the other hand, prior to having any information regarding the consequence of Susharma's attack, the Kaurava forces attacked the kingdom of Virata and stole his sixty thousand cows. Duryodhanana's intention was to subjugate king Virata i.e. the realm of the Self with the assistance of other cardinal passions. He knew it well that the task was not an easy one to accomplish and he had to steal secretly. But the news of the theft reached the palace timely. Till then the king had not returned from the battlefield and the mentionable male member in the palace was the adolescent prince Uttaro. Spurred with emotion he began to brag that had he got a good charioteer he could have defeated the Kauravas. However, following Sairindhri's advice he finally got a charioteer — Vrihannala, the hermaphrodite.

When the followers of Kama (desire) strive to make the traits and propensities of manhood inactive, it becomes imperative on the part of Virata who is the lord of them all, to stave them off and then faith (Shraddha), vital energy (Prana), temperance (Vahih samyama) and restraint (Antara Samyama) come forward to co-operate with him. But when Kama (desire) commits the same crime then to repel him there needs the active role of neuter tejas. Only tejas can stave him off.

Having Vrihannala as his charioteer Uttaro reaching the battle-field became terrified and awe-struck in keeping with the usage. He wanted to leave the battle-ground to save his life, but Vrihannala opposed his bid. Time had come now to reveal himself after expiry of the term for the exile unrevealed and by that revelation to expose to the hostile opposition the inception of the future great war. So there was a great difference between the necessities of Vrihannala and Uttaro.

After bringing down the weapons from the silk-cotton tree by Uttaro, Arjuna divulged his identity to Uttaro but that appeared to be unbelievable to him. The extent of belief of beings is very narrow. But after providing evidence to his liking, he finally believed that actually his charioteer was Arjuna. Then he agreed to act on the advice of him and also became his charioteer.

We know of two offsprings of Virata in the tale, the son Uttaro and the daughter Uttara. The difference between the two is in sex only. Both are Uttaro — meaning the solution to a question and also the future. The question we ask regarding the world around and the life of beings to Virata (the exalted one) and the reply we get is understood by us commensurate with our understanding that becomes not so clear to us in most cases. So the answer appears to be weak and the weakness in understanding is our life-long companion. This weakness becomes obvious in front of tejas which appropriates it.

So we find the vaunting prince in the palace seeing the Kaurava army in the battle-field becomes enterprising to save his life discarding his boastfulness. This is the natural behaviour of beings. The fear that is at the root of this behaviour needs to be done away with tejas and being encouraged by tejas uttaro becomes free from fear.

On expiry of the period of the exile unrevealed to expose his own identity to the enemies was imperative on the part of Arjuna. So he had to assure and encourage the frightful prince to be his charioteer. On the other hand, when the prince was fleeing from the battle-field and catching him up Vrihannala was imploring him to be the charioteer and not the fighter, the Kaurava generals assumed that the charioteer was Arjuna but could not make out why and when Arjuna became a neuter person. As the Kaurava heroes were curious about his being asexual Arjuna made his identity known to them by blowing his conch-shell and twang of the Gandiva, that their assumption was not wrong at all.

When the beings rush towards the realm of the Self to be established there, the six cardinal passions, eight bondages etc. become restless to make an all out effort to create impediments to their way so that the beings cannot succeed.

For this reason alone stealing of Virata's cows takes place and his kingdom is attacked. If Virata be kept otherwise busy and encumbered in his kingdom, he would not be able to assist those aspiring souls to be established in this kingdom. Hence Kama and his associates are now present in Virata's kingdom, defying all morality, all regulation to steal the property of others and in that act there are the heroes like Bhishma, Drona and Karna. The wise grandsire Bhishma renouncing his all sense of morality and vast knowledge of scriptures is present here to assist Kama in this ignoble battle.

Where Kama is frenzied and indomitable, there the ego is its servile assistant. The savour of Kama (eros) cannot be enjoyed without active participation of ego. They both are so powerful that none of them is subject to natural death; one is to die at his own will and the other has an armoured body and the weak part of his body is only known to Guru and none else. As desired by Kama and under the guidance of the ego the Kurus are assembled here in the battle-field.

When the generals and warriors were discussing on Arjuna, the ego following his characteristic nature reminded them that their immediate duty was to resist Arjuna and not to research on him. So they were required to fight unitedly. In the perspective of the ego's warning prejudicial notion opined that by no means Kama should come within the bound of tejas. The notional prejudice, avarice et al being the associates of Kama are ready to fight against tejas.

But tejas announcing his presence saluted the notional prejudice and sent a message also to him. When Duryodhana was confirmed that completing the term for the exile unrevealed Arjuna had revealed himself, his instant reaction was to fight and not to return the kingdom. Knowing of the reaction of Duryodhana Asmita (ego) arranged to divide the army to guard Duryodhana, to keep watch over the stolen cows led to Hastinapura and array the rest to fight against Arjuna.

Right now Arjuna's target was not the grandsire but Duryodhana — Kama. To have the right to the realm of the Self the primary duty of an aspirant is to subdue Kama. So long he had been deprived of the right to the realm of the self by Kama who today had designed to steal away the traits of manhood. So repelling that Kama tejas sought to rescue those traits of manhood. But Arjuna could not find Duryodhana in the assemblage of the Kurus and surmised that Duryodhana was running towards Hastinapura and needed to be halted at once. With this end in view as Arjuna was advancing to that direction, understanding Arjuna's intention Karna came forward to fight with him and within a short while left the battle-field being injured. To ensure the security of Duryodhana Karna came and fought and fled away. After his flight from the battle-field, the subdued bondages and traits who were his followers tried their best to protect Duryodhana fighting with Arjuna with a view to resist him. Firstly came the imagination of the mind (Kripacharya) and then one by one the notional intelligence (Dronacharya), the reflection of notional intelligence (Ashvathama) and all of them fled from the battle-field being defeated. Then again came avarice (Karna). The avarice is the principal hostile opposition to an austerer. This time also Karna was defeated and became senseless. After Karna became inactive Arjuna attacked the ego (Bhishma). At this time all the traits (other Kuru fighters) came forward to fight but they too became senseless being defeated. Senseless Bhishma was carried away by his charioteer. Now Kama (Duryodhana) came forward to fight but was compelled to flee away. Tejas cleft off his diadem — his residual glory then mixed up with the earth.

Under these conditions the Kaurava forces had no alternative but to flee from the battle-field. Letting them flee, Arjuna rescuing the stolen cows arranged to return to the capital. The message reached the capital that Uttaro was victorious over the Kauravas. Vrihannala taught the prince to tell that this victory was his own on return to the palace. Then both of them reached the silk-cotton three and kept the weapons as before; then Arjuna became the charioteer of Uttaro.

Victorious Virata on his return from the battle-field after defeating Susharma, could know that the prince set out to fight against the Kauravas and his charioteer was Vrihannala. He became anxious for the safety of Uttaro and ordered that those who returned with him unhurt should remain in the palace as security for the prince. He then ordered "the rest of the army should immediately go to see as to whether the prince was alive or not and having the information let me have it. I think as he has gone with a hermaphrodite charioteer, he is not living at all."

At this time Yudhisthira told Virata, "O king as today Vrihannala has gone with the prince being his charioteer, nobody can steal your herd of cows."

Meanwhile the couriers brought the news, "...Prince Uttaro is coming with his charioteer and rescuing the herd of cows defeating the Kaurava forces." Yudhisthira said at one, "He whose charioteer is Vrihannala, he is sure to be victorious."

Paying no heed to his words, Virata after giving orders for welcome to the prince, asked Kanka to play the game of dice to which Yudhisthira said, "It is heard, to play with the delighted and sly person is improper and utterly condemned." In reply Virata said, "Today my son has easily defeated the Kaurava forces." But even after it Kanka praised the role of Vrihannala as a charioteer and angry Virata struck Kanka with a dice and blood began to trickle down from his nostrils and at this moment the usher announced the prince with this charioteer was present at the gate. Yudhisthira asked him to lead the prince only to the court. Uttara came and saw Kanka was bleeding and wanted to know who had done it. Virata replied that Kanka was unnecessarily praising Vrihannala and hence he had struck Kanka. Uttara asked him to apologise to Kanka and when the king did so, Yudhisthira said he had already forgiven him.

Then the prince said, he had not won the battle but a son of a god. But he could not be presented before the king to day; tomorrow or the day after that would be possible.

Next day prior to the formal session of the court Virata saw that five Pandava brothers and Draupadi after washing were seated in six thrones wearing new clothes and ornaments and he asked angrily why the king's courtier was sitting on the king's throne. Arjuna replied disclosing their identity. The king being satisfied then proposed to marry his daughter Uttara to Arjuna who politely declining said to accept her as his daughter-in-law and the king agreed.

As with the revelation of the identity of the Pandavas at the court of Virata ended their exile for thirteen years likewise after the conclusion of a waiting began another waiting. The first waiting was for the end of the exile and the second one for retrieval of the lost kingdom. The first and the second waiting were actually single one that bore the ray of hope auguring the marriage of Abhimanyu.

The Pandavas being defeated in the game of dice were compelled to accept twelve year's exile and another year's unrevealed exile. Again after the death of Kichaka when the queen Sudeshna asked Sairindhri to go elsewhere leaving the palace she pleaded for thirteen more days' time. So it is seen that the number thirteen has some importance. But why? We have said it earlier that the time from birth to death constitute one aeon (Yuga i.e. twelve years) and a year's stay in the mother's womb (i.e. in a state of completely absorbed in self-knowledge). This life-span of beings is not meant for squandering in food, sleep and coition only but to enrich it with the realization of Truth in life being disciplined and restraining the senses notwithstanding the acceptance of food, sleep and coition in day to day life. To make this life of pain and pleasure, smile and tears, separation and union meaningful, there are four wishes — Dharma (spiritual attainment). Artha (earning of wealth), Kama (fulfillment of desires) and lastly Moksha (emancipation). The life of beings revolves round these four wishes. There are three gunas viz. Sattva, Rajas and Tamas. Each of the wishes manifests itself multiplied by three gunas. Then the total be twelve. This is the term for exile of beings in this world. This life influenced by these twelve is sure to lose the vision of aim and needs to have its fixed vision of aim for which it should strive by reaming unrevealed in the mother womb (i.e. in the realm of the Self).

In the life of beings the element of 'twelve' and then that of 'one' are unavoidable and to establish this truth the author has used the allegory of 'exile' and the 'exile unrevealed'.

Is it not astonishing?

The Embassy Of Krishna In The Kaurava Court

Nobody expected of Duryodhana being inspired by his sense of morality would return the kingdom to Yudhisthira heartily. So when the celebrations of the wedding were over Krishna proposed before Virata, Drupada and other kings and relatives to send an emissary to the Kaurava Court and Krishna proposed to shoulder the responsibility Himself to go to the Kaurava court. In this part of the tale the Lord holds the centre-stage and delineated a preamble to one of the chapters of His Leela.

The Leela of Krishna is divided into three — the first one is the chapter of Vrindavana and the characteristic of this one is to manifest the charming beauty of Love. There were an adolescent boy, a seventeen year old girl and a host of women of Vraja (Vrindavana) whose interaction on the emotion of love that manifested six modes of it viz. (1) the feeling of amorous attraction even before acquaintance with the lover (Purvaraga), (2) the attachment of love (Anuraga), (3) the separation (Viraha), (4) the Union (milana), (5) the worried suspense for love (utkanthita), (6) the repulsive feeling for love (Viprakarsha).

The melody of this Leela is dependent upon twelve realities, viz. five senses, five sense-organs, the individual self and the Supreme Self. The time for continuity was twelve years.

The next part of His Leela continued for a century and the place of occurrence was Mathura. It is of a disciplined life restrained in every respect. But the previous Leela at Vrindavana and the ensuing Leela at Mathura are not two water-tight compartments; rather there were influences of the preceding one upon that of the subsequent. Hence we see at the outset the Mathura Leela that the beauty of the previous Leela is manifest in the next one which is evident in the episode of Kuvza, an eighty year old ugly and foul-mouthed woman whose body skin used to hang loosely, in which a pleasant conclusion was drawn by the Lord turning her into a charming and beautiful lass of sixteen and made her the queen consort of Him at Mathura. Yet there was not the graceful charm of love of the Vrindavana Leela. There Krishna was the king, a Kshatriya warrior. There was no scope for gracefulness in observing the duty of a king and in warfare also. Here in the restrained life, the aim was to be united with Atman making ineffective the seeds of enjoyment of sense-objects one by one by the way of Yoga. It is assumed there are six lotuses in six nerve-centre of the spinal cord which have one hundred petals each of which contains a seed of a mental trait. Owing to the influence of these traits the beings become victims of suffering, creating a distance between Atman and individuals. To do away with this distance, the seeds of enjoyment need to be made ineffective and the union between the individual self and Atman is possible. The Yogis desire this union.

The third phase of His Leela was extended while He was residing at Dvaraka. There are thirteen elements of it; they are the four desires (varga) multiplied by three gunas and the singular vision. The four desires multiplied by three gunas cannot enable the beings to be beyond maya (delusion) and ignorance nor can they establish the beings in singular vision that needs the establishment in wisdom. Until you are wise you cannot have the singular vision. As in the first phase of His Leela He manifested the sweet elegance and had shown to render the mental traits ineffective in a disciplined and restrained life, likewise in the third phase of the Leela He has shown us how to be established in the dharma of man — manhood, rising beyond the mind thoroughly subdued by Kama (desire).

We have said it earlier that the physical creation is controlled by Kama and hence the other three desires (vargas) get influenced and regulated by it. The desire (Kama) alone represents the other three vargas (desires). Hence our virtuosity and philosophy of life pertain to have sense-objects, preserving sense-objects and enjoying them being guided by the unbridled Kama (desire). The beings are devoid of the energy that needs to control this indomitable Kama. He has that energy who is the Creator and none else. He as Guru inspires the beings to control desire (Kama) and to establish this truth Krishna shouldered the responsibility of embassy which made the demonic side obliged to accord the due importance to Him.

It would be easier to perceive the nature of the conflict between the divine and demonic sides if we could know of the same in our body. In a body of twenty-four elements, the five primary elements and Krishna are on the divine side while the six cardinal passions are on the demonic side and they are antagonistic to each other. Those who are on the divine side are not jealous and honestly perform their ordained duty, stick to their own dharma, in other words, they exhibit discipline. On the other hand, the demonic side is expert in robbing of what belongs to other, dislodging others from their rightful possessions, procrastinating and idle in performance of ordained duty and unparalleled in seeking sense-objects, in other words, extremely indisciplined in thought and action.

The demonic side once appropriated the Pandavas' kingdom with impropriety and now after fulfillment of all their conditions, they were not up to return the kingdom and hence there was the necessity of embassy.

Duryodhana was bound by his own promise to return their kingdom. Now it is not clear whether honouring his promise he is to return the kingdom to the Pandavas. So Krishna proposes to send an emissary to the Kaurava court and taking the cue from Krishna's proposal Drupada preferred war to treaty and according to his proposal it was decided to send his priest to the Kaurava court. From end to end of the body arterial energy conveys messages and it is not astonishing that the priest of the arterial energy would be that emissary.

On the other hand, on happy ending of the nuptials in the Matsya kingdom the guests returned to their places. Krishna too went to Dvaraka while the Pandavas and Kauravas considering the possibility of war began their preparations. Both camps sent their emissaries to different kingdoms to bring the kings there in their own camps. On the same day Duryodhana and Arjuna went to Dvaraka to have Krishna with them. First reached Duryodhana and saw Him asleep. So he had to wait being seated on a throne placed at His head side. Arjuna came a little later and began to wait being seated on an ordinary seat at His leg side. Rising from sleep He first saw Arjuna and then Duryodana and asked to know of their mission. Duryodhana replied that he sought His help in the impending war notwithstanding His equal relationship with them and the Pandavas but his demand should be of greater import as he had come earlier. Krishna said he would help them both but he had seen Arjuna first and the claim of the youngest should have the priority. He addressed Arjuna saying, "One hundred million warriors equal to Me in the skill of fighting, would fight on one side" and He Himself was to join the war unarmed. Arjuna might opt for any between the two. Arjuna gracefully accepted Him knowing well that He would remain unarmed without taking any active part in the war. Duryodhana left Dvaraka happily having one hundred million Narayani soldiers. Prior to it, having met with Balarama he could know that Balarama wanted to fight in favour of Duryodhana but as willed by Krishna, he would remain impartial.

In the life of light and darkness, right and wrong, discipline and indiscipline, on the demonic side there are six main players consisting of six cardinal passions and on the divine side the same number of players are there and they are five Pandava brothers and Krishna Himself.

The conflict is between those two sides that pertains to the authority to rule the human body consisting of twenty four elements which ought to have been vested with the divine side but that has been taken away by the demonic side by their deceitful design. They are bound by the promise to return that right on fulfilling their conditions but they are now not agreeable do that. So the preparation of war and also the effort of embassy were necessitated to solve the crisis. On the other hand, Krishna was equally related to them all, but his cordiality with the Pandavas was greater and the third Pandava was His friend. Now, it was rather embarrassing to select a side judiciously while both of the sides sought His participatation. But His impartiality had to be maintained. In this perspective He devised a plan which could not be questioned knowing that Duryodhana and Arjuna were coming to seek His help. His will was fulfilled. The first caller was Duryodhana. He was older than Arjuna of the other side and as he came first, he occupied the better seat kept near his head. Arjuna came later, he took the seat on the opposite — His leg side. So long Arjuna did not come he remained asleep and woke up after Arjuna's arrival. The import was to see Arjuna first after His waking up and to grant his prayer prior to that of Duryodhana; hence this arrangement.

Krishna is the Consciousness encased in the body. He is Immutable, Actionless and the Mute Witness. But he is Guru too. He is the Creator of the vile as well as the refined and both of them are made vigorous by Him. Both of them had to be satisfied in order to give a shape to His own Will to fulfil the aim. Hence this inaction.

Duryodhana is dull-headed but arrogant and indefatigable in seeking and having sense-objects. Krishna was well aware of this aspect of his character and so he first said of the one hundred million of indefatigable warriors said to be born of the person of Krishna himself, who would fight on one side and he himself would remain on the other unarmed and would not fight. Instantly, gladdened Arjuna prayed for him to be on their side. But Duryodhana knew that to win a war a powerful army was necessary and one hundred million strong an army was not a matter of joke. So he sought for his band of soldiers and happily left Dvaraka but failed to foresee the outcome of the war to be fought that was decided there at that moment. After his departure Krishna asked Arjuna as to why did he accept him on their side knowing that he would remain unarmed and expected not to fight yet he accepted him on their side. Arjuna replied he knew that Krishna alone could kill the sons of Dhritarastra. But Arjuna desired to kill them. If Krishna did not fight then he would get the chance to do it. Secondly, unbiased and neutral Krishna could easily be approached for the job of a charioteer and he asked Him to be his charioteer. Krishna agreed.

A short drama was enacted in the palace of Dvaraka to decide on which side he would remain and at the root of it all was the conflict between the Kurus and Pandavas. On the one side there were six cardinal passions viz. (1) Kama (Desire), (2) Krodha (Wrath), (3) Lobha (Avarice), (4) Moha (Delusion), (5) Mada (Assertiveness) and (6) Matsarya (Ego) and on the other side there were six excellences viz. (1) Shama (Restraint of external senses), (2) Dama (Restraint of internal senses), (3) Titiksha (Forbearance), (4) Uparati (Abstinence), (5) Shraddha (Faith) and (6) Samadhana (Solver). Krishna is the solver. One side is to appropriate unrighteously the kingdom of the other while the rightful owners are up to have it returned which has not yet been possible. So the conflict ensues. As the warring sides are there in the human body likewise Consciousness encased in the body is there with its energy of attraction, cultivation and detraction. Krishna is on one side but he is not to fight being impartial though he will remain amidst the war. But why?

Behind the creation of beings there is a particular aim of the Creator and that aim is to establish them in their own nature attracting them towards the culmination. Should we then assume that the beings are not established in human nature? No, not at all; had that been true, the question of the possibility of a war would not have been arisen. The nature of man is manhood and the Divine Leela is meant for endowing him with his manhood. This is the reason for his becoming the charioteer of the reality of tejas to remain within the conflict but not take part in it.

In course of discussing the birth of the Pandavas we have said earlier that téjas brings about harmony between two subtle elements viz. the ether and air and two physical elements viz. the water and earth and this act of synthesis reveals a complete existence. This singular role of tejas cannot be played by any other elements and he is the friend of the Lord, — none of the other elements. So when the request of becoming his charioteer came from tejas, the Lord accepted it instantly because making a medium of tejas he was to reveal a greater part of the third phase of His Leela with a view to establish the future generations in manhood incanting the mantra so that the intonation of it resonates deep into the human heart inspiring them to ensure to create a society beyond all conflicts, free from malice and violence, endowing them with the vigour to transform this assurance into a firm faith. Now starts his role as Guru.

Knowing that a war was impending between Pandavas and Kauravas, Shalya, the king of Madra set out for the Matsya kingdom with a large army to join Yudhisthira's side. Having this news Duryodhana caused to stop him in the midway and felicitated him in many ways to accept the post of a commander on his side and Shalya agreed. But before formally joining the Kaurava camp he pleaded to have a meeting with Yudhisthira. Duryodhana complied but he reminded him not to forget his promise to him.

Shalya came to the Matsya kingdom and met with Yudhisthira who told Shalya, "O uncle, you have done a very good job accepting the proposal of Duryodhana. But for my sake you are to do a misdeed; ....you are to destroy the vigour of Karna by accepting the call to be his charioteer to save Arjuna for our benefit while they two will be fighting a duel. Uncle, we know it is a wrong doing but you are to do it for our good."

Shalya agreed. He said, "...I'll do that what you have said by agreeing to be his charioteer. He estimates me to be equal to Vasudeva in the battle-field ... I'll give him harmful and contrary suggestions while he will be fighting and I think thus he will be robbed of his arrogance and vigour. Then you may easily kill him."

Shalva was the thorn of obstacle to austerity and the king of Madra, Shalya was also a thorn for extraction of the thorn pricked into the way of austerity. The avarice and the aspiration for performing duty in earthly consideration — both are very powerful in life. The first one is a cardinal passion and other is the trait of mind and both of them are serious obstacles to austerity. It needs some skilful tricks to do away with them. Not only these two but to kill other cardinal passions also you are to espouse the same course as you cannot kill them justly in frontal fight. You are to depend upon your skill to play tricks to kill them. To kill Karna the role of such a one was necessary whom he could trust beyond all questions nor could he have even an iota of doubt in his ill advices and contrary steps in the battle-field and he would put an end of his own self. Shalya was such a skilled warrior that Karna used to compare his prowess to be equal to that of Krishna. So there was no scope for being skeptical of Shalya.

Hence Yudhisthira conferred the great responsibility upon the right person and the sole credit of it should go to Duryodhana. Had he not invited Shalya to join the Kaurava camp, all this would not have happened and he too could not help in killing Karna.

Meanwhile, the preparation of war was on in both camps. The priest of Drupada once went to Hastinapura with a proposal for an alliance. Listening to the priest Bhishma opined, "As promised the Pandavas are now the owners of their parental kingdom." Paying no heed to Bhishma's words Karna boastfully and arrogantly said, "King Duryodhana may give away the whole world, but if threatened, he will not give any land measuring a single foot-mark even to the enemy .... So the Pandavas should not adopt any unrighteous means." Bhishma retorted, "Surely Karna has not forgotten that Arjuna alone defeated six generals in the battle-field." Dhritarastra too rebuked Karna and said, the proposal of Bhishma was beneficial to us and the Pandavas too and considering that it would be good for the world, I'll send Sanjaya to the Pandavas."

Sanjaya was sent in embassy to the Matsya kingdom. There in course of conversation with Yudhisthira he could learn that relying upon Krishna Yudhisthira was to abide by the advices of Krishna. Then Krishna said, "I desire an alliance between the Kauravas and Pandavas and I do never advise them otherwise. In presence of other Pandavas king Yudhisthira had said of alliance several times — I have heard it. But Maharaj Dhritarastra and his sons are very much avaricious; so to enter into an alliance with the Pandavas will be very hard for him. Therefore it is not surprising that the hostility will grow more and more". Then

Krishna said to Sanjaya that He Himself would go to Hastina so that they enter into an alliance. Sanjaya should report there that the Pandavas were ready either to serve them or fight against them.

After Krishna had finished Yudhisthira asked Sanjaya to tell Duryodhana that "they would be satisfied to have a part of the kingdom; so you please make a gift of five hamlets to your brother viz, Kushasthali, Vrikasthala, Makandi, Varanavata and another one" "...I am ready for any alliance and conflict too."

On his return to Hastina Sanjaya had no diffidence to rebuke Dhritarastra : To him all that which was antagonistic to righteousness, import and contrary to civilized behaviour was Dhritarastra's action. Reproved by Sanjaya Dhritarastra became weak a little and called for Vidura for his counsel. Vidura imparted many a good advice and said lastly. "...you please enter into an alliance with the Pandavas who are relying on truth. So dissuade Duryodhana from armed conflict." Having the advices of Sanjaya and Vidura Dhritarastra began to think in favour of entering into an alliance.

In the conflict between the demonic and divine sides within the body, arterial energy is the medium of exchanging news and views. So the priest of Drupada took the charge of embassy in favour of the Pandavas and went to Hastina. In the Kaurava court the ego (Bhishma) realizing the worth of the message said that the Pandavas were now rightful owners of their father's kingdom meaning thereby to return the kingdom to them. But the avarice (Karna) could not share this view at all. It is obvious that where there arises the question of returning any property grabbed unlawfully, being inspired by righteousness the sense of duty avarice wakes up to oppose the effort creating a mesh of intrigues. So Karna boastfully opposed the views of Bhishma. Glorifying Duryodhana and debasing the Pandavas, expressed his views while Bhisma reminded him of the fact that Arjuna alone made six generals senseless in the battle-field and Karna should not forget it nor was his grandiloquence befitting him. Dhritarastra rebuked him and said the views of Bhishma were beneficial. He sent the exhaustive knowledge to the Pandavas as his ambassador.

Now it is evident that howsoever the mind is entangled in sense-objects, at times it becomes righteous under the influence of Consciousness adrift upon the part of its inner existence that makes it thoughtful of righteousness. And in the tale that part of Consciousness is Vidura. So being moved by his advice Dhritarastra decided to send exhaustive knowledge (Sanjaya) to the Pandavas. The materialistic mind, for the time being, desires to be correlated to the Pandavas through the exhaustive knowledge but that is a far cry. Who but does Guru know this truth? It is evident in the fact that when Yudhisthira opened his mind to Sanjaya, after his arrival at Viratnagara in embassy, that in all respects he was dependent upon Krishna, then Krishna exposed the hollowness of the proposal of Dhritarastra saying, "Moharaj Dhritarastra and his sons" were very much avaricious of money and to enter into an alliance with the Pandavas was highly critical, rather it was impossible and the conflict would be growing. He asked Sanjaya to tell the Kaurava court that the Pandavas were ready for both alliance and war. At this time Yudhisthira said to Sanjaya to tell Duryodhana that they would be satisfied to have five hamlets only and they (Kaurava) might enjoy the rest of the kingdom. Now, why did Yudhisthira asked for five hamlets only instead of the whole kingdom?

The five hamlets are the five nerve-centres (chakra) of the spinal cord and they are known to be (1) Muladhara, (2) Swadhisthana, (3) Manipura, (4) Anahata and (5) Vishuddha. Each of these nerve-centres is the home to each of the five elements e.g. the Muladhara nerve-centre is the home for the reality of earth; the Swadhisthana nerve-centre is the home for the reality of water, Manipura is the home of the reality of tejas. The next nerve-centre, Anahata is the home to the reality of air and the Vishuddha nerve-centre is the home to the reality of ether. These five nerve-centres exert immense influence in conducting the body and they contain the seeds of mental propensities and traits that condition the human behaviour. Hence having the right of these nerve-centres one may rule over the body without being its king.

Duryodhana was very much agitated lest the rebuke of Sanjaya and advices of Vidura could change the mind of Dhritarastra; so he began to narrate the prowess of the Kaurava heroes to his blind father saying, "Father, we three, Karna, brother Duhshasana and me, no doubt, will make the Pandavas fall down." Proud Duryodhana said even more that, "If so necessitates we will give up our life, all our wealth too but not to live with the Pandavas unitedly. I shall not give them that measure of land which be pricked by the end of a needle."

When the intervening distance was being widened owing to pride and boastfulness between one and the other among the Kuru warriors, listening to the description of the intimate friendship of Arjuna and Krishna, narrated by Sanjaya, Dhritarastra said to Duryodhana, "Son, Sanjaya is our well wisher; so please go to Keshava (Krishna) to have his refuge." But Duryodhana cared two figs for his father's advice.

Dhritarastra is the king, Sanjaya is his charioteer. One is the king and the other is an ordinary employee of him, — a charioteer (the old version of modern driver). Such an ordinary employee is criticizing his master, the king of the land in scathing terms in the open court but the addressed person, the king endures the rebukes as a mute listener. The courtiers too hear them but remain silent and the charioteer is not fired. Such an instance is inconceivable in modern times, but it happened in the distant past. But why? The relation between Dhritarastra and Sanjaya cannot be weighed upon the scale of either nobility or of the connexion between the lord and his servant. We should keep in mind that this humble charioteer was given the charge of embassy when the royal family was in a crisis and none raised any question regarding his competence in that job. We have already said that Sanjaya is the exhaustive knowledge. On the other hand, Dhritarastra is the king of the body but blind i.e. ignorant. Depending upon the cardinal passions, bondages the king plods the dark way of ignorance. But Sanjaya? He treads the path of righteousness and virtue. Not only Dhritarastra but the persons having a vast knowledge of scriptures like Bhishma, Drona, Karna etc. also did not dare criticize him at any time. The mind has five natures viz. frenzied, indiscreet, distracted, resolute and dissolved. The distracted mind at times becomes resolute, even dissolved. The exhaustive knowledge carries the resolute mind to be dissolved. Until the exhaustive knowledge carries it, the mind can never be resolute nor can it be dissolved. Hence Sanjaya is the charioteer of Dhritarastra and he has the authority to animadvert upon Dhritarastra but none has the authority to censure Sanjaya.

At Viratanagara in course of conversation with Yudhisthira Krishna said for the benefit of both sides He Himself would shoulder the charge of embassy and go to Hastina. Having this news when the discussion regarding his reception was on, Duryodhana in presence of Bhishma revealed his desire to imprison Him saying "...I'll make a captive of Him and then the Vrishnis, Pandavas and the world will be under my control." Hearing this, angry Bhishma left the conference.

Krishna reached Hastina. There he met with Kunti. She opined in favour of war. Duryodhana invited him to a luncheon which He declined and became a guest of Vidura.

In the court of the Kauravas He addressed Dhritarastra, "O Bharata. I am to say that there should be an alliance between the Kauravas and Pandavas so that there should be no destruction of the valiant warriors. I have come here to pray this to you. There is no necessity to advise you anymore; you are aware of what is to be known." Speaking on the benefit of alliance for a while, Krishna said, "Now considering the well-being of both sides I am speaking to all of you, let the subjects be not fallen from dharma, wealth and happiness. Your sons are regarding a trifle to be of great import and the import is regarded to be a trifle, you please subdue them. In fine, Pandavas are agreeable to both alliance and conflict; do whatever you like."

On hearing the proposal Dhritarastra said that although the proposal of Krishna was virtuous and conformed to justice as he was not independent, his desires remained unfulfilled. He requested Krishna to make Duryodhana understand the merit of His proposal. Being requested by Dhritarastra, Krishna addressed Duryodhana. "Brother, to enter into alliance with the Pandavas is desired by your father and also by the courtiers. Now please approve of it. Adding something more He said to honour the words of the well-wishers, to enter into an alliance with the Pandavas and to return them the half of the kingdom and by doing all this he would live in peace and self-esteem being loveable to the friends for all the time to come.

After Krishna, Bhishma and Drona endorsing the speech of Krishna requested Duryodhana to enter into an alliance with the Pandavas. Paying no heed to their request he addressed Krishna, "O Vasudeva, it is your duty to consider well what you say, but without doing that you are seriously reproaching me, ...but I find not an iota of fault of mine even by meticulously analyzing my behaviour. But yet you all are bearing malice against me.... I do not find such a Kshatriya who can defeat us in fight. Even the gods can not defeat Bhishma, Drona and Karna, not to speak of the Pandavas. However, if we relying upon our own dharma breathe our last lying on the bed of arrows in the battle-field, we will attain heaven. It is the dharma of Kshatriyas." Later he said, "What more, I am not to give them that measure of land which can be pricked with the end of a needle."

Having Duryodhana's views Krishna said to him, "Duryodhana, you will surely have your coveted heroic bed in the battle-field along with your courtiers. Wait, the great war would ensue in a short time. Then describing him as a disgrace to the family, he said how becoming envious of the wealth of the Pandavas in league with Shakuni he appropriated that wealth of the Pandavas defeating them in the deceitful game of dice, how he persecuted Draupadi and passed acrimonious remarks to the Pandavas etc. He finally said, "Beatitude shall never visit you."

At this time Duhshasana opined in favour of alliance but to no avail. Being reproached by Krishna Duryodhana began to confer with Karna, Shakuni and Duhshasana. There they decided to imprison Krishna with a view to render the Pandavas weak. "The enterprise of the Pandavas and the Somakas would be impaired if he is imprisoned." Krishna could know of it at the right time. At a time he addressed Duryodhana, "It is your illusion that you are planning to defeat and imprison Me taking Me to be alone? Then laughing aloud he showed His Universal Form to the present ones including Bhishma, Drona, Vidura, Sanjaya even Dhritarastra too with his divine eye bestowed by Krishna.

In the Kaurava court Krishna's embassy failed.

The cardinal passions in restrained and disciplined state act in favour of manhood, but in unrestrained state they are antagonistic to manhood, dharma and truth. As the king of the body is blind, the indomitable Kama (desire) thinks, he is unconquerable being puffed by assertion. When the discussion was going on regarding the reception to be accorded to Him considering His dignity, Duryodhana opened his mind saying, had He been imprisoned the Pandavas would be weak and his kingdom would be free from troubles. The ego (Bhishma) could not tolerate this impertinence and withdrew from the conference. Howsoever dull witted Duryodhana be, he clearly understood that Krishna was their sole patron and had He been made a captive, his way would have been free of thorns. This suggestion was given to him by his maternal uncle Shakuni i.e. delusion. Kama under delusion loses his judgment and is conducted to evil course. Because he was deluded, he failed to understand that Krishna was not the patron of the Pandavas only but of the whole of humanity and he knows that identity of Him, who likes to have it. He who is the source of every energy, cannot be imprisoned by physical strength. He is bound by Bhakti but Kama is not upto that.

Krishna came to Hastina and spoke of the alliance to Dhritarastra. Krishna is the Consciousness encased in the body and the mind is its perverted form. Born of perversion the mind is not free from perversion, hence it thinks, it is the lord of the human body. But the real lord of the body is Consciousness encased in the body and as this Consciousness is actionless, the charge of conducting the body has been given to the mind and it is His Will. This mind is Dhritarastra and he is blind. Owing to his blindness his eldest son, Kama born of attachment (Gandhari) has taken up the king's mace to rule Hastina. Dhritarastra is the king by name only but not in action. So having the proposal of Krishna Dhritarastra says His proposal though justified and virtuous but the power to administer is not in his hands, so he cannot act following Krishna even if he descries it. If Krishna can make Duryodhana agreeable then it will be good for all.

As requested, Krishna did so knowing well that His efforts would not yield a positive result and had that been happened His Leela would have been impeded. Yet such a dramatic scene had to be enacted. In reply to Krishna proud Duryodhana boastfully declared that his heroes could not be defeated by the Pandavas nor by the gods even. He then was oblivious of the fact that a few days back his six generals were defeated by Arjuna alone at Viratanagara and they returned to Hastina alive owing to his kindness. Who could know better than Krishna how much hollow was the boasting of Duryodhana? Ignoring Krishna he went to confer with associates to devise the means to imprison Him. Krishna could know of his intention and laughing loudly he revealed His universal Form.

Due to ignorance Duryodhana took Krishna for an ordinary fellow and with this cognizance he plotted to imprison Him. This step of him was unjust, immoral and unexpected. So to make him know of His identity He showed His Universal Form. But dull as Duryodhana was, he took it to be a magic show failing to form an idea of His Divine Entity. Some others also visualized it but their reaction was not similar to that of Duryodhana. Even Dhritarastra too saw this unearthly scene and formed an idea of His divine entity and accorded importance to it as he could do. Others also did so. Only Duryodhana failed. Krishna's embassy also failed.

The possibility of the armed conflict became greater.

www.ingramcontent.com/pod-product-compliance
Lightning Source LLC
LaVergne TN
LVHW061539070526
838199LV00077B/6837